Stéphane Mallarmé

Updated Edition

Twayne's World Authors Series

French Literature

David O'Connell, Editor

Georgia State University

TWAS 52

STÉPHANE MALLARMÉ
(1842–1898)
Photograph courtesy of H. Roger Viollet

Stéphane Mallarmé

Updated Edition

By F. C. St. Aubyn

University of Pittsburgh, Emeritus

Twayne Publishers
A Division of G. K. Hall & Co. • *Boston*

Stéphane Mallarmé, Updated Edition
F. C. St. Aubyn

Copyright 1989 by G. K. Hall & Co.
All rights reserved.
Published by Twayne Publishers
A Division of G. K. Hall & Co.
70 Lincoln Street
Boston, Massachusetts 02111

First edition © 1969, Twayne Publishers, Inc.

Copyediting supervised by Barbara Sutton.
Book production by Janet Z. Reynolds.
Book design by Barbara Anderson.

Typeset in 11 pt. Garamond
by Compset, Inc., Beverly, Massachusetts

Printed on permanent/durable acid-free paper
and bound in the United States of America

Library of Congress Cataloging-in-Publication Data

St. Aubyn, Frederic C. (Frederic Chase), 1921–
    Stéphane Mallarmé / by F.C. St. Aubyn. — Updated ed.
        p.   cm. — (Twayne's world authors series ; TWAS 52. French
    literature)
    Bibliography: p.
    Includes index.
    ISBN 0-8057-8254-0
    1. Mallarmé, Stéphane, 1842–1898—Criticism and interpretation.
I. Title.   II. Series: Twayne's world authors series ; TWAS 52.
III. Series: Twayne's world authors series. French literature.
PQ2344.Z5S2   1989
841'.8—dc19   89-30568
                                                                CIP

To my parents

Contents

About the Author

F. C. St. Aubyn received his B. A. from Southwest Missouri State University. After serving in the U.S. Army Air Force in World War II, he earned his M.A. and Ph.D. degrees at Yale University. He has taught at Yale, the State University of New York at Binghamton, the University of Delaware, and Elmira College. From 1972 to 1976 he was chairman of the Department of French and Italian at the University of Pittsburgh. Professor St. Aubyn is also author of the Twayne's World Authors Series volumes *Arthur Rimbaud, Updated Edition* and *Charles Péguy.* Coauthor of two textbook editions—one of the play *Les Mouches* by Jean-Paul Sartre and another of *Trois Pièces Surréalistes* by Cocteau, Aragon, and Vitrac—his numerous articles on modern French literature have been published in the United States, Canada, England, France, Italy, and Australia. He has published more than eighty book reviews and in 1967–68 was the recipient of a fellowship from the American Council of Learned Societies. In 1976 he was named Outstanding Alumnus by Southwest Missouri State University. That same year he was invited by the Australian government to lecture for eight weeks at the University of Queensland in Brisbane. The University of Pittsburgh named him professor emeritus of French in 1986, and in that year his undergraduate alma mater published the catalog *The William J. Jones Collections: Rimbaud—Butor,* which contains 1,818 items by and about Rimbaud that Professor St. Aubyn collected and donated to the university. The French government honored St. Aubyn by naming him a *chevalier* in the *Ordre des Palmes Académiques* in 1987.

Preface

This book is intended as a general, analytical, and critical introduction to the poetry of Mallarmé for students and teachers in high schools and colleges as well as for the general public. No attempt has been made to oversimplify the enormous complexity of the subject. The attempt has been to present, within the limits of vocabulary, syntax, and prosody, the most immediate, if not the most obvious, interpretation so that the reader can unravel some of the finer subtleties for himself.

Because of space limitations, fourteen of the poems generally included in the *Poésies complètes* have not been considered; the occasional pieces and the works in prose except the twelve poems in prose, *Igitur,* and *Un Coup de Dés,* have also been omitted. It is hoped that the reader will have in hand a copy of the text that interests him. The original French has usually been provided in parentheses immediately after a quotation from the poetry only, thus permitting the discussion of a greater number of works.

Because the American reader may not be familiar with Mallarmé's life, a chronology and brief biography have been provided. I have outlined the evolution of his poetic concepts to help orient the reader to the poetry. The youthful works are discussed because they reveal the growth and development of Mallarmé and pertain to his later poems. Although it is hoped that the reader will arrive at his own conclusions before the final chapter, I have provided a brief summary in an attempt to assay Mallarmé's accomplishments and influence. A critical bibliography of over one hundred items is offered as a guide to further study and enjoyment of the poetry of Mallarmé.

I should like to take this opportunity to express my profound gratitude to the late Professor Henri Peyre for his unfailing consideration and encouragement. He first introduced me to Mallarmé and warned me not to make too much of a crossword puzzle of his poetry. I am not sure I have entirely succeeded, but to the extent that I have, I must thank Professor Peyre.

I should also like to thank the administration of Elmira College for the opportunity it provided to write this book, and my colleagues and students for the inspiration they afforded.

Only William B. Monroe and I know how much this book owes to him.

F. C. St. Aubyn

University of Pittsburgh, Emeritus

Chronology

1842   18 March, Etienne (called Stéphane) Mallarmé born in Paris, son of Numa-Florence-Joseph Mallarmé and Elisabeth-Félicie Desmolins; father, Deputy Chief Clerk in the Registry and Public Property Office.

1847   Mother dies.

1848   Father marries Anne-Hubertine Mathieu.

1857   Younger sister Maria dies at age thirteen.

1860   After first failing in August, Mallarmé receives his baccalaureate in November from the lycée at Sens.

1861   Friendship with the young teacher, Emmanuel des Essarts.

1862   Publishes first poems and first article; travels to London with future wife, Maria-Christina Gerhard.

1863   Father dies; returns to London and begins translating Poe; 10 August, marries Maria; appointed deputy teacher of English at Tournon.

1864   Begins "Hérodiade"; publishes first poems in prose; 19 November: daughter Geneviève born.

1865   Begins work on *L'Après-Midi d'un Faune*.

1866   Publishes eleven poems in *Le Parnasse Contemporain*; appointed professor of English at the lycée in Besançon.

1867   Professor at the lycée in Avignon.

1869   Publishes a fragment of "Hérodiade" in the second *Parnasse Contemporain*, which does not appear until 1871 because of the war; begins *Igitur*, published in 1925.

1870   Granted leave of absence from teaching.

1871   16 July, birth of son Anatole; appointed teacher of English at the Lycée Fontanes in Paris.

1872   Begins to publish translations of Poe.

1874   First vacations at Valvins near Fontainebleau; publishes eight issues of his review, *La Dernière Mode*.

1875   Moves to 87, rue de Rome, in Paris.

1876   *L'Après-Midi d'un Faune* published, illustrated by Manet; Manet paints his portrait.

1877   "Le Tombeau d'Edgar Poe" published.

1878   Textbook, *Les Mots anglais*, published.

1879   Son Anatole dies at age eight.

1880   *Les Dieux antiques* published; begins his "Tuesdays."

1883   Named officer of the Academy; Verlaine publishes *Les Poètes mauditis*.

1884   Named professor of English at the Lycée Janson-de-Sailly.

1885   Professor at the Collège Rollin.

1886   Publishes three poems in prose in the first issue of *La Vogue*; begins to publish "Notes sur le Théâtre."

1887   *Album de Vers et de Prose* published in Bruxelles; *Poésies* published in Paris.

1888   Translation of Whistler's "Ten O'Clock" published.

1890   Lectures in Belgium on Villiers de l'Isle-Adam.

1891   *Pages* published in Bruxelles.

1893   *Vers et Prose* published in Paris.

1894   Retires from teaching; lectures at Oxford and Cambridge.

1896   Elected Prince of Poets.

1897   *Un Coup de Dés* and *Divagations* published.

1898   9 September, Mallarmé dies at Valvins.

1913   "Le Cantique de Saint Jean" published.

1925   *Igitur* published.

1926   "Ouverture ancienne" published, now appears as the opening section of *Hérodiade*.

1959   *Les Noces d'Hérodiadae* published.

Chapter One
Introduction: A Poet's Life
The Uneventful Life

The life of Stéphane Mallarmé, who was born in Paris in 1842, was deceptively dull. Outwardly nothing much happened. His biographer wrote: "The destiny of Mallarmé was pure, simple, uneventful."[1] Yet that same biographer needed almost 800 pages to recount the uneventful life of this poet whose renown rests on less than fifty poems.

Mallarmé was born into the most narrowly bourgeois of all French classes, that of the petty functionary, the small cog in the vast bureaucratic machinery that has kept France going through untold upheavals and disasters at least since the time of Philip II in the late twelfth and early thirteenth centuries. In this stable and secure but not very wealthy world, however, Mallarmé's mother died when he was five. His father remarried the next year. Mallarmé and his younger sister Maria found themselves separated. He remained with his father and stepmother, although most of the time he lived at boarding school. Maria was kept by their maternal grandparents, the Desmolins, an even more typical petty functionary and his kind but bourgeois wife who lived in the suburbs of Paris. Again death struck. Maria, Mallarmé's closest companion, died in 1857 at the age of thirteen. His earliest poems date from this period and indeed the lost sister haunts his poetry for years to come.

Mallarmé finally, not without some difficulty, received his baccalaureate in 1860 from the lycée at Sens, a town seventy miles southeast of Paris where his parents were then living. He spent the next two years as a dutiful apprentice in his grandfather's office. In the meantime he had become the friend of a young teacher, Emmanuel des Essarts. He had read Baudelaire and Poe. In 1862 he published his first poems and his first article. That year he met his future wife, Maria-Christina Gerhard, seven years his senior, employed as the German companion to a wealthy family. Considering her name and age Maria seems to be a replacement for the lost mother–sister in Mallarmé's life. Mallarmé announced to his grandfather that he wanted to become a teacher of a foreign language, the foreign language being English. With Maria he left for London to perfect his English and to learn to read Poe better.

Difficulties soon developed between the young lovers, and Maria returned to France late in 1862. Mallarmé himself returned to France in 1863. Just after he reached his majority in March and could claim his modest inheritance from his mother, his father died. He continued his courtship of Maria; they returned to London and were married on 10 August. The following month he received his teaching certificate and late in the year he was named deputy teacher of English in the little town of Tournon, lost in the provinces 370 miles southeast of Paris. There his daughter, Françoise-Geneviève-Stéphanie, called "Vève," was born on 19 November 1864.

Thus began Mallarmé's undistinguished teaching career, which was to last for thirty years, broken only by moves from Tournon to Besançon to Avignon, and at last in 1871 to the Lycée Fontanes—today the Lycée Condorcet—in Paris. The reports of his superiors and the remarks of his students, as well as Mallarmé's own admissions, all seem to indicate that he was something of a failure as a teacher. Certainly few men were less qualified to teach than Mallarmé. His refined manners, his distracted air, his soft voice made the maintenance of discipline in the classroom practically impossible. From his own point of view, he had, as his grandfather had warned him, exchanged one routine job for another and lost a great deal in the bargain. The work in his grandfather's office may have been monotonous, but after hours there were no lessons to prepare and no papers to correct and grade. In the office there were no unruly boys to create mayhem and bedlam all day long and his evenings would have been his own. The only time Mallarmé found for poetry was late at night after his academic chores were finished and his little family had retired. The lamp became a frequent theme in Mallarmé's poetry.

While still living in the provinces, Mallarmé was successful in having eleven of his early poems published in Paris in *Le Parnasse Contemporain,* edited by his good friend, the poet Catulle Mendès. Their appearance marked the beginning of Mallarmé's renown at the age of twenty-four. Almost every year after that Mallarmé published poems, poems in prose, articles, essays, criticism, translations, and prefaces, in addition to the few books that appeared at greater intervals.

On 16 July 1871, the year Mallarmé reached Paris, his son Anatole was born, destined to live only eight years. Plagued all of his life by poverty, Mallarmé nevertheless vacationed for the first time in 1874 in the little town of Valvins on the Seine near Fontainebleau. There he rented a small country house overlooking the Seine and spent much of his later life, with or without his family and friends. The following year the Mallarmé family moved to its final abode in Paris, the famous apartment at 87, rue de Rome, where they lived for twenty-three years. He began his "Tuesdays," which became one of the great phenomena of French artistic life during the last twenty years of the nineteenth century, in 1880 on the rue de Rome. Few written and few oral invitations were extended. By word of mouth, old and young, artists, writers, and musicians, heard of the reunions and dropped in. As a rule, only Mallarmé spoke in his quiet voice while standing by the fireplace smoking his eternal cigarette. He evidently enchanted his listeners with his thoughts, ideas, and ruminations. The "Tuesdays" continued almost up to his death and practically a whole generation of writers was influenced by them. Everyone who attended agreed they were unforgettable, yet no one was ever truly successful at re-creating their essence.

The popularity of the "Tuesdays" demonstrated that Mallarmé, who had not yet published a single volume of poetry, and who was not to do so until 1887 when he was forty-five years old, was slowly becoming better known. Three important events took place in 1883: he was named an officer of the Academy by the government; Verlaine published his series of articles entitled *Les Poètes maudits* in which Mallarmé figured as one of the subjects; and his friend Manet died, leaving Mallarmé the few hours he had formerly spent in the artist's atelier to spend with one of Manet's acquaintances, Méry Laurent. If any event ever occurred that might have marred the purity of Mallarmé's life, it was his friendship with Méry Laurent. In the past she had vaguely been an actress and she was now "a kept woman," with a luxurious apartment conveniently located near Mallarmé's on the rue de Rome. The friendship lasted for years; certainly Méry Laurent was one of the three most important women in his life. His wife Maria perhaps knew more about Mallarmé's homey, homely needs than about his poetry. Méry probably knew more about his poetry than Maria and certainly she knew more about male vanity and Mallarmé's social needs, which were not so homey and far from being homely. Yet Mallarmé's daughter probably knew more about her father's genuine needs as well as his poetry than either of the older women. In any event, all four remained friends and the purity of Mallarmé's personal life does not seem to have been compromised.

The following year Mallarmé was transferred to the Lycée Janson-de-Sailly in the suburbs of Paris, and in 1885 to the Collège Rollin in Paris itself, where he stayed until 1893 when he asked for a leave of absence for reasons of health, and from which he was allowed to retire early in 1894. The *Album de Vers et de Prose* had been published in Bruxelles and the *Poésies* in Paris, both in 1887. In 1890 Mallarmé toured Belgium where he lectured about his friend, Villiers de l'Isle-Adam. Upon retiring, in 1894, Mallarmé spoke at both Oxford and Cambridge, but after thirty years of teaching the language he was still not able to give a lecture in English. In 1896 Mallarmé was elected Prince of Poets, the latest in a succession that had included Victor Hugo, Leconte de Lisle, and Verlaine. Just two years later Mallarmé died at Valvins on 9 September at the age of fifty-six.

One wonders what was so unusual about this impoverished man who spent thirty years doing a relatively poor job of teaching and who actually published only one volume of poetry containing about sixty poems. Modest even in his transgressions, Mallarmé would hardly seem the type to exert so much influence on French literature of the twentieth century. Aside from the *Poésies* perhaps only the "Tuesdays" and his election as Prince of Poets give some intimation of all that lies hidden in the story and personality of Mallarmé. This bare outline of the life of Mallarmé is only deceptively dull.

The Eventful Life

The last thirty years of the nineteenth century constituted a period of unparalleled foment for all of the arts in France, a country known for its long and rich tradition of artistic innovation and achievement. Impressionism in painting was moving away from an earlier realism, naturalism, and romanticism. Impressionism in music was moving away from romanticism and neoromanticism. All impressionism led in a direction that could only result in the radical experiments of this century. In poetry symbolism was vying with the Parnassian School, preparing the way for the twentieth century's most important movement, surrealism. Naturalism had gone far beyond realism in the novel. Little magazines were born by the dozens and died in droves. Militant manifestoes in literature, art, and aesthetics were proclaimed on all sides. Even the Decadents had their day. In the midst of it all was Mallarmé valiantly trying to find the time and courage to put pen to paper.

Mallarmé knew literally all the poets, writers, and editors of his day, both first and second rank. Among the older generation and the precursors and founders of the Parnassian movement he knew Théophile Gautier, Leconte de Lisle, Théodore de Banville, and Villiers de l'Isle-Adam. He even knew the great Provençal poet Frédéric Mistral. In his own generation he knew well the Parnassian, Catulle Mendès, and the symbolist, Verlaine, perhaps less so François Coppée and José-Maria de Heredia. Among the younger generation he encountered Arthur Rimbaud about whom he wrote a famous article, as well as Emile Verhaeren, Jules Laforgue, Henri de Régnier, and Vielé-Griffin. He could count among his disciples and successors many of that generation born around 1870 including Pierre Louys, André Gide, Paul Valéry, and Paul Claudel. He had as a student in his class the poet Léon-Paul Fargue. Among foreigners he knew at least slightly the Irish-English poet and dramatist Oscar Wilde and the German symbolist poet Stefan George.

Among novelists Mallarmé was acquainted with the Goncourt brothers of an earlier generation. In his own generation he knew particularly well Joris-Karl Huysmans, the hero of whose novel, *A Rebours,* provided Mallarmé with the inspiration for one of his most enigmatic poems, "Prose pour des Esseintes." Alphonse Daudet, Anatole France, and Émile Zola were also of his generation, while Guy de Maupassant was ten years his junior, Maurice Barrès twenty, and Marcel Proust thirty.

His acquaintances among artists and painters were almost as numerous. Among the older generation he knew the muralist Puvis de Chavannes. His closest friends included Edouard Manet, who painted his portrait in 1876. In addition to this famous portrait there hung at the same time on the walls of his humble apartment an oil painting by Manet's sister-in-law Berthe Morisot, of the little yawl he used on the Seine at Valvins; a painting by Constantin Guys that had belonged to Baudelaire and had come to him by way of Théodore de Banville; a portrait of Geneviève by Whistler; a Monet; and Manet's "Hamlet." Mallarmé translated into French and had published Whistler's lecture entitled "Ten O'Clock." He was also instrumental in the purchase by the Louvre of Whistler's celebrated portrait of his mother. At one time Mallarmé was going to collaborate on a book illustrated by Berthe

Morisot, Renoir, Monet, and Degas, but unfortunately it was never realized. Renoir painted Mallarmé's portrait as did Edvard Munch and Gauguin. Whistler did a lithograph of him. Mallarmé knew Pissarro and Odilon Redon as well as the sculptor Rodin. In a younger generation he was acquainted with Vuillard.

Among musicians and composers, Debussy attended some of the "Tuesdays" and set a few of Mallarmé's poems to music. In 1871 Mallarmé heard Camille Saint-Saëns play one of his own compositions on the organ at the funeral of Mallarmé's painter friend, Henri Regnault, killed in the Franco-Prussian War. He heard the première of Debussy's *Prélude à l'Après-Midi d'un Faune* in 1894, a work inspired by Mallarmé's poem, which proved to be one of the seminal compositions in the history of modern music. Mallarmé heard Gabriel Fauré play the organ at Verlaine's funeral in 1896.

Among men of the stage, Mallarmé was associated with Lugné-Poe who, as director and producer, was destined to exert a profound influence on the course of all subsequent French theater. Mallarmé knew Alexandre Dumas *fils* and was a friend of the greatest symbolist dramatist, Maurice Maeterlinck. Mallarmé attended the première of Alfred Jarry's *Ubu Roi* in 1896, which can be called, without too much exaggeration, the first play of the twentieth century.

All of which meant that Mallarmé was in constant contact with the literary, artistic, and musical currents of his day. If his early poems reveal the inevitable influence of romantics like Victor Hugo and Lamartine, then his more mature works show a striking affinity with those of the Parnassians like Théophile Gautier and Théodore de Banville. Baudelaire and Poe appear throughout his works. In many respects he resembles less, oddly enough, the two poets usually grouped with him as symbolists, Verlaine and Rimbaud. In fact, his theory and practice resemble more those of the impressionist painters. Mallarmé's poetic theory goes exactly counter to that of the realism and naturalism rampant in the novel of his time.

His many friendships meant that Mallarmé, in moving to Paris and leaving behind the loneliness and isolation of the provinces, was hard put to find time to write. In the summer of 1893, he wrote to Méry Laurent,[2] he had received at Valvins no less than sixty books, all of which had to be acknowledged with comments demonstrating that he had read them. Caught up in the innuendoes of the day, amidst the attacks and counterattacks, claims and counterclaims, Mallarmé strove to remain above and beyond the melee, to remain friends with everyone. Practically pilloried on the one side and almost apotheosized on the other, he maintained a calm that belied the intensity of his inner emotions. Luckily Mallarmé had long since, and in the depths of the provinces, begun to forge the poetic doctrine that would, with few alterations, last him all his life and forever set off his creations from poetry before and after. In the end his poetic doctrine, as exemplified by his poetry, was his true life.

The True Life

Mallarmé's poetic doctrine has been thought to be impossibly arcane and hermetic, infinitely abstract and obscure, his poetry "a vacuum," as a recent critic put it, where "we breathe pure nothingness thinly disguised in ghostly veils and magic arabesques."[3] Nothing could be further from the truth. Mallarmé's doctrine and poetry are solidly based on the concrete. Indeed, one is amazed at how many of his poems are occasional pieces, that is, poetry occasioned by an idea, a sentiment, an object, or an event. A careful analysis of his doctrine as it evolved over twenty years leads me to agree that "Mallarmé is a difficult poet but it is doubtful whether he can properly be called an obscure one."[4]

In formulating his doctrine and in writing his poetry, Mallarmé began with the basic tool common to all poets; the word. He is reported to have replied to a friend, "But, Degas, it is not with ideas that one makes poetry . . . *It is with words.*"[5] In his preoccupation with words Mallarmé evolved a concept of purity and beauty unsurpassed for the singleness of its purpose, the eminence of its goal, and the perfection of its execution.

Mallarmé confronted the problem that exists for all modern poets, a problem that, as Sir Herbert Read put it, "Mallarmé was the first to formulate and attempt to overcome—the evident fact that the language of our western civilization had become too corrupt for poetic use."[6] Sir Herbert describes this corruption as "a state of exhaustion or evisceration, and the consequential resort, in any process of verbalization, to the cliché." Mallarmé, speaking of the task of the true poet in the sonnet "Le Tombeau d'Edgar Poe," expressed it in one alexandrine: "To give a purer meaning to the words of the tribe" (*Donner un sens plus pur aux mots de la tribu*). The problem of how to give this "purer meaning" to words is fundamental to Mallarmé's doctrine.

When Mallarmé began to compose "Hérodiade" in October 1864, he realized he was attempting something that had never been tried in poetry. In a famous letter to his friend Henri Cazalis he described his endeavors: "I am inventing a language which must necessarily arise from a very new poetics which I could define in these two words: *To describe not the thing, but the effect it produces.*"[7] As surprising as the idea itself is the fact that the great romantic-realist Stendhal had already said precisely the same thing thirty years earlier: "I do not pretend to describe things in themselves, but only their effect on me."[8] Mallarmé could not have found the idea in Stendhal's fictionalized autobiography since the book was not published until twenty-five years after Mallarmé had begun to delineate his doctrine. Stendhal may only have been hunting excuses for the inaccuracies and slips of memory in recounting his life. The coincidence does reveal, however, the filiation between Mallarmé and his predecessors, between symbolism and romanticism.

Mallarmé's statement also reveals his early affinity with the impressionist school of painting. What he says seems to contradict what has been said previously about his preoccupation with the word: "Therefore, the verse must not in this case be composed of words, but of intentions, and all words must give way to the sensations." The individual word, as an object itself and like the object, must disappear in the impression created. To avoid the cliché, to create such an effect, words must be used in a radically new way.

The separate word means just what it has always meant. Only by unusual juxtaposition, by the unexpected context can it take on a new and richer meaning. Being so placed that it seems misplaced "the word does not echo the thing but other words."[9] In this relationship of word to word the word no longer refers either to the thing or to an idea. In fact, Mallarmé's originality lay, according to one of his earliest and best critics, in "transferring to words themselves the totally allusory function of ideas."[10] Too much has been made of Mallarmé's Platonism. In Mallarmé's poetry neither the word nor the poetic image nor the symbol is the equivalent of the Platonic idea. They do not represent or stand for something else. They are so ordered as to re-create an effect, evoke a mood. This they can do only through syntax. In manipulating syntax Mallarmé admittedly does violence to the sentence. Most connectives and many verbs are gradually suppressed, leaving only juxtaposition and separation.

Within this apparent disorder "anacoluthon and syllepsis are, for Mallarmé, not figures of rhetoric, but the very basis of his style" (p. 324). A poem for Mallarmé "is not a grouping but a succession" (p. 312), and within that succession he "proceeds by envelopment rather than by development" (p. 325). The poem, then, is not a description of anything, not even a symbol of something. The poem is a mood and within this mood the word means primarily itself in relation to other words and groups of words and "the poetic image means primarily itself in relation to the poem"; it is an emotion and the emotion *"is* the poem, not something else still behind it."[11] The denotation of the individual word thus becomes suggestion and the total suggestion becomes the poem.

Such an unusual ordering of words within the sentence is also closely allied in Mallarmé's mind with the ordering of words on the page. Not only the black of the ink of the poem on the page is important but also the unused white of the page. The page can represent purity, and purity can mean sterility. The poet needs all his strength to sully the white page with a poem he knows cannot be perfect. This idea is expressed as early as the poem "Brise marine" of 1865. Purity and perfection unite to create one of Mallarmé's great mental blocks to the creation of poetry, an attitude that can, of course, result in sterility. Haunted all his life by the ideal of perfection, Mallarmé was also haunted by the fear of sterility. His poetic output was limited to the few poems he was finally able to set down on paper. His typographical experiments continued throughout his life and culminated in the amazing eccentricities of the long poem *Un Coup de Dés* written in 1897, the year before his death.

From a preoccupation with the poem as a two-dimensional object, Mallarmé moved to the possibility of the poem in three dimensions. While working on "Hérodiade" he began to compose a poem completely different in nature, *L'Après-Midi d'un Faune.* Although the second part of "Hérodiade" is in dialogue form and entitled "Scène," it is hardly scenic. In writing to Cazalis in 1865 concerning *L'Après-Midi d'un Faune* Mallarmé said, "I am making it absolutely scenic, not *possible in the theater,* but *needing it."*[12] Twenty years of meditating on the relationships between poetry and the drama resulted in Mallarmé's essays "Hamlet" of 1886, "Notes sur le Théâtre" of 1886–87, and "Crayonné au Théâtre" of 1887. Mallarmé does not hesitate to declare in the last of these essays that "The Theater is of a superior essence," that it is "Our only magnificence, the scene, to which the combination of the various arts united by poetry attributes . . . some religious or official character."[13] Although Mallarmé was to retain this high opinion of the theater throughout his life, his talent was basically lyric rather than dramatic. His affinity for the theater should be kept in mind, however, in any attempt to interpret his poetry, particularly the longer poems.

In addition to and in conjunction with this idea of the synthesis of poetry and the theater came the idea of a synthesis of all the arts. In the letter of 1865 quoted above, Mallarmé described the truly poetic as "a deep study of sound and color, of music and painting." As early as 1866 he was writing to a friend of his desire to attempt simply "the work."[14] By the time Mallarmé was replying to Verlaine's request for biographical information in 1885 "the work" had become "the Book." After denigrating his early works Mallarmé wrote to Verlaine:

I have always dreamed and attempted something else, with the patience of an alchemist, ready to sacrifice to it all vanity and all satisfaction, as men used to burn their furniture and roofbeams to feed the furnace of the Great Work. What work? It is difficult to say: a book, quite simply, in many volumes, architectural and premeditated, and not a collection of chance inspirations no matter how marvelous they may be . . . I will go further, I will say: the Book, convinced that basically there is only one, attempted without knowing it by whoever writes, even by Geniuses. The orphic explanation of the Earth, which is the poet's only duty and the true function of literature: for the very rhythm of the book, impersonal and alive down to its pagination, would then be juxtaposed to the equations of this dream, or Ode.[15]

Mallarmé's concept of the synthesis of the arts had been affected by his acquaintance with the ideas of Wagner. Five months before replying to Verlaine, Mallarmé had written an essay entitled "Richard Wagner, Rêverie d'un Poète français," in which he spoke of the "Monster-Who-Cannot-Be."[16] The monster is impossible because in such a synthesis one of the arts must necessarily be slighted. As much as Mallarmé admired Wagner's theory, the word would still have to come first although Mallarmé aspired as ardently to realize this ideal as did Wagner. First and foremost, however, Mallarmé aspired to "the Book" that would explain the world to man.

According to some of his biographers, while still at Tournon, Mallarmé is supposed to have suffered a traumatic experience regarding his profession as poet. This was on the night of 2 March 1866. Mondor has demonstrated that in a letter to his friend Aubanel, on 3 March, Mallarmé noted the night but without indicating much that was unusual. He had not come to any sudden illumination about the nature of poetic creation. In "his insomnia and his insatiable meditation"[17] he had, however, come to grips with some of the problems presented by "Hérodiade."

In Besançon, Mallarmé continued to mold with painful effort his concept of poetry. There he came face to face with nothingness in all its horror. There he also discovered the mirror, so to speak, with all its possibilities and implications. From this time the concepts of nothingness and the mirror were to play a fundamental role in his poetic creativity. In a letter to Cazalis of 14 May 1867, Mallarmé put it his way:

I confess, moreover, but to you alone, that I still need, so great have been the humiliations of my triumph, to look at myself in this mirror in order to think, and if it were not in front of the table where I am writing this letter, I should again become Nothingness. That is to inform you that I am now impersonal and no longer the Stéphane whom you knew, but an aptitude which the spiritual universe has of seeing and developing itself through that which was I.[18]

His "Thought has thought itself and arrived at a pure Conception" (p. 240). Certainly this idea shares something with the romantic conception of the poet as prophet and guide expressed so often and in so many different ways by Victor Hugo and others. Musset's nocturnal muse of divine inspiration also hovers over much of what Mallarmé wrote. Mallarmé's unfinished story *Igitur,* of 1869, with its midnight sights and sounds is more romantic than the romantics themselves.

Yet Mallarmé's idea shares more in this instance with Rimbaud's concept of the poet as "seer" expressed in his amazing letters of 13 and 15 May 1871.[19] With Rimbaud it was "a long, immense, and reasoned *deranging* of all the *senses.*" Somewhat like Mallarmé in front of his mirror, Rimbaud maintained that "It is false to say: I think. One should say: I am thought." For him, as for Mallarmé, the "I is another." He too is attempting "To find a language" and "This language will be of the soul for the soul, summing up all, perfumes, sounds, colors." Here, Rimbaud echoes Baudelaire just as Mallarmé has done before him. While for Rimbaud it is a question of "changing life" (p. 216) as he put it in *Une Saison en Enfer,* for Mallarmé it is an attempt, as has already been quoted, at an "orphic explanation of the Earth." Each is straining to arrive at the unknown through some sort of cosmic communion with the world. Instead of harking back to the romantics, however, Mallarmé and Rimbuad seem to foreshadow the surrealists and the existentialists. Their point of view is much more profoundly and seriously psychological than that of the romantics. While the anguish of the earlier poets was at least as sincere, that of Mallarmé and Rimbaud seems more closely akin to the angst of the mid–twentieth-century philosophers. Out of his torment Mallarmé forged his concept of beauty that remains the epitome of his thought and his poetry. He outlined it in the same letter of 14 May 1867, to Cazalis: "There is only Beauty;—and it has only one perfect expression—Poetry. All the rest is a lie—except for those who live by the body, love, and, that love of the mind, friendship . . . For me, Poetry takes the place of love, because it is enamored of itself, and because its sensual delight falls back deliciously in my soul."[20] Beauty was the be-all and end-all for Mallarmé while poetry was his primary mode of expression. He did not communicate very well within his family. His slight indiscretions outside the family seem more of an excuse to extend the range of his sensibilities to be put to the use of poetry rather than an immediate physical satisfaction. Such an exalted idea of beauty has it dangers, however, and for six or seven years, between 1867 and 1873, Mallarmé produced little poetry.

The role of Poe in the formation of Mallarmé's aesthetic doctrine is difficult for the contemporary American to understand. At a young age the tintinnabulation of the bells can produce a certain titillation, but with any luck, a little education, and the passage of time, that exhilaration quickly fades. The insistent rhymes become a clamor to the English ear and the persistent rhythms a sickening singsong. If Poe's poetry has fallen out of fashion, at least for the moment, his less well-known poetic doctrine still holds an important place in the development of American literature. Its place in the history of French literature was consecrated for Mallarmé and other French writers by Baudelaire's translations. Mallarmé's biographer has pointed out how much Mallarmé's above-quoted statement on beauty owes to Baudelaire's translation of Poe's essay on *The Philosophy of Composition*.[21]

A perceptive critic has stated that Poe interested so many Frenchmen because he was "the only modern poet of the English language who had a rationally and even dogmatically formulated poetics."[22] The same critic attributed Baudelaire's "cult of poetry for itself," "his views on the music of poetry," "the indispensable brevity" of poetry, and "the primordial role accorded the imagination and the conception of poetry as power of suggestion," to Poe rather than to any of his French predecessors. Mondor saw Mallarmé conquered by Poe because of the latter's "penetration, his analytical profundity, the rigor, the resources, the strangeness of his art, the calculations and extraordinary sonority of his music."[23] Many of these ideas appear in one form or another in Mallarmé's reply to Jules Huret's inquiry on "The Evolution of Literature" of 1891.[24] Even there, however, Mallarmé came back to one of his dominant ideas, that "the world was made in order to result in a beautiful book."

Before deciding on the best approach to Mallarmé's poetry one other element of his doctrine should be mentioned: the dance. Two articles, one entitled "Ballets" of 1886 and the other "Les Fonds dans le Ballet" of 1893, reveal the importance Mallarmé accorded this art form. In the former he maintained that "One art holds the stage, historical with the Drama; with the Ballet, another, emblematic. To be allied, but not to be confused."[25] Mallarmé saw the moving dancer as a symbol, "a Sign," and "the visual incorporation of the idea."

The second essay, written after having seen Loïe Fuller perform, is one of the most beautiful evocations of the dance ever conceived. It conjures up Louis Comfort Tiffany's magic representation in glass of the same dancer, or the bronzes by Pierre Roche and Raoul Larche. According to Mallarmé there is in the dance "A pensive delicacy as achieves for example the pleasure found in the reading of poetry." Never exhausted for Mallarmé are "the subtle means included in the arcanum of the Dance." In this synthesis of the arts one has the impression that the "perfect poem" for Mallarmé would be the reading of his "Hérodiade" by Vera Zorina while Martha Graham danced to the music composed by Paul Hindemith for the poem and for Miss Graham. Or it could be Rudolf Nureyev dancing Nijinsky's choreography to Debussy's *Prélude à l'Après-Midi d'un Faune* while the late Gérard Philippe recited Mallarmé's poem. Exciting as the prospect is, one must return to the two-dimensional poems.

All these elements of Mallarmé's poetic doctrine should be kept in mind while reading his poetry. Their evolution is the true life of Mallarmé. The problem is that Mallarmé's poems do not "mean" any one thing. They should be read like music, perpendicularly as well as horizontally, with all of the various possibilities constituting the harmony and with the lyric lines nothing more than an impression or an intention. Mallarmé himself suggested an approach to his poetry while writing to Cazalis in July 1868, of an early version of the sonnet "Ses purs ongles . . .": "The meaning, if it has one (but I would console myself with the contrary thanks to the amount of poetry it contains, it seems to me), is evoked by an internal mirage of the words themselves. In

letting oneself go while murmuring it several times one experiences a
rather cabalistic sensation."[26] This does not mean that the approach
should be fuzzily impressionistic, depending upon blurred outlines to
conceal its lack of "meaning." It does mean that one should concentrate
on this "internal mirage of words" until it produces a sensation and
then proceed to analyze that sensation as far as it is logically possible.
One does not end with a single explanation nor the only "correct"
interpretation. An impression will not necessarily be more "right" than
another but it should be consistent with the vocabulary, syntax, and
prosody of the given poem.

To experience this occult and mystical, in short, cabalistic, sensation
one has to look at the poem until an impression takes shape and at that
moment, that verbalized impression will be the poem. As Thibaudet
wrote, "a poem by Mallarmé is so constructed as to solicit the creative
activity of the reader and to develop itself through it."[27] One has to
exercise all his creative activity to arrive at a satisfying interpretation
of Mallarmé's difficult poetry, but the results are worth the effort. In
the struggle one lives, in a sense, and for a few moments, the true life
of Mallarmé.

Chapter Two
The Road to Parnassus
Early Gleanings

In the "Autobiography" Mallarmé wrote on 16 November 1885, in reply to a request for biographical information from Verlaine, he stated that as a schoolboy he had had "a secret desire to replace, one day, Béranger"[1] because he had met the poet in a friend's home. The project proved impossible although he had "long attempted [it] in a hundred little notebooks which were always confiscated." One is amused and amazed by the fact that Mallarmé should have chosen as his idol Pierre-Jean de Béranger, who is remembered today as a once popular third-rate poet now read, if at all, only in courses in the history of French poetry. The literary historian is also attracted by the possibility of what those "hundred little notebooks" might reveal about Mallarmé's formative years.

Two prose pieces by the twelve-year-old Mallarmé still exist: "La Coupe d'or" and "L'Ange gardien" of 1854. The latter is readily available in the *Oeuvres complètes* (pp. 1,383–84). His earliest poem is probably one of thirty-five lines written in 1855 or 1856.[2] His earliest prose work, which might be called a poem in prose, was written perhaps between 1855 and 1858,[3] although from internal evidence another critic would date it from 1859 or 1860.[4] For a long time only four of Mallarmé's poems of 1859 were known: "Pépita," "Mélancolie" (*Oeuvres complètes*, pp. 1,384–86), "Sa Fosse est creusée! . . . Sa Fosse est fermée" and "La Prière d'une mère" (*Oeuvres complètes*, pp. 4–14). Then in 1944 or 1945 Mallarmé's faithful biographer, Henri Mondor, turned up almost by accident four of the hundred little notebooks mentioned by Mallarmé. One of them, entitled *Entre quatre murs*, contained forty-one poems in addition to two which had been crossed out, written by Mallarmé in 1859 and 1860, with the titles of twelve others that were missing. The additional three notebooks each bore the title *Glanes* (*Gleanings*) and the date 1860. In them Mallarmé had copied down some 800 lines by his favorite poets from Villon to Baudelaire. Mondor finally published his findings in 1954.[5] From the standpoint of influ-

15

ences the notebooks revealed what might have been expected, but there were other revelations also.

After the somewhat mawkish religiosity of Mallarmé's earliest prose, the poems of *Entre quatre murs* reveal the teenage turbulence of the young poet. Idylls, elegies, and ballads abound, filled with heaving bosoms and half-glimpsed thighs. Victor Hugo's influence is found from beginning to end with that of two other great romantic poets, Lamartine and Musset, appearing less frequently. Evidences of the later Parnassian school can be noted although they become more obvious in subsequent poems. The schoolboy had also read the Neoclassical poetry of André Chénier of the end of the eighteenth century and in one poem, "Sur la tombe de Béranger," he bids farewell to the poet who had died in 1857.

Classical allusions and romantic dreams, Spanish señoritas and seductive Bohemians, and satans and will-o'-the-wisps alternate with erotic visions and blasphemous impieties. Roses and lilies (*La rose aime le lys* in "Billet du matin"), the swan and the nymphs and the faun (*cygne au col neigeux* and *Les nymphes en riant fuient un faune lascif* in "Loeda"), and the azure in the tree branches (*L'azur se rit dans la ramure* in "Sourire") make their appearances. The alexandrine, the octosyllable, and the decasyllable are all tried. Even experiments with alternating lines of six and four syllables, to be used seriously later only in the "Cantique de Saint Jean," are essayed. Most important, this single notebook reveals that Mallarmé must have written in the one year of 1859 almost 2,000 lines of poetry,[6] and that from a writer who was soon to create his own legend of sterility.

The three notebooks of *Glanes* reveal that in 1860 Mallarmé read and translated Poe literally and at length and copied down more than 800 lines of Baudelaire, Sainte-Beuve, Hugo, and many other poets from the sixteenth to the nineteenth centuries. Such intense and voluminous activity is strangely at odds with the slender volume of poetry that was to be Mallarmé's lifetime production. While a longer and more detailed study of these four notebooks could be very informative, I shall limit myself to analyses of those poems that are easily and readily available in the *Oeuvres complètes*.

Further Gleanings

The earliest poem in Mallarmé's *Oeuvres complètes* is appropriately enough an occasional piece, since he wrote many such works throughout his life. The "Cantate pour la première communion," dated July 1858, is composed of a Chorus of six lines and three Verses, also of six lines. The Chorus asks the angels, those "Children of heaven," to celebrate "The joy and the happiness / Of the children of the earth!" The first Verse expresses the desire for the vows to mount to heaven "On the wings of Hope" and compares them to the incense "which is exhaled at the foot of the altar." Both this earliest poem, and the latest, which was not included by Mallarmé in his *Poésies* of 1887, treat Hope with a capital. The first line of the second Verse begins and ends with two forms of the same word, *Enfant—enfance,* a device Mallarmé would use frequently in later poems. The First Communion is a "mysterious wedding / Of strength and weakness," a "sweet drunkenness! / A prelude to heavenly joy." In the last Verse it has become the day to pray for mother, for those who revile us, for everyone. The final Chorus asks the angels to celebrate "The glory and the happiness" of these earthly children. The poem, whose sentimental banality cannot be denied, nevertheless exhibits a certain control of form and one is interested to note the word *azur* rhymed with *pur* in the first two lines of the Chorus, as it does in "Adieu" of July 1858, "Chant d'ivresse" of January, "Le Nuage" of March, and "Causerie d'adieu" of November 1859 in *Entre quatre murs,* where it is also rhymed twice with *obscur* and once with *sur.*

The second poem is really two poems, "Sa Fosse est creusée . . . ," dated June 1859, and "Sa Fosse est fermée" of 11 July the same year. In *Entre quatre murs* the former is dated 1 July and the latter simply July 1859. A note by Mallarmé indicates they were written in memory of a young American, Harriet Smyth, who died in England of tuberculosis during the summer of 1859. Mallarmé's younger sister Maria had died just two years earlier and certainly her memory is also evoked in the poems.

"Sa Fosse est creusée . . ." is composed of three sections, the first containing eleven quatrains of alexandrines. The second section includes ten lines of eight syllables, followed by a quatrain of alexandrines. The third section contains six quatrains in the *Oeuvres complètes,* seven quatrains of which one lacks a last line in *Entre quatre murs.* In both editions the last two quatrains are irregular, the next to the last ending in a hemistich and the last in a line of eight syllables. The figure of speech in the first line, *les épis d'or,* which could be translated "golden spikes" or "sheaves," returns in the third quatrain of the last section to give some unity to the poem. *Azur* again rhymes with *pur.*

Throughout the poem the monosyllables like *Hier* are pronounced as two syllables, dieresis in poetic license, augmenting the lugubrious tone. In the last section we learn that the young girl had never known her mother, which makes us think of Mallarmé's sister. The weeping brothers and sisters and the somber father of the last section are stock figures in such poetry.

The second poem, "Sa Fosse est fermée . . . ," is composed of 123 alexandrines in rhymed couplets except for line 27, which has no rhyme, obviously to emphasize the expression *un baiser du Très-Haut!* The idea of *La fleur rit aux épis* is taken up in the seventh line and brought back in lines 90 and 108. The young maiden sleeps under the weeping willow so dear to the romantics and to Shakespeare, whose England is evoked as Albion. *Azur* is rhymed twice with *pur* in twenty-six lines. The archangel hovers over both poems, as does the Hugo of the poems "Charles Vacquerie," "Claire," and "A Villequier" in his *Contemplations*.[7]

"L'Enfant prodigue" of 1861 is, on the other hand, the first poem to reveal the influence of Baudelaire. The metaphor involving the orange in the first of the five quatrains comes directly from the first poem of Baudelaire's *Les Fleurs du mal*, "Au lecteur." The vocabulary of the "Infinite" and the "Gulf" can be attributed to Hugo as well as Baudelaire, while "ecstatic perfumes" is more reminiscent of the latter. The expression *tes pieds qui calmeraient la mer* will become *mes pieds qui calmeraient la mer* in "Hérodiade" a few years later.

"Galanterie macabre," also of 1861, shows traces of the influence of Théophile Gautier in its opening lines as well as of Baudelaire in its closing stanzas.[8] Its twelve quatrains of alexandrines describe a squalid city suburb where the narrator saw "a funereally grotesque tableau," a very young, very poor, very dead woman. For the first time the wax of the candle is said to have wept (*la cire a déjà pleuré plus d'un mort*), a figure to be used later. In speaking of death Mallarmé says that "She intoxicates with azure our eyes" (*Elle enivre d'azur nos yeux*), an expression that also presages things to come. Romeo is there in company with the Demon, Satan, and Vice, while in the narrator's heart "ennui hangs its funereal flags" and memory is a sarcophagus with "unguents penetrating the gloom." Baudelaire would have approved.

Théodore de Banville would no doubt have approved of the twenty quatrains of lighthearted octosyllables in "A une laveuse blonde," again dated 1861. In his description of the pretty little washerwoman, Mallarmé goes back to the Cythera of the court of Louis XV and Madame de Pompadour. Boucher and Watteau depicted this site, which Baudelaire used for his own infernal purposes in "Un Voyage à Cythère." Here precious stones enter Mallarmé's poetry (*un vieux dauphine / Qui pleure à flots des pierreries*), as well as the old book (*ton livre aux écussons d'or*), the fan (*un éventail baigné d'écume*), and the swan (*le cygne câlin, cygne onduleux*). Someone is humming Gluck; and Chloe, Diana, Venus, under the name of Cypris, Leda, and even Eve, are all there. The poem is a charming description, worthy of Banville.

In "A un poète immoral" Mallarmé probably addressed himself to his new friend, the young teacher Emmanuel des Essarts. The twelve quatrains are precisely dated 11 December 1861 in the first two lines. The dream is mixed with cigar smoke, to which poetry is compared, an idea Mallarmé will use later in expressing his poetics. The Eve of all poets is there, painted this time by Watteau. Terpsichore and the fan (*un fol éventail*) are there as well. Another charming description equally worthy of Banville.

The sonnet in alexandrines, "Contre un poète parisien" of 1862, is dedicated to des Essarts. The belaureled Dante is contrasted with the naked Anacreon, while in the first tercet "the grand Bohemians" are described as "mad with azure." In the last tercet the Muse's "nimbused fleece" is compared to a monstrance (*la toison nimbée a l'air d'un ostensoir*), a vocabulary that recalls Baudelaire and Mallarmé's later images.

In the first of the four stanzas of "Soleil d'hiver," published 13 July 1862, the Parnassian *vermeil* rhymes with *sommeil* as it had in "L'Enfant prodigue" and "A un poète immoral." The same rhyme was used in "Heir. Aujourd'hui. Demain" of March 1859, and in "Poisson d'avril" and "Sourire," both dated April 1859, in *Entre quatre murs.* Such rhymes tend to disappear in Mallarmé's later works. Phoebus and the drunken, sleeping fauns (*O faunes ivres dans la mousse*) with their grapes are there. The sun god "with his red peruke," who in summer is a veritable swashbuckler, becomes in winter "nothing more than a bald Guritan," the comic character from Victor Hugo's *Ruy Blas,* who lets escape "a rusty ray." The note of humor, as in this poem, is afterwards confined to the numerous little occasional pieces Mallarmé wrote.

Another poem of 1862, "Mysticis umbraculis" (which might be freely translated as "Secret Bower"), carries the subtitle "Prose des fous," prose being used here somewhat in the ecclesiastical sense of a Latin hymn composed of rhymed lines without regular meter. Mal-

larmé later used the word in the title of one of his most famous poems.
The alexandrines are disposed in two tercets, each with one rhyme.
This extremely erotic poem describes a sleeping woman whose finger,
which by synecdoche stands for the whole hand, "without amethyst,"
unconsciously raises the batiste of her nightgown to reveal her stomach
which is like snow where has "Fallen the mossy nest of a gay
goldfinch."

Another poem in somewhat the same erotic vein is the "Sonnet" of
1862 or 1863. Mallarmé gives all the humorous reasons why some
nincompoop might one night "rub his tassled nightcap" against "his
cold and dry" wife's white bonnet, a night from which, "Oh Shakespeare and thou, Dante, there can be born a poet!"

The last of Mallarmé's youthful poems is "Le Château de l'Espé-
rance," probably of 1863, which he at one time considered including
in his *Poésies*. The title may have been suggested by Théophile Gautier's "Le Château du Souvenir,"[9] but certainly the image in the opening stanza, the first of four quatrains in octosyllables, came directly
from Baudelaire: "Your pale hair ripples / Amid the perfumes of your
skin." The hair becomes a flag with which the narrator storms the
castle only to find that "Hope rubs the wrong way and smooths down
/ Without a pale star shooting forth / The Night black as a black cat."
Night as a black cat and electricity as a star recall Baudelaire, while
the double use of *noir* at the beginning and end of the final line (*La
Nuit noire comme un chat noir*) will be repeated often. The image of the
star also will make frequent appearances. The broad, very rich rhymes
in -*ondoie* and -*apeau* of the first stanza are followed by the equally broad
-*lots* and -*once* in the second. In the third the first rhyme is the acute
-*ivre* while in the last stanza the sharp sibilant -*isse* contrasts with the
broad -*oir*. Rhymes in *i* and -*oir* will be favorites of Mallarmé. All in
all, a poem almost worthy of being included in the *Poésies*.

In these early gleanings we find many of the images, subjects,
themes, and literary devices that Mallarmé employed later in his mature poems. We can also understand why he did not care to include
them in his one published volume. The influences are too obvious.
Most quickly shed were the borrowings from Hugo and the other romantic poets. The Parnassian influence was more difficult to shake
and, like that of Baudelaire, perhaps never totally escaped. Enormous
effort was necessary to "de-Baudelaire-ize" as well as bowdlerize his
style and content. A certain preciousness, indigenous perhaps to

French poetic expression and language, remained with him forever. Mallarmé chose to publish only four poems that predated the one that appeared in *Le Nouveau Parnasse Satyrique* of 1866 and the eleven that were published in *Le Parnasse Contemporain,* also of 1866. In these sixteen poems, however, Mallarmé slowly but surely became his own poet, with a vision unique in French poetry and world poetry.

Chapter Three

Parnassus Conquered

The Way Up

Although one cannot claim that Mallarmé was totally unknown before his poems appeared in *Le Parnasse Contemporain* of 1866, one can say that their publication brought the twenty-four-year-old poet to the attention of the French literary elite. His first published poem was "Placet futile" of 1862, but the young teacher was condemned to spend five more years exiled in the provinces after his appearance in *Le Parnasse Contemporain* before his definitive return to Paris in 1871. After 1866 Mallarmé published something almost every year of his life.

For the edition of his poems that Mallarmé was preparing at the time of his death, he chose to greet his readers with a sonnet of 1893 entitled "Salut." By its nature the poem is well suited for the task but because it belongs to a later style I shall discuss it along with other poems of its period.

The first of the "First Poems" is "Le Guignon" ("The Jinx") which dates from 1862 and was reworked considerably fifteen years later. The title, the subject, and the form owe a great deal to Théophile Gautier and Baudelaire. Even traces of Gérard de Nerval have been found.[1] The poem in its final form is, however, completely worthy of Mallarmé.

Its twenty-one tercets of alexandrines, plus one line to complete the rhyme, are in terza rima. The classical caesura is observed for the most part with little, if any, enjambment. The subject of this first poem is, appropriately enough, the fate of the poet, the successful as well as the unsuccessful.

All poets are "beggars of azure" (*mendieurs d'azur*), visionaries, above the common herd but suffering from all the human faults and frailties. They go through life without its necessities, "Biting the golden lemon of bitter ideal" (*Mordant au citron d'or de l'idéal amer*), sucking at the breast "of sorrow as they did at that of dreams" (*Ils tettent la douleur comme ils tétaient le rêve*). But for every successful poet there are a hundred failures, those "Equals of Prometheus who lack a vulture!"

(*Egaux de Prométhée à qui manque un vautour!*). They suffer "under the whip of a raging monarch, / The Jinx" (*Ils courent sous le fouet d'un monarque rageur, / Le Guignon*). In the end these "Ridiculous martyrs" (*Dérisoires martyrs*), "these unobtrusive gods" (*ces dieux effacés*), "These harassed heroes" (*Ces héros excédés*), can only "hang themselves ridiculously on the lamp post" (*Vont ridiculement se pendre au réverbère*).

Mallarmé's vision has some of the sweeping movement of Hugo's "Les Djinns," some of the ghoulish, macabre atmosphere of many of Baudelaire's poems. The conclusion of "Le Guignon" recalls the sad suicide of Gérard de Nerval in 1855. This first poem foretells Mallarmé's lifelong preoccupation with the role and function of the poet and poetry.

The second poem, "Apparition," probably dates from 1863 but was not published until twenty years later. Its sixteen alexandrines contain inversions of word order and enjambments more characteristic of the later poetry. The sad moon, the weeping seraphim, the "white sobs" (*blancs sanglots*) drawn "from the dying viols" (*de mourantes violes*), anticipate Verlaine and the somewhat Pre-Raphaelite portrait of "Ophélie" by Rimbaud. "The azure of the corollas" (*l'azur des corolles*) and the "perfumed stars" (*étoiles parfumées*) are Mallarmé, however, while this bittersweet vision of "the blessed day of your first kiss" (*le jour béni de ton premier baiser*) stands in quiet contrast to the lugubrious vision of the poet that precedes it. The line "The plucking of a Dream from the heart that has plucked it" (*La cueillaison d'un Rêve au coeur qui l'a cueilli*) with its double *cueillaison—cueilli* again foretells Mallarmé's use of the same device while making us think of the beautiful line to come in "Hérodiade," "Rare limpidity of a heart that dreamt it" (*Rare limpidité d'un coeur qui le songea*).

The charming and somewhat precious sonnet in alexandrines of 1862 entitled "Placet futile" ("Useless Petition") was Mallarmé's first published poem and continues the tone and the subject matter of "Apparition." The poet speaks to his blond princess, comparing her to Hebe, the goddess of youth and cupbearer to the gods before Ganymede, begging her to "name us shepherd of your smiles" (*nommez-nous berger de vos sourires*). Her "divine coiffeurs are goldsmiths" (*les coiffeurs divins sont des orfèvres*), foreshadowing Hérodiade's metallic locks. But her "raspberry laughter" (*ris framboisés*) shares nothing with that melancholy princess although Love is "winged with a fan" (*ailé d'un éventail*), an object that will reappear later. Both Debussy and Ravel set this sonnet to music.

The most enigmatic of the four early poems is the sonnet "Le Pitre châtié" ("The Punished Clown"), which dates from 1864 but was reworked considerably and not published until twenty-three years later. The subject of the poet as clown may have been suggested by Baudelaire's prose poem "Vieux Saltimbanque" of 1861. One of the most startling details of the poem is the opening apposition "Eyes, lakes" (*Yeux, lacs*). Such concision and condensation exemplify Mallarmé's mature style.

Like the later poems this sonnet does not at first seem to make sense. After several readings, however, an idea begins to take shape. In the first quatrain the clown compares someone's eyes to lakes, speaks of his desire to be "reborn / Other than the actor [I] who by a gesture evoked / . . . the ignoble soot of the [stage] lamps" (*renaître / Autre que l'historien qui du geste évoquais / . . . la suie ignoble des quinquets*), and goes on to say that he has made a hole, a window, in the canvas of the circus tent, obviously in an attempt to escape his profession, his destiny as a clown. Although several ambiguities arise, the first person singular of *J'ai troué* must be the same as the first person singular subject of *évoquais*. The expression *Comme plume* suggests diverse alternatives: the sooty smoke may be rising from the oil lamps as the plume rises from the actor's hat since we know that Mallarmé associated the Hamlet of the second quatrain with a hat topped by a feather.[2] The actor may evoke the stage with his gestures as the writer does with his pen,[3] or one of the actor's gestures may be the movement of the feather caused by the shaking of his head. As we shall discover in analyzing Mallarmé's poetry, such alternatives are almost never mutually exclusive but generally totally inclusive, making possible a wealth of associations.

In the second quatrain the first-person narrator has become a "limpid, traitorous swimmer" (*limpide nageur traître*) in the lakes of the first quatrain, traitorous precisely because he wants to renounce "the bad / Hamlet" (*le mauvais / Hamlet*) he has been. The idea that the swimmer, with his "remultiplied bounds" (*A bonds multipliés*), compares his action to innovating "A thousand sepulchers" (*Mille sépulcres*), the thousand that can also refer to the numberless waves, brings us back to the idea in the first quatrain of being reborn, for to be reborn one must die. The swimmer would plunge into the tombs bathed, cleansed, baptized by the water, thus "virgin" (*vierge*).

The first tercet compares the sun to the "Hilarious gold of the cymbal beaten by fists" (*Hilare or de cymbale à des poings irrité*), adding sound effects to the visual and tactile. The sun becomes the reality of day striking the clown's "nakedness / Which, pure, exhaled itself from my mother-of-pearl freshness" (*la nudité / Qui pure s'exhala de ma fraîcheur de nacre*). The lines remind us of those we shall hear from Hérodiade in which she speaks of her "white shudder" of nakedness which must be hidden from "the tepid azure of summer" lest she die.

In the final tercet the sunny purity of the clown's cleansed nakedness is contrasted with his usual state, the "Rancid night of the skin" (*Rance nuit de la peau*), the disagreeable second skin of makeup he must wear. When it has been washed off, the realization comes that the makeup was the clown's true reality, his only genius, his whole art (*tout son sacre*). The water of the lakes of the first line becomes in the last line "the perfidious water of glaciers" (*l'eau perfide des glaciers*), pure, cold, unbearable. Thus is the clown punished for wanting to foresake the art that is his true self.

The key word of the poem is *sacre*. By its use Mallarmé extends the limits of the sonnet from those of the vision of the clown who, in renouncing for whatever cause—and that cause is not made clear in this final version—his role as symbolized by his makeup, has renounced his true self. The role of the clown is extended to the role every artist—and with Mallarmé we think first of the poet—must play. The conventions, the discipline, the sacrifices implicit in every art must become so much a part of the artist that he is no longer himself without them. All of the harsh rhymes, *-aître, -ais, -té, -acre,* emphasize the agony of the artist who in thinking to seek himself would lose himself. The dilemma of the artist has perhaps never been expressed in such explicit and yet such general terms. The poem remains one of Mallarmé's great creations.

The View from the Top

These four poems among Mallarmé's "First Poems" are the only ones he was willing to include in his *Poésies* of 1887 but not, for some reason, in *Le Parnasse Contemporain* of 1866. He did include in the *Poésies* one poem that had appeared in *Le Nouveau Parnasse Satyrique du dix-neuvième siècle,* also of 1866, the eleven poems that appeared in *Le Parnasse Contemporain,* and one poem that dated from 1865 but that was not published until 1883. These thirteen poems illustrate Mallarmé's manner before and during the time he lost himself in the two long compositions, "Hérodiade" and *L'Après-Midi d'un Faune.* After purging himself, so to speak, with these enormous undertakings, he returned to shorter forms.

While the first of these poems, "Une négresse . . . ," belongs to the extremely erotic vein already witnessed in "Mysticis umbraculis," we must remember that it is satirical in nature, having been published in *Le Nouveau Parnasse Satyrique*. Although some of its figures are commonplace, others reveal a sense of the comic completely unexpected amidst the high seriousness of the majority of Mallarmé's poems. They also forewarn us to expect the erotic that may be half-hidden in the more difficult poems.

The comparison in the first quatrain of the Negress to the somewhat comical *goinfre* or glutton sets the tone of the poem. The description in the second quatrain of the movement of her boots continues the humorous vein: "She darts the dark shock of her boots / Like some tongue" (*Elle darde le choc obscur de ses bottines / Ainsi que quelque langue*). One most frequently finds the verb *darder* used in its figurative sense, as "the sun darts its rays" or "to dart a furious look at someone." We must also remember that the noun *dard* is used to designate the harmless tongue of a serpent. The comparison here of the movement of the boots to "some tongue unskilled in pleasure" (*quelque langue inhabile au plaisir*) conjures up the vision of the feet wobbling wildly in the air while the figure itself is salaciously suggestive.

The comparisons with animals in the third quatrain, "the frightened gazelle-like nudity" (*la nudité peureuse de gazelle*) and "like a crazy elephant" (*tel un fol éléphant*), juxtapose incongruously these two denizens of the jungle. On the other hand, the comparisons to the mouth and the shell in the final quatrain are not very original and thus something of a letdown. They do, however, emphasize the eroticism of the poem. When the critic gets too carried away by the arcane hermeticism of the later poems, he should return periodically to this sensual vision of humorous but human reality.

The first poem in *Le Parnasse Contemporain* was "Les Fenêtres" ("Windows") of 1863, written in London. Its sources have been traced to Sainte-Beuve and through him to the English poet William Bowles.[4] The poem is divided exactly in half. In the first five quatrains of alexandrines a dying old man whose mouth is "voracious for the blue azure" (*d'azur bleu vorace*) drags himself painfully to the hospital window. There he forgets the horrors of illness and death, "and when evening bleeds among the [roof] tiles" (*et quand le soir saigne parmi les tuiles*) his eye "Sees golden galleys, beautiful as swans, / Sleeping on a river of purple and perfumes" (*Voit des galères d'or, belles comme des cygnes, / Sur un fleuve de pourpre et de parfums dormir*).

In the last five quatrains the narrator, "seized by disgust for man with his hard soul" (*pris du dégoût de l'homme à l'âme dure*) and vulgar appetites, would flee to the window where one can turn his back on life and see himself transformed into an angel. He would, like *"Le Pitre châtié,"* be reborn, "But alas! Here-below is master" (*Mais, hélas! Ici-bas est maître*) and there is no way of avoiding life except "At the risk of falling throughout eternity" (*—Au risque de tomber pendant l'éternité*).

Seven of the twenty rhymes of this poem are based on the harsh sound *i* and five on the equally acute *é*. *Azur* again rhymes with *sûr* and in one line of twelve syllables there are five nasal *m*'s: *Je me mire et me vois ange! et je meurs, et j'aime.* Even more important is the symbol of the window. Its glass is described as "bathed by eternal dews" (*lavé d'éternelles rosées*), gilt by "the chaste morning of Infinity" (*Que dore le matin chaste de l'Infini*). "Whether the window be art or mysticity" (*Que la vitre soit l'art, soit la mysticité*), the glass becomes "crystal insulted by the monster" (*le cristal par le monstre insulté*) of the narrator's own reflection. He would in the end like to break through it in order to flee, but such evasion is impossible. Mallarmé's preoccupation with mirrors and glass culminates in the letter of 1867 quoted in chapter 1 and in the extensive symbolic use in "Hérodiade" and other later poems.

While the little poem "Les Fleurs," of 1864, undoubtedly owes something to Hugo,[5] it is also a perfect example of Mallarmé's Parnassian period. The "golden avalanches of old azure" (*Des avalanches d'or du vieil azur*), "the eternal snow of the stars" (*la neige éternelle des astres*), "the swans with their slender necks" (*les cygnes au col fin*), the "Vermilion" or "Vermeil" (*Vermeil*), "the modesty of trampled dawns" (*la pudeur des aurores foulées*), the hyacinth, the myrtle, and "the cruel rose" (*la rose / Cruelle*) are all there. For the first time Mallarmé introduces Hérodiade into his poetry and along with her "the sobbing whiteness of lilies" (*la blancheur sanglotante des lys*), "the blue incense of pale horizons" (*l'encens bleu des horizons pâlis*), "the weeping moon" (*la lune qui pleure*), the cithern and the censers, and "great flowers with the balmy Death" (*De grandes fleurs avec la balsamique Mort*). The conclusion includes the significant word *las*, "For the tired poet whom life weakens" (*Pour le poète las que la vie étiole*). We have already seen the word in the opening of the preceding poem, *Las du triste hôpital . . .* , and we shall see it again three poems later in "Las de l'amer repos. . . ." The word reveals a great deal about Mallarmé's pessimism of the period, his fa-

tigue, his fear of sterility, his difficulties with creating poetry. All the
flowers of the world hardly recompense the suffering poet.

The little sonnet of 1862, "Renouveau" ("Renewal"), continues the
same theme. "The sickly spring" (*Le printemps maladif*) is contrasted
with "Winter, the season of the serene art, lucid winter" (*L'hiver, saison
de l'art serein, l'hiver lucide*), while the poet laments his impotence. His
skull is bound by "a circle of iron . . . like an old tomb" (*mon crâne /
Qu'un cercle de fer serre ainsi qu'un vieux tombeau*) and he wanders "after a
vague and beautiful dream" (*j'erre après un rêve vague et beau*). Again he
is "tired" (*las*) and waits "for his ennui to rise" (*J'attends, en m'abîmant
que mon ennui s'élève*), but "the Azure laughs on the hedge" (*l'Azur rit
sur la haie*) and the poet is left to his fate. The double *L'hiver—l'hiver*
is used again while interior rhymes like *cercle-fer-serre-j'erre* will be employed later. Obvious opposites like *m'abîmant—s'élève* will be implied
rather than stated. The impotence (*impuissance*) and boredom (*ennui*) of
the poem as well as the skull bound by a circle of iron recall both Poe
and Baudelaire.

Still another sonnet, "Angoisse" ("Anguish") of 1864, owes something to Baudelaire.[6] "The incurable boredom" (*l'incurable ennui*), "the
unknown curtains of remorse" (*les rideaux inconnus du remords*), and the
"dark lies" (*noirs mensonges*) all suggest Mallarmé's great predecessor.
The idea that "Vice, eating away my native nobility" (*le Vice, rongeant
ma native noblesse*) has marked the poet with sterility, as well as the
vision of the poet as "pale, wasted, haunted by my shroud" (*pâle, défait,
hanté par mon linceul*), suggest Baudelaire. Just as in "Les Fenêtres" and
"Renouveau," the poet attempts to flee without success.

A much better poem is "Las de l'amer repos . . ." of the same year.
Its twenty-eight alexandrines are divided into stanzas of ten and eighteen lines. In many respects the poem sums up Mallarmé's life at this
point and recapitulates his poetic theory at this stage of his
development.

In the first stanza he speaks of his idleness that is an insult to the
fame for which he gave up his "adorable childhood" (*l'enfance / Adorable*)
spent in "woods of roses under the natural / Azure" (*des bois de roses avec
l'azur / Naturel*). The circular movement of the first stanza is maintained by the reintroduction of roses twice in the next to the last line.
Azur rhymes with *dur* while the lugubrious images of sterility and
death utilized in "Angoisse" are continued. The poet is again "seven
times more tired" (*plus las sept fois*) of the "harsh pact" (*pacte dur*) every
creator must make if he is to write. During his long evening vigils he

must hollow out a new grave "In the cold and avaricious terrain" (*Dans le terrain avare et froid*) of his brain, which is a "Grave digger without pity for sterility" (*Fossoyeur sans pitié pour la stérilité*). In spite of himself his brain keeps working while each night lost is another step toward the grave. What will he be able to say to Dawn when the cemetery or death unites all these "empty holes" (*trous vides*), which are his wasted, unproductive evenings? The double *roses*—*roses* as well as the ambiguities of the last three lines are indicative of Mallarmé's style at this time. The conclusion reads:

> —What can I say to this Dawn, O Dreams, visited
> By roses, when, out of fear of its livid roses,
> The vast cemetery unites the empty holes?—
> —*Que dire à cette Aurore, ô Rêves, visité*
> *Par les roses, quand, peur de ses roses livides,*
> *Le vaste cimetière unira les trous vides?*—

Both *visité* and *peur* can refer either to the speaker or the cemetery. Are these pale roses his hopes or dreams or are they dawn or are they the wasted spot of light given off by his lamp, wasted because unproductive? They could be all of these.

In the second stanza the poet wants to forsake "the voracious Art" (*l'Art vorace*) of his "cruel land" (*pays / Cruel*), constantly reproached as he is by his "friends, the past, genius, / And my lamp" (*mes amis, le passé, le génie, / Et ma lampe*), the lamp that has witnessed his agony throughout the long, painful nights while he waited for inspiration. He would like to turn to the art of Chinese painting on porcelain cups where the roses of childhood of the first stanza reappear but this time "bizarre" and "transparent," a veritable extension of the soul. In such an art death becomes the wise man's only dream. Such an artist can choose, serenely, to paint a young landscape. The five lines which follow are an admirable statement of Mallarmé's ideas about symbolism at this stage of his development:

> A line of thin and pale azure would be
> A lake, amid the sky of naked porcelain,
> A bright crescent destroyed by a white cloud
> Soaks its calm horn in the waters' ice,
> Not far from three great eyelashes of emerald, reeds.
> *Une ligne d'azur mince et pâle serait*
> *Un lac, parmi le ciel de porcelaine nue,*

Un clair croissant perdu par une blanche nue
Trempe sa corne calme en la glace des eaux,
Non loin de trois grands cils d'émeraude, roseaux.

The repetition of the hard *c* followed by the liquid *l*'s and *r*'s in *clair croissant* and *corne calme* conjure up the icy waters mentioned in the conclusion of "Le Pitre châtié," just as the abrupt apposition of *cils d'émeraude, roseaux* reminds us of the opening of that poem. While symbolism is still a one-to-one relationship for Mallarmé in this poem, the delicate, fragile beauty of the creation will be found in many of his later poems.

The little sonnet "Le Sonneur" ("The Bell Ringer") was published in 1862 and was thus among Mallarmé's first. In it he speaks again of the poet's plight, comparing it this time to that of the bell ringer who after all his efforts hears only a far-off tinkling. The poet in his "anxious night" (*nuit désireuse*) pulls the rope "to ring the Ideal" (*à sonner l'Idéal*), but all he gets is "a faithful plumage of cold sins" (*De froids péchés s'ébat un plumage féal*) frolicking about and a voice that reaches him only "in snatches and hollow" (*par bribes et creuse*). The poet, "tired of having pulled in vain" (*fatigué d'avoir en vain tiré*), will remove the stone from the end of the rope and hang himself, a fate that recalls the conclusion of "Le Guignon," also of 1862.

Baudelaire and, to a much lesser extent, Musset[7] are to be found in Mallarmé's sonnet "Tristesse d'été" ("Summer Sadness") of 1864. The narrator regards his sleeping loved one on the sand under the sun. The mixture of hair and water images recalls Baudelaire: "the gold of your hair" (*l'or de tes cheveux*) in which the sun "heats a languorous bath" (*chauffe un bain langoureux*) and "your hair is a tepid river" (*ta chevelure est une rivière tiède*). The same sun consumes "the incense" (*l'encens*) on her "hostile cheek" (*joue ennemie*). "The immutable calm of this white blaze" (*De ce blanc flamboiement l'immuable accalmie*) also made her say, "We shall never be a single mummy / Beneath the ancient desert and the happy palms!" (*Nous ne serons jamais une seule momie / Sous l'antique désert et les palmiers heureux!*). In her hair the narrator would like "to drown without shivering the soul" (*noyer sans frissons l'âme*) that possesses them both and "find this Nothingness" (*trouver ce Néant*) she does not know. He will taste "the makeup wept" (*le fard pleuré*) by her eyelashes to see if it has "The insensitiveness of the azure and of stones" (*L'insensibilité de l'azur et des pierres*). Like this consuming but enduring love that would make of the two lovers a thing, a single mummy lost beneath the desert, here burning indifference could give to the stricken heart the insensitiveness of things, "of the azure and of stone," the high and low, the ineffable and the material, the far away and the near at hand. Mallarmé expresses here the nostalgia of love and of the lover in a brief, sad, summer song.

Mallarmé's preoccupation with *azur* finally exploded in the poem entitled "L'Azur" of. 1863–64. He wrote to his friend Cazalis that its nine quatrains of alexandrines had cost him a great effort.[8] Part of the problem was, as he put it, that while "banishing a thousand lyric graciousnesses and beautiful lines which ceaselessly haunted my brain, I wanted to remain implacably within my subject." Only by doing so could he rid himself of this haunting *azur,* which intruded on so many of his thoughts and found partial and unsatisfactory expression in so many of his poems. After "Hérodiade" Mallarmé freed himself little by little from this paralyzing preoccupation although the fear must have stayed with him until his dying day.

In his own analysis of the poem Mallarmé hints at his theory of composition that took its final form in his letter of October 1864 to the same friend quoted in chapter 1: "To describe not the thing, but the effect it produces." The circular movement of the poem goes from the opening phrase *De l'éternel azur* to the final word *l'Azur.* As Mallarmé wrote:

. . . the first word, which expresses the first idea, in addition to the fact that it contributes to the general *effect* of the poem, also serves to prepare for the last [idea].

The *effect produced,* without a dissonance, without a frill, even an adorable one, which distracts,—that's what I'm hungering for. (C1:103–4)

And that is what Mallarmé accomplished.

In the first stanza "the serene irony of the eternal azure" (*De l'éternel azur la sereine ironie*) overwhelms "the powerless poet" (*Le poète impuissant*) lost in "a sterile desert" (*un désert stérile*). Even though he shuts his eyes in the second stanza he can feel its look as intense as "crushing remorse" (*remords atterrant*) on his "empty soul" (*âme vide*) and he asks, "Where to flee?" (*Où fuir?*). In the third he begs the fog to rise up and with its "monotonous ashes" (*cendres monotones*) and "long tatters of mist" (*longs haillons de brume*) to blot out the azure. In the fourth he prays "Dear Boredom" (*Cher Ennui*) to stop up "the great blue holes wickedly made by the birds" (*Les grands trous bleus que font méchamment les oiseaux*). That he prays to boredom "confirms my powerlessness," as Mallarmé wrote to Cazalis (C1:104). In the fifth stanza he asks that the chimneys continue to smoke and that "a wandering prison of soot blot out . . . the sun" (*de suie une errante prison / Eteigne . . . / Le soleil*). By the sixth stanza "The Sky is dead" (*Le Ciel est mort*). He asks matter, the last resort of the powerless, "the joy of the Powerless" he wrote to Cazalis, to grant "Forgetfulness of the cruel Ideal and of Sin" (*L'oubli de l'Idéal cruel et du Péché*). He also wrote to his friend: "Tired of the evil which gnaws at me, I want to taste the ordinary happiness of the crowd." In the seventh stanza he compares his brain to an empty "pot of makeup lying at the foot of a wall" (*le pot de fard gisant au pied du mur*). The reference to makeup recalls "Le Pitre châtié" and the conclusion of "Tristesse d'été." His brain no longer possesses the art of "decking out the sobbing idea" (*attifer la sanglotante idée*), is no longer capable of giving voice to thought.

In the last two stanzas defeat is acknowledged. As Mallarmé wrote to Cazalis, "The enemy is a spectre, the dead sky *returns*." "The Azure triumphs" (*L'Azur triomphe*) and he hears it singing "In the bells" (*Dans les cloches*). It has become a voice which "issues forth from the living metal in blue angeluses" (*Du métal vivant sort en bleus angélus*). In the final stanza its sound "rolls through the mist" (*roule par la brume*) and "goes through / Your native agony like a sure sword" (*traverse / Ta native agonie ainsi qu'un glaive sûr*). The last line is one final outcry: "*I am haunted. The Azure! the Azure! the Azure! the Azure!*" (*Je suis hanté. L'Azur! l'Azur! l'Azur! l'Azur!*). The word resounds like ringing bells. As Mallarmé wrote to Cazalis: "All of this poignant revelation was necessary in order to motivate the sincere and bizarre cry at the end" (C1:105). His effort had been "to combine, in perfect harmony, the dramatic element hostile to the idea of pure and subjective poetry with the serenity and the calm of lines necessary for the Beauty." The poem becomes a sort of poetic art for Mallarmé, or as he modestly put it, "a very poorly written and formless sketch of an article on art." Almost every poem he writes becomes an illustration, direct or indirect, of his theory of art. He never strays far from his true subject, creation, and more specifically poetic creation. "L'Azur" is one of the more powerful early revelations of the anguish of the poet haunted by beauty and perfection, sterility and ennui.

The first line of "Brise marine" ("Sea Breeze") of 1865 has become one of the most often quoted of Mallarmé and of all French literature:

"The flesh is sad, alas! and I've read all the books" (*La chair est triste, hélas! et j'ai lu tous les livres*). The question of "Where to flee?" of "L'Azur" has become a nostalgic exclamation "To flee! to flee yonder!" (*Fuir! là-bas fuir!*). The idea of suddenly leaving one's loved ones for an exotic land had been expressed by Baudelaire[9] among others, but the treatment of the subject is Mallarmé's.

The sixteen alexandrines are divided into two stanzas of ten and six lines. The boredom expressed in the first line of the first stanza is repeated by the word "A Boredom" (*Un Ennui*) of the first line of the second. In his tedium the narrator can feel the joy of the birds "amidst the unknown foam and the skies" (*parmi l'écume inconnue et les cieux!*). Nothing, neither the well-known gardens reflected in the narrator's eyes, nor the bright glow shed by his lamp, nor the young mother feeding her infant can restrain this heart once it has soaked itself in the sea. The empty paper on the poet's desk remains so because the narrator cannot bring himself to diminish its purity, its whiteness, no matter how much he is attracted to it by the desire to write. The desire to flee, "I shall depart!" (*Je partirai!*), will be echoed conditionally by Hérodiade, *J'y partirais*.

The narrator begs the steamer to lift its anchor for "an exotic nature" (*une exotique nature*), for in his weariness he still believes "in the supreme good-bye of handkerchiefs" (*l'adieu suprême des mouchoirs*), supreme because they are last to be seen in separation. The possibility exists that these very masts will invite a storm, leaving one stranded without so much as a desert isle. In spite of the danger the heart of the fifth line is asked in the last line to listen to the sailors' song. The rhymes in the last stanza are the broad liquid sounds of -*oirs, -rages,* and -*lots,* while *mâts* is repeated three times in three lines, twice in a single line. The rhythm of the last two lines expresses very well the combination of danger and nostalgia:

> . . . the shipwrecks
> Lost, without masts, without masts nor fertile isles . . .
> But, oh my heart, hear the song of the sailors.
> . . . *les naufrages*
> *Perdus, sans mâts, sans mâts, ni fertiles îlots . . .*
> *Mais, ô mon coeur, entends le chant des matelots.*

While the last line recalls the rhythm of the closing line of Baudelaire's "Recueillement," the poem with its allusion to the poet at his work table before the white paper combined with the desire to flee is a genuine expression of Mallarmé's obsessions. The little ten-line poem "Soupir" ("Sigh") of 1864 recalls both Baudelaire and Sainte-Beuve.[10] Mallarmé himself called it "an autumnal reverie,"[11] All of the elements of autumn are here. The poet's rising soul is compared to the water in a fountain that mounts to the sky, "sighs towards the Azure" (*soupire vers l'Azur*), "the compassionate Azure of pale and pure October" (*l'Azur attendri d'Octobre pâle et pur*). *Azur* rhymes with *pur* while being reflected in the great basins where fallen leaves wander. The *errant* of line 3 becomes *erre* in line 9, while all disappears in a long ray of yellow sunlight. Opposites, the sky and the water, the high and the low, the "infinte languor" (*langueur infinie*) and "the still water" (*l'eau morte*) and "the wild agony" (*la fauve agonie*) are contrasted as well as the falling of the leaves and the rising of the water in the fountain. Such variations play an important part in Mallarmé's longer poems to come. The poem is as suave as anything Verlaine wrote but without his sentimentality.

In addition to "Le Guignon," Mallarmé wrote a second poem in terza rima, "Aumône" ("Alms"). Although it dates from 1862, Mallarmé revised this poem several times until it arrived at its present state in 1887. The eight tercets, plus one line to complete the rhyme, express ironically the horror and futility of almsgiving. In the first tercet the beggar is compared to the "Senile nursling of an avaricious nipple" (*Sénile nourrisson d'une tétine avare*), avaricious because the beggar has so little to eat. He has wheedled the alms only in order to stretch out his life "coin by coin" (*pièce à pièce*). Mallarmé uses the unusual figure of straining (*égoutter*) as if the beggar were attempting to lengthen his life drop by drop at the same time as coin by coin. The two ideas are combined with a third, the tolling of the death-knell (*en égoutter ton glas*), as if the beggar were attempting to space out the inevitable tollings of the bell.

The beggar is exhorted to draw "from the dear metal some bizarre sin" (*Tire du métal cher quelque péché bizarre*), to kiss it, to blow on it "a burning fanfare" (*une ardente fanfare*) until it writhes. If he spends the money on tobacco all of these houses can become like a church with its incense. Just as prayers mount to heaven on the incense, so the tobacco, "cradler of a blue rift [in the clouds]" (*berceur d'une bleue éclaircie*), can "wordlessly roll forth orisons" (*Le tabac sans parler roule les oraisons*). *Eclaircie* can mean a break in the clouds or the fog, a spell of sunny weather, or figuratively a bright period in life. Tobacco could do all that, and if it is as powerful as opium it could "smash the pharmacy" (*Et l'opium puissant brise la pharmacie!*), that is, make all other drugs seem weak in comparison, render the rest of the pharmacy useless. Perhaps the beggar would prefer to buy a drink. In line 11 the narrator addresses the beggar, asking if he wants to tear the satin, dresses, and skin (*Robes et peau, veux-tu lacérer le satin*), or it could mean *do you want* to tear the satin of the fine dresses and the carefully tended skin of the inhabitants of "the princely cafés" (*les cafés princiers*) in front of which he waits for morning. Does he want "to drink in the happy saliva inertia" (*boire en la salive heureuse l'inertie*), that is, find forgetfulness in the beery foam? Inside the café, beautifully decorated as it is, "the people throw a banquet to the beggar at the window" (*On jette au mendiant de la vitre, un festin*).

When the drunken beggar at last issues forth, shivering in his wretched clothing, dawn has become "a lake of golden wine" (*l'aurore est un lac de vin d'or*) and he "swears he has stars in his throat" (*Et tu jures avoir au gosier les étoiles!*). If the beggar does not bother to count up his treasure, he might even buy a plume for his hat or a candle at compline for some saint in whom he still believes. These are not foolish suggestions, since life is long for those who are hungry (*La terre s'ouvre vieille à qui crève de faim*). The giver hates to think of another alms and wishes to be forgotten. His final word to the beggar is "And above all, brother, don't go buy bread" (*Et surtout ne va pas, frère, acheter du pain*). The poet, like the beggar, has his dreams; like the clown, his sad moments. None can live by bread alone. Even the beggar cannot always be practical.

The last poem Mallarmé included in his *Poésies* before "Hérodiade" was "Don du poème" ("Gift of the poem"), probably written in 1865, at the same time he was composing the longer poem, but not published until 1883. Exegetes have gone back to Vergil's *Georgics* to find Idumea and palms mentioned in one line and traced them to Boileau's *Satires* in classical French literature.[12] One critic found Idumea used as a rhyme by Vigny among the romantic poets.[13] In any event, Hérodiade was a princess of Idumea, and the poem recounts the birth of a poem, probably "Hérodiade," in fourteen dense alexandrines. The poem is like a "child on an Idumean night" (*enfant d'une nuit d'Idumée*), born of the darkness, brought forth by the poet alone. The night and black of the first two lines contrast with the whiteness and azure of the last two lines. At first *Noire* seems to refer to night, but reading further one finds it modifying dawn, described as having "a place and bleeding wing bereft of feathers" (*à l'aile saignante et pâle, déplumée*). The association of dawn with wings and feathers is used at greater length by Mallarmée in "Hérodiade." As in the latter poem, dawn shines "Through the glass burned with spices and gold" (*Par le verre brûlé d'aromates et d'or*) on the inside, "Through the window panes icy and mournful" (*Par les carreaux glacés, hélas! mornes encor*) on the outside. One commentator finds the "glass burned with spices and gold" to be the oil-filled glass of the lamp with the spices suggesting the household odors. His development of the idea of natural versus man-made light is an interesting one.[14]

The light of dawn meets the light of "the angelic lamp" (*la lampe angélique*), angelic because it was witness to the birth of the poem. The effect is like "Palms!" (*Palmes!*) when the rays of the lamp spread out like palm leaves in the dark. The *elle* seems at first to refer either to dawn or the lamp, but it actually refers to the solitude of this early moment, blue with cold and sterile in spite of the birth that has just taken place. As the moment reveals to the father "this relic" (*cette relique*) of the perfect poem the poet aspired to create, the solitude shuddered at the sight of such a pitiful creation and the father was already "attempting a hostile smile" (*essayant un sourire ennemi*), a smile because the poem is his flesh and blood, hostile because the poem is so much less than the poet had hoped for.

In the concluding six lines the poet asks the woman nursing her daughter to welcome this "horrible birth" (*horrible naissance*). *La berceuse* with her daughter could refer to Mallarmé's own wife and daughter Geneviève with their innocence and cold feet, innocent because untouched by the cares of the poet, cold because of poverty and the early morning hour. *La berceuse* could also refer to the solitude that cradles and nurses the poet into creation. She could also be the female element that must now receive the poem-child and nurse and nurture it at her breast "From which woman flows in sibylline whiteness / For lips made hungry by the air of virgin azure" (*Par qui coule en blancheur sibylline la femme / Pour les lèvres que l'air du vierge azur affame*). The only sound is that of the woman's voice "recalling viol and harpsichord" (*rappelant viole et clavecin*), the voice by which she soothes and lulls the newborn infant into life. On another level the virgin azure symbolizes the pure ideal that haunts the poet even after his most perfect creation. The poem remains the poet's only gift, imperfect though the poem may be.

The seventeen poems just discussed are a prelude to two longer and larger works that were to occupy Mallarmé for years and, in the case of "Hérodiade," all of his life. In the early poems one finds echoes and reminiscences of Mallarmé's predecessors but occasionally and most frequently in those poems he reworked later, the reader finds the true Mallarmé, enigmatic but not hermetic, difficult but not impossible. The beauties revealed by these poems are only a suggestion of the beauties to come. As Mallarmé becomes more surely himself, his poetry becomes more distinctly a voice and an expression never heard before, or after, in French literature.

Chapter Four
The Shadow of a Princess

The subject of Hérodiade, or Salomé as she is better known in English, has been a popular one ever since the Bible. Her story was told both by Matthew (14:1–11) and Mark (6:17–28) and represents all that is Eastern and exotic, strange and cruel, voluptuous and evil, morbid and decadent. It is, in addition, the classical tale of revenge through trickery. Consecrated as it is because it appears in the Bible, the incident takes on an aura both holy and heroic, involving that infallible element of a good story, martyrdom.

The Many Salomés

In the biblical story Salomé remains unnamed and innocent. Her stepfather, Herod Antipas, tetrarch of Galilee, had thrown John the Baptist in prison because he had dared to say that it was not lawful for Herod to marry his sister-in-law Hérodias, Salomé's mother. Herod was afraid, however, to have John put to death because the people considered him a prophet. At Herod's birthday feast Salomé danced before Herod and his guests and so pleased the old man that he swore to give her anything she wanted. This was just the occasion for which Hérodias had been waiting. She instructed Salomé to ask for John's head on a platter. Herod immediately regretted his impetuous generosity but because of the oath sworn before his guests, he fulfilled Salomé's request. She in turn presented John's head to her mother. Thus she was guilty only of being a dutiful daughter. In addition to the great similarity of names, this mother–daughter complicity has caused great confusion among artists and writers between Hérodias and Hérodiade.

That a Jewish princess would have danced before her father and his guests is highly improbable historically, but it makes a good tale. The biblical Salomé nevertheless also belongs to history. We know that she was the granddaughter of Herod the Great and the daughter of Herod Philip and Hérodias. Not only was her stepfather her uncle but also the man she first married, the Tetrarch of Trachonitis, who was her uncle on her father's side and her great-uncle on her mother's side. Such a marriage would hardly seem destined to last. Salomé later married her first cousin, Aristobulus, king of Armenia Minor and ultimately king of Chalcis, and she died probably around 90–95 A.D. The great Jewish historian, Flavius Josephus, gave Salomé her name in his *Jewish Antiquities* of the first century. The Church Fathers of the fourth century, including among others Eusebius of Caesarea, Saint John Chrysostom, and Saint Jerome, found it advantageous to make an evil woman of Salomé in their interpretations of religious history. Thus we find Salomé portrayed much later in St. Mark's Cathedral in Venice, in the cathedral at Rouen in France, at Hildesheim in Germany, and at Ely in England, to name only a few. Salomé really came into her own, however, as a subject for painters and sculptors, when John the Baptist was adopted by the city of Florence as its patron saint.

There Andrea Pisano sculpted her story in bas-relief on the baptistery doors of the cathedral in the fourteenth century. Giotto, Lorenzetti, and Masolino da Panicale all depicted her in one way or another and just a hundred years after Pisano, Donatello created another famous bas-relief of Salomé. In the fifteenth century Giovanni di Paolo, Fra Filippo Lippi, and an unknown artist of the School of Leonardo painted her. Above all, Benozzo Gozzoli did a charming little oil now in the National Gallery in Washington. Later Lucas Cranach, Titian, and Caravaggio all did well-known portraits.

With the early artists Salomé was of course only incidental to the story of the martyrdom of John the Baptist, their real subject. Slowly, over the centuries, Herod and Hérodias, their guests, and the dance all fade from the picture, leaving generally only Salomé with a companion who could be her mother, her nurse, or her maid, and the head of John. Thus she is portrayed in Titian's painting, a reproduction of which Mallarmé possessed.

Salomé did not fare so well in the seventeenth and eighteenth centuries, but early in the nineteenth she appealed enormously to the romantic temperament. The greatest French romantic painter, Eugène Delacroix, depicted her on the ceiling of the Palais Bourbon, today the Chamber of Deputies in Paris, between 1838 and 1847. Stendhal compared beautiful Italian women several times to Leonardo da Vinci's "Hérodiade." Unfortunately, there is no "Hérodiade" by Leonardo. Critics think he must have been referring to the painting by Bernardino Luini. Nevertheless, Mathilde de la Mole in Stendhal's novel *Le*

Rouge et le noir (1830) kisses the severed head of her lover, the first heroine I have found who did so, thus setting the scene for Oscar Wilde's *Salomé* late in the century. In 1841 the German lyric poet Heinrich Heine wrote a series of satirical poems, subsequently translated by the author into French, under the title *Atta Troll* in which Hérodias got her due. She, too, kisses the severed head.

The immediate influence upon Mallarmé, in addition to Baudelaire's sonnet "Avec ses vêtements ondoyants et nacrés," was in all probability Flaubert's long short story of 1862 about the daughter of Hamilcar, Salammbô. Many critics have pointed out the resemblances between the two aloof and mysterious heroines, their hair, their jewelry, their virginity, the incense, the azure plains, the lions, the mirror, the dialogue with the nurse. Something of the same heroine is to be found in Villiers de l'Isle-Adam's philosophical novel *Isis* of the same year. Flaubert was so fascinated by the subject that he published another long short story in 1877, this time about Salomé's mother, entitled *Hérodias*. He had seen the famous relief of Salomé dancing on her hands in a tympanum of the cathedral at Rouen. His description of Salomé's dance remains one of the classics of French writing.

Mallarmé's earliest mention of Hérodiade comes in his poem "Les Fleurs" of 1864, discussed in chapter 3. It is fortunate for us that Mallarmé did choose Hérodiade because during the symbolist and Decadent period there were almost more Salomés than there are in biblical history.[1] Mallarmé gave his reason for choosing the name Hérodiade instead of Salomé twice. In *Les Noces d'Hérodiade* he wrote: "I kept the name Hérodiade in order to differentiate it clearly from the Salomé, I will say modern or exhumed with its archaic news item, the dance."[2] In his correspondence he also noted: "The little inspiration I have had, I owe it to this name, and I believe if my heroine had been called Salomé, I would have invented this somber name, and red like an open pomegranate, *Hérodiade*."[3]

In 1870 Mallarmé's good friend Henri Regnault painted the famous Salomé to be found in the Metropolitan Museum. That same year Théodore de Banville wrote a sonnet dedicated to Regnault entitled "La Danseuse," which was published in Banville's *Rimes dorées*. The same poet drew another portrait of her in a sonnet in his volume *Princesses* of 1874. Around 1876 Gustave Moreau did a series of paintings of Salomé in some of which Herod is barely distinguishable but in others of which the head of John the Baptist makes a sudden apparition. Jules Massenet composed a flaccid but occasionally beautiful opera entitled *Hérodiade* in 1881 in which Salomé becomes, of all things, a chaste woman who in her remorse commits suicide. Mallarmé's friend Huysmans published his novel *A Rebours* in 1884 in which the hero owns two of Moreau's paintings of Salomé. Jules Laforgue returned to the satiric vein of the romantics in his *Moralités légendaires* of 1886, and also had Salomé kiss the severed head of John the Baptist.

But none of these Salomés is the one most of us remember. She is rather, and this we tend to forget, the *Salomé* that Oscar Wilde wrote in French and published in 1894 in an English translation by Lord Alfred Douglas with the art nouveau illustrations by the precocious Aubrey Beardsley. Actually the Salomé most of us really remember is the one presented by Richard Strauss in his opera of 1905, but we forget that the libretto is simply Oscar Wilde's play translated into German. Who can forget the Dance of the Seven Veils and the grisly kissing of the severed head? That Wilde has Salomé killed in the end by Herod's soldiers does not quite accord with history but it is the only possible conclusion to all that the spectators have witnessed.

The New Old Overture

Mallarmé's Hérodiade shares something with many of these Salomés and yet his poem endures because his heroine remains a creation quite distinct and different.

Although Mallarmé began "Hérodiade" in 1864, the poem was on his desk at his death, still apparently unfinished. No other poem cost him so much effort and anguish. No other poem represents such a clearcut continuation of the Parnassian tradition while offering such a radical departure from almost all of the French literary past. After "Hérodiade" Mallarmé's poetry takes on its own unique configuration and never again resembles anything but itself.

Today "Hérodiade" is almost always published as a triptych including the "Ouverture ancienne d'Hérodiade," the "Scène," and the "Cantique de Saint Jean." This was never the case during Mallarmé's lifetime but the three poems do constitute a logical suite and much can be gained from considering them together. I have called this section "the New Old Overture" because the "Ouverture ancienne" was actually composed after the "Scène" had been started and represents a radical stylistic departure for Mallarmé. Its tone is infinitely more dense and opaque than anything Mallarmé had previously written. He called the overture an "Incantation." It acts as a prelude, a prologue, and an introduction to the scene that follows. The poem is, rather, an invocation in which the nurse conjures up the vision of Hérodiade. The poem consists of ninety-six alexandrines divided into four parts of nineteen, eighteen, twenty, and thirty-nine lines. The alexandrines are arranged according to the classical French pattern of rhymed couplets with alternating feminine and masculine rhymes, more than two-thirds of which are rich. The alexandrines only seem classical, however, because Mallarmé has so dislocated the interior rhythm that they are difficult to distinguish orally. The classical hemistich or 6–6 division of the line has almost completely disappeared. The romantic ternary division of 4–4–4 is almost never employed either. The first eight lines, for example, show the following disposition: 3–6–3, 3–3–6, 3–9, 4–6–2, 6–6, 6–4–2, 6–6, 1–8–3. The division into alexandrines is almost completely arbitrary, however, for according to the meaning the rhythm falls into the following pattern: 3–6, 6–3–6, 3–9, 4–6, 8–6, 6–4, 8–6, 1–8–3. Enjambment is thus so frequent that only the rich rhymes are left to give some feeling of the alexandrine.

In the first part the nurse sets the exterior scene. She is standing at a window describing what she sees. The time is dawn in autumn. The rising motion symbolized by dawn contrasts with the falling away indicated by autumn and these contradictory movements of rising and falling create the inner tension of the poem. In addition, both the dawn and autumn are dying away. The last traces of dawn in the sky are described as a wing, "heraldic plumage" (*plumage héraldique*), reflected in the water of the pool, so that the high and the low, the sky and the basin, the bird and the water, all become one element. The house itself is a "cinerary and sacrificial tower" (*tour cinéraire et sacrificatrice*), a "Heavy tomb" (*Lourde tombe*), a "pale mausoleum" (*pâle mausolée*), "the manor-house of fallen and sad lands" (*des pays déchus et tristes le manoir*), so that while a tower by its nature rises, all terms used to describe it imply a sad deterioration, a heavy dying and fading away.

If the color of dawn is a "crimson space" (*espace cramoisi*) and the colors of autumn are "its torch" (*son brandon*), both are being extinguished in the water of reality and the water of time. The plumage of dawn was only vainly black because the light of day has come to chase away the night. All is silence and isolation and desolation. Even the water "is no longer visited by the plume" (*Que ne visite plus la plume*), which by synecdoche has become the dawn itself "or by the unforgettable swan" (*ni le cygne / Inoubliable*) omnipresent in Parnassian and symbolist poetry. Slowly throughout the first sixteen lines the bird becomes the central image so that as "the water reflects the desolation / . . . / Of the swan" (*l'eau reflète l'abandon / . . . / Du cygne*), the "pale mausoleum" may be the bird itself floating on the water. The swan has tucked its head under its wing as if "distressed / By the pure diamond of some star" (*désolée / Par le diamant pur de quelque étoile*), which again brings the high and low, the near and far away, the bird, and the star, together. The star may have been some other sun because it was "Earlier" (*Antérieure*) and "has never shone" (*ne scintilla jamais*). On the more symbolic level it may be a hope or a dream, an idea or an ideal never realized.

The reader cannot forget that this is after all the prelude to a tragedy, to crime, decapitation, and death. The word "Abolished" (*Abolie*) begins the poem and is repeated in the second line. The wing of dawn is "frightful" (*affreuse*), the water in the pool is "tears" (*larmes*) and reflects "alarms" (*alarmes*), fears, uncertainties. The water itself is somber and gloomy. Of the ten rhymes four are based on one of Mallarmé's favorite sounds, the acute French *i,* which results in a sharp and agonizing tonality. Near the end the sudden line, "Crime! pyre! ancient dawn! torture!" (*Crime! bûcher! aurore ancienne! supplice!*), announces all that will happen. The "Purple of a sky" is reflected by the "Pool, accomplice of the purple" (*Pourpre d'un ciel! Etang de la pourpre complice!*), which is in turn reflected in the rosy panes of the open window at which the nurse stands. The double *pourpre—pourpre* and the opposition *ciel—Etang* are by now familiar to the reader. The glass through which the nurse is looking may be stained glass illuminated by the rays of the rising sun.

By means of the dawn reflected first in the pool and then in the window, Mallarmé by the use of his mirror has projected us into Hérodiade's room. The chamber, seen as through a frame, is bizarre with all its "pomp of a warring century" (*attirail / De siècle belliqueux*) and "faded goldwork" (*orfèvrerie éteinte*). It "has the snowy yesteryear for antique tint" (*A le neigeux jadis pour ancienne teinte*). The tapestry, "with its mother-of-pearl luster" (*au lustre nacré*), is a series of "useless / Folds with the shrouded eyes / Of sibyls offering their aged nails to the Magi" (*plis / Inutiles avec les yeux ensevelis / De sibylles offrant leur ongle vieil aux Mages*). The disparate elements of the prophetess and the fingernail will return in Mallarmé's poetry. "Offering" in the sense of "showing their aged fingernails" on the part of the sibyls to the Magi does not make for a strong reading. Knowing that the word *onyx* comes from the Greek word for fingernail is not much help here either, although an offering of onyx might be more impressive. Pointing to the Magi as future prophets might be more satisfying, since sibyls are generally associated with the earlier pre-Christian era. The fingernail as synecdoche for the finger or the hand is undoubtedly the clearest interpretation with the connotation of some kind of offering. The important connection is, however, that between the sibyls and the nurse: one of the sibyls through a series of transformations introduces for the first time the sense of smell into the poem.

Through a confusion or an intermixing or an association of the tapestry with the nurse's own dress one of the sibyls "with a past of branches / On my robe" (*avec un passé de ramages / Sur ma robe*) seems an aroma. *Passé* can mean both "past" and "satin-stitch embroidery" and here the echo of the former in the latter may well be intended. The bird is introduced again and so is the element of imprisoned movement. In the tapestry or on the dress the sky is "strewn with birds amidst the tarnished silver" (*Au ciel d'oiseaux parmi l'argent noir parsemé*). The sibyl, "costumed and phantom-like" (*costumée et fantôme*), seems to take off in flights into this sky. The rising of the flight and the rising of the aroma are one but their sources are different. Hérodiade's bed, hidden heretofore by "a blownout candle" (*un cierge soufflé*), is empty and the aroma carried by the sibyl is that "of cold bones hovering over the sachet" (*Un arôme d'os froids rôdant sur le sachet*). These flowers were "foresworn to the moon" (*parjures à la lune*) and one of them is still dropping its petals "in the dead wax" (*A la cire expirée*). Both "the long regret" (*le long regret*) of their dying and their stems "Steep in a lone glass of languished brilliance" (*Trempent en un seul verre à l'éclat alangui*). The motionless flight, the empty bed, the extinguished candle, the dead wax, the dying roses, the odor of cold bones, all continue and intensify the mournful overtones of the opening part of the poem.

The last line of this part takes us in a circular movement back to the beginning of the first part, for here too "A Dawn was dragging its wings in the tears!" (*Une Aurore traînait ses ailes dans les larmes!*). Mallarmé creates circles within circles, however, for in one instance he uses one word to begin and end a single line: "An aroma which carries, O roses, an aroma" (*Un arôme qui porte, ô roses, un arôme*). He repeats the word *arôme* three times in three lines and makes it rhyme with *fantôme*, the sound of which accentuates the mystery of the poem. In another line he uses a sort of modified chiasma: "Of which the long regret and the stems of which" (*De qui le long regret et les tiges de qui*), to heighten the feeling of useless circular movement, all of which ends in tears.

At the beginning of the third part the nurse hears a voice and realizes that it is her own. The reflection of the dawn in the water is a "Magic shadow with symbolic charms!" (*Ombre magicienne aux symboliques charmes!*). Only by having read the "*Scène*" beforehand could we find this shadow to be Hérodiade since only there in the first line is she described as "the shadow of a princess." The nurse's voice is a "long evocation of the past" (*du passé longue évocation*), thus repeating the word "past" of the previous section. The useless folds of the tapestry have become "the yellow folds of thought" (*les plis jaunes de la pensée*) and will become "the stiff folds / . . . / Of the shroud" (*les plis roidis / . . . / Du suaire*). The nurse wonders if it is her voice "ready for in incantation" (*prête à l'incantation*).

In this section Mallarmé makes some of his boldest poetic leaps. On the one hand, a subject is separated from its verb by ten lines. On the other, Mallarmé repeats a whole hemistich, "the old veiled brilliance" (*le vieil éclat voilé*), at the end of one line and at the beginning of another, separated only by one line. The voice is described as loitering or languishing "in the yellow folds of thought." The actual verb used is *Traînant*, which repeats the *traînait* of the preceding section. There then begins an extended metaphor of five and half lines in which the voice arises through the confused thoughts, as "an incense-laden cloth" (*une toile encensée*)[4] permits "the old veiled brilliance" to shine through the "pure lace" (*les dentelles pures*) and "beautiful embroideries" (*ses belles guipures*) covering a "confused pile of cold monstrances" (*un confus amas d'ostensoirs refroidis*). The religious vocabulary suggests Baudelaire while the figure of speech suggests Victor Hugo. The poetic daring is, however, clearly Mallarmé's.

The final question is: Will this voice, even though it is "the musical response to petitioning verses" (*l'antienne aux versets demandeurs*), waste its splendors and go unheard in the final hour of anguish? In the last three lines of this part Mallarmé indicates that because of the "force of silence and black shadows / All returns equally to the ancient past" (*force du silence et des noires ténèbres / Tout rentre également en l'ancien passé*), thus recalling the *passé* of the second line of this section. In the last line "the water of the ancient basins resigns itself" (*l'eau des bassins anciens se résigne*), thus repeating the *ancien* of two lines before and at the same time the idea of the resigned water of the first part.

Mallarmé has so separated the poem that each of the last three sections shares a rhyme with its predecessor, linking them together orally. The final and longest part shares the rhyme *résigne—signe* already used

in the first part. After the exterior and interior descriptions and the
realization on the part of the nurse that it is her own voice speaking
and evoking the mournful scene, she at last arrives at Hérodiade.

The omens are not good. The opening *Elle* of this section is both
the *Elle* of the voice of six lines earlier and Hérodiade. She has been
singing incoherently, "a lamentable sign" (*signe / Lamentable!*). The bed
of the second section is mentioned again, and this time the metaphor
is that of the book. The unused bed is "useless and so claustral" (*inutile
et si claustral*), precisely because unused. Because Hérodiade has abandoned it, the bed "no longer has the dear spellbook of dreams in folds"
(*Qui des rêves par plis n'a plus le cher grimoire*). Just as the empty book of
magic no longer contains dreams in its folded pages, so the unused
sheets of the bed no longer emit "The perfume of the sleeping hair"
(*Le parfum des cheveux endormis*). Here the folds of parts 2 and 3 are
repeated as well as the aroma of part 2. More important, the hair figure
that will play such a significant role in the "Scène" has been
introduced.

Indeed, the nurse wonders if Hérodiade has been to bed at all since
she wanders morning and night, "In the morning shivering with flowers . . . / And when the spiteful evening has cut the pomegranates!"
(*Au matin grelottant de fleurs . . . / Et quand le soir méchant a coupé les
grenades!*). The red of the pomegranate is the red of the sun and the
day that night effectively eliminates. With the mention of morning
and night the water-time image of the first part is reintroduced. The
crescent of the moon moves across the sky as time moves across the face
of the clock. The clock is a waterclock that weeps time teardrop by
teardrop, and as the water slowly drips the counterweight slowly rises,
bringing with it Lucifer, a name that means "bringing light" used by
the ancients to indicate "the morning star" or Venus, thus combining
Satan and Venus, the rebel archangel and the goddess of love, in one
image. As in almost every image, the rising and falling motion continues. Hérodiade wanders forsaken, "and on her shadow not / A single
angel accompanies her inexpressible step!" (*délaissée, elle erre, et sur son
ombre pas / Un ange accompagnant son indicible pas!*), inexpressible because
unknown, unspeakable, indecipherable, ineffable.

In the following eight lines a king and a father are evoked, who
must be the father-king of Hérodiade. The king had long ago hired
the nurse to care for Hérodiade. If she was a wet nurse then, her milk
has dried up long since. The father was abandoned in Rome by Hérodias and has no way of knowing the fate of Hérodiade. The image of

the glacier, frozen water, is introduced, and just as the glacier is im-
mobile, so the father does not come to the aid of his daughter. The
glacier, as frozen water, reflects the fate of the father, as the water
symbolizes the fate of the daughter. Just as the glacier melts into the
atmosphere, so the sound of the father's trumpets expires in the sky,
just as the odor of the pines fades in the air. The rising movement is
counterbalanced by the slow sinking of a glacier and the fallen pile of
coffinless cadavers, coffins that would have been made of pine. The call
of his trumpets recalls Roland's useless and too-late sounding of the
horn in *La Chanson de Roland*. The trumpets are of the same silver
mentioned in part two and the silver is again dark, but this time *obscur*,
as was the drop of the water clock nine lines earlier. The nurse's question is, "Will he come back one day from the Roman side of the Alps!
/ Soon enough?" (*Reviendra-t-il un jour des pays cisalpins! / Assez tôt?*).
For the tragedy of Hérodiade is about to take place and "all is omens
and bad dreams!" (*car tout est présage et mauvais rêve!*).

Again "fingernail" is used as synecdoche for finger and as the hand
was raised at the window in the conclusion of part one, the raised finger
here recalls the raising of the trumpets four lines earlier and at the
same time is changed into a candle by the reflection of the sun's rays
on its tip or nail, an "envious" (*envieux*) candle because only reflected.
But the red of dawn will soon be the "red of sad dusk" (*rougeur de triste
crépuscule*), the red of dying day which "Will penetrate the body's
shrinking wax!" (*Pénétrera du corps la cire qui recule!*). Just as sunset
signals the lighting of the candles whose wax will be melted away, so
the passing of time signals the melting away of the body. This is not,
however, the red of dying day but the red of breaking day and what is
more "The rising of the last day which puts an end to everything"
(*Lever du jour dernier qui vient tout achever*). The struggle is so sad that
one can no longer tell what time it is, "this prophetic time which
weeps / On the child" (*ce temps prophétique qui pleure / Sur l'enfant*).

With the mention of the child we have returned to Héroidade and
in the "time which weeps" we have the tears and water and time of the
water clock all gathered into one image. And just as the swan of the
first part hid its head in its feathers so Hérodiade is "exiled in her
precious heart" (*exilée en son coeur précieux*). The first *allée* in the fourth
from the last line is a past participle modifying *enfant* as does *exilée*.
The solitary swan-princess-child has "gone / From the feather anguish
into the eternal alley / Of her hopes" (*allée / De la plume détresse, en
l'éternelle allée / De ses espoirs*), with the alley as a narrow way at best. In

the final image of the poem we return to the stars and diamonds of part one to which her hopes are compared. But this is "a dying star, and one which no longer shines" (*une étoile mourante, et qui ne brille plus*). The movement of the poem has thus been from the star "which has never shone" (*qui ne scintilla jamais*) to the star "which no longer shines" (*qui ne brille plus*). From no hope we have progressed to a hope which is no longer. In the interval there was the life and the beauty and the potential of Hérodiade. If on one level she represents youth that feeds on age—the nurse, on that same level she represents youth which becomes that on which it feeds—old age. All passes and is destroyed. On another level, all that is left is the ideal, an ideal of the perfect work of art that Hérodiade personifies. Out of the past come the traditions and the forms, the heritage, and the lifeblood. And into the past they slowly and surely recede. All that is gained is time, a new and different time that will in turn be lost. Out of this cycle of rise and fall comes art, not art for its own sake only, but an art that is pure and perfect and that has for its subject itself, an art that turns on itself, but in so doing involves all that is human in the creation of something superhuman, since men die and art, which is their creation, lives.

A Faraway Shadow

The "Scène" is a dialogue between Hérodiade and her nurse. Of the 134 alexandrines more than three-fourths are spoken by the heroine. Although cast in the form of a dialogue the scene is not theatrical. The overall impression is static, yet underneath this motionless exterior a moving drama, interior and psychological, unfolds. Mallarmé has caught Hérodiade at the most decisive moment of her life. She is still youthful, an innocent virgin, but she faces a choice whose consequences are both inevitable and tragic. In the anguish of choosing she reveals all that she has been and all that she will be. Although the choice is not actually made in Mallarmé's poem, Hérodiade's sad fate is clear, if unknown, and in the end she is resigned to it.

The nurse is interrupted in her mournful musings of the "Ouverture" by the sudden appearance of Hérodiade and the "Scène" begins. The nurse has talked herself into such a state that she is surprised to find Hérodiade still alive, so surprised that she says: "You are alive! or do I see here the shadow of a princess? (*Tu vis! ou vois-je ici l'ombre d'une princesse?*). The image of Hérodiade as a shadow permeates the whole poem. The nurse's use of the familiar *tu* reveals the extent of her surprise since in her second speech, she reverts to the more polite *vous*. The *tu* also reveals that the nurse's fundamental attitude toward Hérodiade is that of the nurse toward the child. Similarly, Hérodiade in her surprise at first uses *vous* to the nurse when she reacts with her opening word, *Reculez,* but by line 11 she reverts to *tu* and thereafter the pronouns never change.

Three actions on the part of the nurse combined with three violent reactions on the part of Hérodiade constitute the movement of the scene. In the second line, upon seeing Hérodiade, the nurse offers to kiss her hand. In line 31 she proffers perfume, and in line 53 she stretches forth her hand to replace a fallen lock of hair. Hérodiade's reaction in each instance is exactly the same. She recoils inviolate from this human touch. Strangely enough, the first two actions elicit long responses from Hérodiade in both of which she talks about her hair, although the first has to do with her hand and only the second might have to do with putting perfume on her hair. In reply to the third gesture, where it is a question of actually touching her hair, Hérodiade at last speaks in a general way of her distaste at being touched.

Mallarmé maintains the circular movement of the scene as he did in the overture. The nurse in the second line speaks not only of Hérodiade's fingers but also their rings, which imply metals and precious stones. The last word of the poem is *pierreries,* jewels or precious stones. Both metals and gems become a fundamental image of the poem. Kissing the hand suggests a royal reverence, while kissing the rings has religious overtones. The nurse also says: "cease / Wandering in an unknown age" (*cesse / De marcher dans un âge ignoré*), which links the scene with the "prophetic time" of the conclusion of the overture.

In her long reply of twenty-five lines Hérodiade speaks first of her hair, then of the time of the prophets, next of lions, flowers, and water, and finally, and again, of her hair that completes the circular movement of the speech. The final word is "mirror," which recalls the numerous reflections of the overture and opens the way for the many subsequent figures involving the mirror.

The reader may be surprised to learn that Hérodiade is, at least according to Mallarmé, a blonde, but the poet had his reasons. He wrote: ". . . the ideal of a woman,—that is to say of one of the facets of beauty, this diamond,—is not the brunet. Eve was blond; Venus blond. Blondness, that is gold, light, richness, dream, nimbus."[5] The reader is not surprised to note that the language used to describe her hair is filled with figures of speech having to do with water. Her "immaculate hair" (*cheveux immaculés*) is a "blond torrent" (*blond torrent*) that "When it bathes my solitary body chills it / With horror" (*Quand il baigne mon corps solitaire le glace / D'horreur*). In addition, her hair, "embraced by light" (*que la lumière enlace*), is "immortal" (*immortels*). Hair does continue to grow at least for a while after death and in this context one thinks of the powers attributed to Samson's hair in the Bible.

Early in her speech Hérodiade states the theme of the poem, which could serve as the theme for much of Mallarmé's subsequent poetry: "Oh woman, a kiss would kill him / If beauty were not death" (*O femme, un baiser me tûrait / Si la beauté n'était la mort*). Hérodiade, as the symbol of beauty and by extension poetry or the work of art, recoils from the human touch since beauty is at the same time purity and perfection. Both attributes are absolutes and thus inhuman. In this sense, beauty is death. The work of art is an object, a thing, and does not live in the human sense. It is, nevertheless, like Hérodiade, a human creation and lives an "immortal" life of its own. This idea illuminates many of the apparent ambiguities of the rest of the poem.

Hérodiade mixes time, prophets, and water in asking herself what has led her to her present situation, "what morning forgotten by the prophets / Pours, on the dying distances, its sad festivals" (*quel matin oublié des prophètes / Verse, sur les lointains mourants, ses tristes fêtes*). The dawn of the nurse in the overture becomes with Hérodiade the dawn or morning of time. The nurse has seen Hérodiade enter the dungeon where the lions are kept, which Hérodiade calls "the heavy prison of stones and iron" (*la lourde prison de pierres et de fer*). She echoes the idea of the heavy tomb and fallen manorhouse mentioned by the nurse in the overture and at the same time continues the image of stone and metal. The belief was that lions would not harm a virgin, and indeed Hérodiade is safe, her "hands unscathed" (*les mains sauves*). The lions of Hérodiade are old and bring with them the memories of "tawny centuries" (*les siècles fauves*). *Fauves*, as an adjective meaning both "wild" and "tawny," refers more properly to the lions, but its application to the centuries confers upon time the attributes of the animal. Hérodiade walked "In the desert perfume of these former kings" (*Dans le parfum désert de ces anciens rois*), for the caged lions were once kings of the beasts and the forests and the deserts. By evoking their heavy, acrid odor Hérodiade continues the allusions to the sense of smell. Although believing herself safe among the lions, Hérodiade was nevertheless thoroughly frightened.

"Dreaming of exiles" (*rêvant aux exils*), the exile mentioned by the nurse at the conclusion of the overture, Hérodiade stops near the basin of water with its fountain, also mentioned by the nurse, and plucks "the petals, / . . . / Of the pale lilies which are in me" (*j'effeuille, / . . . / Les pâles lys qui sont en moi*). Lilies as a white flower symbolize all that is female, virginal, and pure. The dropping petals, this gradual fading away, "in my reverie" (*à travers ma rêverie*) as Hérodiade calls it, suggest the slow loss of all those attributes of innocence and childhood. The movement will be echoed at the very end of the poem when Hérodiade speaks "Of a childhood feeling amidst the reveries / Its cold precious stones at last detach themselves" (*D'une enfance sentant parmi les rêveries / Se séparer enfin ses froides pierreries*). Again the falling motion of the petals contrasts with the rising motion of the water of the fountain, as in the overture. Mallarmé implies that the lions are almost hypnotized watching this movement and in nineteen syllables the poet manages a cluster of seven *d*'s whose repetition suggests the quiet sound of the falling petals: "while fascinated / To follow with their glance the languid debris / Falling" (*tandis, qu'épris / De suivre du regard les languides débris / Descendre*). The lions, as they brush past her, "draw aside the indolence of my skirt / And regard my feet which would calm the sea" (*de ma robe écartent l'indolence / Et regardent mes pieds qui calmeraient la mer*). Mallarmé has applied to Hérodiade one of the attributes of the Virgin Mary whose feet could calm the sea. The reader also remembers the feet of Lamartine's beloved in his poem "Le Lac."

Hérodiade tells her nurse to be calm, thus repeating the *calmeraient* of the preceding line, and to help her comb her hair. Hérodiade compares her hair to an animal's mane, the lion's mane that so frightens the nurse. Hérodiade wants the nurse to look into the mirror while combing her hair, thus avoiding her direct glance. The actions seem to take place in slow motion, an impression heightened by "the indolence" mentioned earlier and the adverb *nonchalamment,* meaning languidly, listlessly, or idly, in the last line of the speech.

The nurse next offers perfume, wanting Hérodiade "to try the funereal / Virtue" (*essayer la vertu / Funèbre*) of "gay myrrh" (*myrrhe gaie*) or attar of roses. *Vertu* means many things in French; virtue, quality, power, and all are intended here. Mallarmé creates two of his more beautiful lines in speaking of perfume: "If not the gay myrrh in its closed bottles, / Of the essence ravished from the old age of roses" (*Sinon la myrrhe gaie en ses bouteilles closes, / De l'essence ravie aux vieillesses de roses*). The liquid *l*'s, the sibilant *s*'s, the contrasts between *ravie* and *roses*, and the rhyme in *–oses*, simulate the idea being expressed and suggest the volatile essence of the perfume.

Hérodiade recoils violently, in contrast to the relaxed *nonchalamment* of her previous speech. The perfume in her hair would make her drunk. She doesn't want her hair to resemble flowers, which with their sweet perfume cause us to forget our human sorrows. She wants it to resemble gold, "ever virgin of aromatics" (*à jamais vierges des aromates*), thus bringing together the idea of virginity and the purity of metals with the idea of the sullying effect of perfume. She wants her hair to resemble "the sterile coldness of metal" (*la froideur stérile du métal*), hair that has reflected ever since her "solitary childhood" (*solitaire enfance*) the "jewels of the natal wall, / Arms, vases" (*joyaux du mur natal / Armes, vases*). As Hérodiade said in her first speech, she wants her hair to be "immaculate" and "immortal."

The nurse hastily asks her pardon and blames it all on old age, which has caused her to forget. She compares her mind to an old book, "my mind dimmed like an old book or black" (*mon esprit pâli comme un vieux livre ou noir*). The nurse had already used the image of the book when she mentioned in the overture the *grimoire* or book of dreams.

Hérodiade asks the nurse to hold up the mirror and begins an apostrophe to the looking glass, which is again one of Mallarmé's more beautiful creations. Mallarmé plays on sounds when he begins: "Oh mirror! / Cold water," which in French reads *O miroir! / Eau froide*. Because of the repeated sound of *o* one feels that the mirror must be round. Here again the mirror, water, time, and shadow play a role. The mirror is described as "Cold water frozen in its frame by boredom" (*Eau froide par l'ennui dans ton cadre gelée*) which recalls the still waters and the glacier of the overture. Hérodiade has many times spent hours looking into the mirror, "distressed / By dreams" (*désolée / Des songes*). The dreams recall the reveries mentioned earlier in the poem. She was searching for her souvenirs, her memories, which are compared to fallen leaves frozen under the water. The leaves call to mind the falling petals of the lily in Hérodiade's first speech. She appears to herself in the mirror "like a faraway shadow" (*comme une ombre lointaine*), thus repeating the idea of Hérodiade as a shadow first expressed by the nurse. As Hérodiade stared into the mirror, also the "severe fountain" (*sévère fontaine*) of the scene with the lilies, she learned "the nakedness" of her "scattered dream" (*J'ai de mon rêve épars connu la nudité!*). In spite of the horror this knowledge of her fate arouses in her, Hérodiade cannot resist asking, like any lovely young woman, if she is beautiful. The nurse compares her to a star, an image that will return later in the poem, and makes the gesture of replacing the fallen lock of hair. Hérodiade again recoils. She calls the gesture a "crime," and "enormous impiety" (*impiété fameuse*), and asks what all of these actions, "This kiss, these proffered perfumes" (*Ce baiser, ces parfums offerts*), this "sacrilegious" touch might mean. They augur ill for Hérodiade in her tower, the "cinerary and sacrificial tower" of the overture. The omens and bad dreams, also of the overture, make of this day for Hérodiade "a day / Which will not end without disaster" (*un jour / Qui ne finira pas sans malheur*), or as in the overture, "the last day which puts an end to everything."

The nurse attempts to console Hérodiade in the face of her fate, but as she speaks a note of irony creeps into her voice. She agrees that the times are "bizarre" and asks heaven's protection for her ward. She describes Hérodiade, as she had in the overture, as wandering, this time like a "solitary shadow and new fury" (*ombre seule et nouvelle fureur*). Hérodiade's terror results in part from her endless introspection. She is, however, "always as adorable as an immortal" (*toujours adorable autant qu'une immortelle*) and "frightfully beautiful" (*belle affreusement*).

When Hérodiade again accuses the nurse of wanting to touch her, the nurse replies that she would rather not know anything about the secrets destiny has in store for Hérodiade. Being human, the nurse feels sure that Hérodiade hides herself away and keeps her beauty to herself in the hopes that someday the right man will come along. Hérodiade calls upon the stars not to listen to the foolish old woman. The nurse speaks of "obscure / Terrors" (*obscures / Epouvantes*) and asks if Hérodiade in her implacable dreaming, devoured as she is by anguish, can be guarding "the unknown splendor / And the vain mystery" (*la splendeur ignorée / Et le mystère vain*) of her beings as a supplication to the god who is waiting for her—such a man could be no less than a god.

When Hérodiade reveals that it is for herself that she does all that she does, the nurse calls her a "Sad flower which grows alone and has no other emotion / Than its shadow seen listlessly in the water" (*Triste fleur qui croît seule et n'a pas d'autre émoi / Que son ombre dans l'eau vue avec atonie*). Again Hérodiade is no more than a shadow and a reflection observed in the pool. She tells the nurse to keep her pity as well as her irony. The old woman asks when "this triumphant disdain" (*ce dédain triomphant*) will wane. Hérodiade replies with a question: "Who would touch me, respected as I am by the lions?" (*Mais qui me toucherait, des lions respectée?*). She wants nothing human and describes herself as "sculptured" (*sculptée*), an epithet that has led many critics to make of "Hérodiade" a more Parnassian poem than it finally is. The only time her eyes seem "lost in paradise" (*perdus au paradis*) is when she remembers her human source, the nurse's milk that she drank long ago. The nurse calls her a "Lamentable victim offered up to her destiny!" (*Victime lamentable à son destin offerte!*).

Hérodiade, by way of reply, goes into the longest "aria" of the poem, a speech of thirty-two lines, divided roughly into four sections of nine, eight, seven, and eight lines each. In it she gathers together all the themes, images, and symbols of both the overture and the scene up to this point, and makes of them the portrait of herself and her fate. In doing so she becomes the work of art the poem is.

In the first section, Hérodiade maintains that it is for herself that she blooms, thus continuing both the figure of the flower she mentioned in her first speech and that used by the nurse only ten lines earlier. She blooms "forsaken," "deserted," in French, *déserte,* a word that echoes *le parfum désert* of her first speech. The precious stones and metals, "gardens of amethyst" (*jardins d'améthyste*) and "unknown golds" (*Ors ignorés*), hidden away in the earth, know her fate. They retain their "ancient light / Under the somber sleep of a primeval earth" (*antique lumière / Sous le sombre sommeil d'une terre première*). The sibilant alliteration and the repetition of the liquid *r*'s in *lumière* and *terre première* have a melancholy effect. Her eyes are "pure jewels" (*de purs bijoux*) that borrow "their melodious clarity" (*leur clarté mélodieuse*) from the stones, while the metals give to her youthful hair "A fatal splendor and its massive allure!" (*et vous / Métaux qui donnez à ma jeune chevelure / Une splendeur fatale et sa massive allure!*). The word *fatale* echoes the use of the same word in her first discourse when she spoke of herself walking, *fatale,* in the lions' den.

In the second section Hérodiade addresses the nurse and calls her a "woman born in evil centuries" (*femme née en des siècles malins*), echoing the *siècles fauves* of her first speech. She mentions "the wickedness of the sibylline caves" (*la méchanceté des antres sibyllins*), recalling the ominous sibyls of the overture. The nurse, according to Hérodiade, has spoken of a mortal man who "Prophesies that if the tepid azure of summer" (*Prophétise que si le tiède azur d'été*) sees her in her "shivering modesty of a star" (*dans ma pudeur grelottante d'étoile*), she will die. Hérodiade repeats here the idea that a mortal man, that is a man who will die, and who is also a prophet, will come. That man could literally be only John the Baptist. According to this same man, "the white shudder of my nakedness" (*le frisson blanc de ma nudité*) would come forth "from the calyxes / Of my robes, like an aroma of fierce delight" (*des calices / De mes robes, arôme aux farouches délices*). The allusions in these few lines become particularly dense. Mallarmé uses the term *azur* in a way quite different from his earlier concept. "The tepid azure of summer" and "the seraphic azure" of twenty lines later characterize ordinary, human life with all its limitations and restrictions, while Hérodiade is the startling exception, just as in her dance she will be startlingly bold according to the accepted niceties of society. In a parenthetical expression Hérodiade states that "woman naturally unveils herself to it" (*Vers lui nativement la femme se dévoile*), meaning that woman turns almost instinctively to the natural life while her own destiny will be frighteningly different.

The nurse had earlier called her a star. Hérodiade will develop the idea in the following sections of this speech. The use of *nudité* at the end of the alexandrine echoes its similar use when Hérodiade spoke of her "scattered dream." The use of *calices* is ambiguous: it can mean both the calyxes of flowers, which explains the aroma, emphasizing the sense of smell in the poem, and repeats the image of Hérodiade as a flower; and the chalices or drinking cups of church sacraments, heightening the religious overtones of the poem. Her robes could have the form of calyxes or chalices. As the former, they would be consecrated as a regular form found in nature; as the latter, they would be sanctified as a form by the church. In another sense she is the vessel of her destiny.

In the third section Hérodiade states frankly: "I love the horror of being virgin and I want / To live amidst the terror my hair causes me" (*J'aime l'horreur d'être vierge et je veux / Vivre parmi l'effroi que me font mes cheveux*). The couplet with its liquid *r*'s, fricative *f*'s and *v*'s, and its soft rhyme in *-eux*, creates a menacing impression. The next few lines are among the more Freudian Mallarmé wrote. Hérodiade loves her destiny:

> So that, at evening, withdrawn in my bed, like an inviolate
> Reptile I can feel in the useless flesh
> The cold glitter of your pale clarity
> *Pour, le soir, retirée en ma couche, reptile*
> *Invoilé sentir en la chair inutile*
> *Le froid scintillement de ta pâle clarté*

Hérodiade is addressing the "White night of icicles and cruel snow" (*Nuit blanche de glaçons et de neige cruelle!*). The suggestiveness of the figure of the reptile is tempered by the adjective "inviolate," which corresponds to the adjective "useless" describing the flesh. The flesh is useless because virginal. Night is dying. Thus the idea of death is mentioned twice in six lines, recalling that beauty which is death, of Hérodiade's opening speech. The night also "burns with chastity" (*toi qui brûles de chasteté*). Underneath the "cold glitter" of what Hérodiade says, a fire seems to smolder, ready to burst forth at any moment. Much of the tension of the poem stems from the contrast between this cold surface and this inner rage.

In the last section of the speech Hérodiade addresses herself to the moon, night's "solitary sister" (*ta soeur solitaire*), her "eternal sister" (*ma soeur éternelle*). Her dream will rise toward the moon which is, as Mallarmé describes it in one of his most beautiful lines, "already thus, / Rare limpidity of a heart which dreamed it" (*telle déjà, / Rare limpidité d'un coeur qui le songea*). Scientific progress may soon rob us of the capacity to think of the moon as nothing more than, and as something as ineffably beautiful as, a "Rare limpidity" dreamed up by the human heart. Like the moon in the sky above, Hérodiade is alone. She uses the word *seule* twice in five lines to emphasize her solitariness. She is alone in her "monotonous fatherland" (*ma monotone patrie*) where nothing changes and all stands still, where everything "lives in the idolatry / Of a mirror" (*vit dans l'idolâtrie / D'un miroir*), bringing us back to the mirror of her first speech. The glass "reflects in its slumbering calm / Hérodiade with her clear glance of a diamond" (*reflète dans son calme dormant / Hérodiade au clair regard de diamant*).

No exile is more definitive than that in one's own country. Fatherland here suggests the Idumea of "Don du poème," at the same time a geographical part of Hérodiade's fatherland and the source of poetic creativity for Mallarmé. The fact that all "lives in the idolatry / Of a mirror" recalls the lines from Mallarmé's letter to his friend Cazalis, quoted in chapter 1, where he wrote that he needed to look at himself in a mirror "in order to think" and if it were not there he would "again become Nothingness." Hérodiade exists truly only as a reflection in the mirror's "slumbering calm," "slumbering" because the reflection does not live, "calm" because the reflection is fixed within the mirror's frame just as a painting is fixed within its borders. Hérodiade's glance has all the beauty and coldness and purity of the sparkle of a diamond, which is finally a living reflection from a thing. With the last line of this speech, whose opening exclamation takes us back to that of the beginning of the speech, "Oh final charm, yes! I feel it, I am alone"

(*O charme dernier, oui! je le sens, je suis seule*), Hérodiade has calmed herself and seems to resign herself to her fate. This rising and falling of the emotions imitates the rising and falling physical motions mentioned earlier.

When the nurse asks her if she is going to die, she says no and begs the nurse both to leave and to "forgive this hard heart." She also orders the nurse to close the shutters in order to keep out "the seraphic / Azure," "the beautiful azure," which she detests and which "smiles in the deep window panes" (*l'azur / Séraphique sourit dans les vitres profondes*). The light of day, the light of human life, is not for her. The "deep window panes" suggest both the windows mentioned by the nurse in the overture and the looking glass of which Hérodiade has just spoken.

In one last feeble gesture of escape Hérodiade asks the nurse if she knows a country where "the waves / Rock" (*Des ondes / Se bercent*), as opposed to her fatherland where the nurse has described the water as resigned. If "the sinister sky has the hated glances / Of Venus who, in the evening, burns in the foliage" (*le sinistre ciel ait les regards haïs / De Vénus qui, le soir, brûle dans le feuillage*), she would go there. Hérodiade has repeated the adverbial expression *le soir*, which she used earlier when speaking of herself "withdrawn in my bed." The mention of Venus recalls the reference to Lucifer in the overture, the name by which the morning star was known to the ancients. But Venus is also an evening star, sometimes called *Vesper* by the French, *Hesperus* by the ancients. The planet Venus, which "burns in the foliage" just as the night "burns with chastity," as a symbol of the goddess of love, seems to be the source of its own light and contrasts with Hérodiade's "eternal sister," the moon, a mere satellite whose light is only a reflection of the sun. The glances of Venus are hated because they represent the human temptation, as does the azure.

Hérodiade seems totally resigned when she finally asks the nurse to light the candles, "a childish whim" (*enfantillage*). The mention of candles recalls lines from the overture where the wax is described as *expirée*. Here Hérodiade speaks of "these candlesticks where the wax in the light fire / Weeps some foreign tear amidst the vain gold" (*ces flambeaux où la cire au feu léger / Pleure parmi l'or vain quelque pleur étranger*). The repetition *Pleure—pleur* we have seen frequently in Mallarmé's poetry. The figure brings us back to the water symbol and to the falling motion, which in turn parallels Hérodiade's apparent resignation. The gold of the fire is vain because it is only seemingly gold and because it is constantly burning itself away into the atmosphere. The tear is foreign or strange because tears are unknown to Hérodiade.

Hérodiade quietly bids the nurse *Adieu* and appears completely re-signed. Immediately after the nurse departs, however, Hérodiade bursts into one last brief outcry against her fate. She tells her own lips that they lie, addressing them as "Oh naked flower / Of my lips" (*ô fleur nue / De mes lèvres*), thus introducing again the figure of flowers which she used in her first speech with reference to herself, and the idea of nakedness, lack of protection, barrenness, openness, developed throughout the poem. She is waiting for "an unknown thing" (*une chose inconnue*), "the mystery" (*le mystère*) of her destiny of which her lips are unaware just as they are perhaps unaware of their own cries. They may be "emitting the last bruised sobs / Of a childhood" (*Jetez-vous les san-glots suprêmes et meurtris / D'une enfance*). Mallarmé used the adjective *suprême* to indicate "the last good-bye of the handkerchiefs" in "Brise marine" just as these are the final sobs of Hérodiade's childhood. She must now become a woman and live her fate. This is "a childhood which feels amidst the reveries / Its cold precious stones at last detach themselves" (*une enfance sentant parmi les rêveries / Se séparer enfin ses froides pierreries*). The memories of childhood are as beautiful and as precious as precious stones but at a certain moment in life we can only look back upon them as objects detached in the past. We have become what we are and while we are in part our childhood, a child itself is some-thing we can never be again. At a certain moment the innocence and the illusory security of childhood disappear. At just that moment Hérodiade resigns herself to her destiny.

On one level the "Scène" can be interpreted, as I have indicated, immediately and obviously, as the moment before Hérodiade's decision that will make of her life a tragedy and at the same time render her famous forever. On the symbolic level she becomes the poem. The poem becomes itself and its own subject. The creative act becomes not only the symbol of artistic creation, but creation itself. Like the work of art Hérodiade is always herself, a human-inhuman thing, never changing and yet ever becoming. She is exiled, as the work of art is exiled in its own being, as the picture on the wall or the piece of sculpture or the poem is exiled within itself. She is as much a thing as a poem that is words and ink on paper or as a painting is oil and pigments on canvas. The work of art shares with metal its strength and durability, with gold its gleam and purity and rarity, with precious stones their beauty and their value. The work of art, no matter how abstract, is always a reflection of something in the eye of the beholder, be it only a line, a curve, a color, a form, a juxtaposition, a tension. The analogy with music is even more striking. Music, like poetry, is notes and ink on paper, but it requires a performer on an instrument as the poem needs a reader. Music is sound in the ear just as the poem is finally an effect on the senses and an impression in the mind. Just as the listener makes of music what he will, so the reader must make of Mallarmé's poems what he will.

Given that scope a great deal has been made of "Hérodiade." Although Thibaudet remains one of the earliest and best critics of Mallarmé, he felt that Mallarmé had written the poem only "in order to assure himself a small corner in the common Anthology."[6] Thibaudet had, however, already called "Hérodiade" "this sumptuous pyre . . . erected both for the apotheosis and the funeral of the Parnassian School" (p. 200). In this respect Mallarmé's biographer Mondor says that "This poem is still Parnassian, announces Symbolism, and is on the way to surpassing it."[7] He calls Hérodiade "the Muse of Mallarmé" (p. 792) and maintains that "The modesty of Hérodiade, her virginity, her princely solitude, her adornments, are the reserve, the silence, the exile of Mallarmé, his displays of vocabulary, images, and reveries" (p. 202). A well-known Italian critic sees Mallarmé's lines only as "a synthetic portrait of the whole Decadent Movement in the figure of the narcissist-virgin,"[8] while according to him "the poem expresses not so much the external aura of preciosity which surrounds her as the anguish of a sterile, lonely soul, troubled with diseased imaginings" (p. 304). Such a narrow interpretation of the poem's symbolism is surprising in a book whose main purport is precisely an investigation of symbolic meaning. Nearer my interpretation is that of the poem's translator: "In *Herodias* itself he created not only a surface finish which in brilliance of color and hardness of syntax was comparable to a Byzantine mosaic, but an atmospheric effect, an intuitive uncovering of secret psychological processes which was unique for its time as it is today, after Freud.[9]" Gone from this interpretation are Parnassianism, Decadentism, and Symbolism if not symbolism, although Praz's Byzantium still haunts the critic. The real meaning of Mallarmé's "Hérodiade" has been best expressed, however, by the French poet and critic: "Mallarmé, with 'Hérodiade,' will attempt for the last time to suspend the human gesture, to link it with the stars, to resolve in Idea the still too mysterious Racinian heroine."[10] In his poem Mallarmé arrests the human gesture just as every masterpiece is a static and eternal moment in time. While it is ever still, it is ever moving with movement implicit in its repose. Thus the smallest human gesture is concomitant with the movement of the stars, their beauty, their brilliance, their unreachable and unknowable distance. Every work of art is the resolution of an idea into the Idea that it is, not the idea behind it or hidden in it but the Idea it becomes in its being. In this instance the Idea is that of the Racinian heroine of classical French literature. Through her, the greatest tragedies of mankind were expressed with poetry and concision, the most profound emotions with clarity and restraint, the deepest dilemmas with perfection and balance, the gravest human failures with purity and measure. Mallarmé has attempted to express all of these through his mysterious heroine and has succeeded to an extent unequalled since.

A Song of Praise

The last part of the triptych is a short poem entitled "Cantique de Saint Jean." It comes as a brief sigh after the grave alexandrines of the "Scène." The seven quatrains are composed of lines of 6–6–6–4 syllables with the rhymes *a/a/b/b*. With only six or four syllables separating them, the rhymes come thick and fast, recalling Verlaine, this time his "Chanson d'automne" with its serried rhymes, "Les sanglots longs / Des violons / De l'automne." Mallarmé never again attempted this form, which did not seem to suit his poetic talents.

The head of Saint John is speaking just at the moment of decapitation. Mallarmé treats the gory subject with his usual elegance and restraint. In the first quatrain, which acts as an introduction, he compares the movement of the falling head to that of the sun. Just as the sun seems to come to a "supernatural halt" (*halte / Surnaturelle*) at the height of the summer solstice around June 22—Saint John's feast day is June 24—and then "Forthwith redescends / Incandescent" (*Aussitôt redescend / Incandescent*), so the head of John the Baptist seems to pause in its flight. Just as the halt "exalts" (*exalte*), raises high the sun, so John's head is exalted in martyrdom. The quatrain recalls nothing so much as Gustave Moreau's painting "L'Apparition" in which the incandescent head of John appears high above a frightened Salomé. Six sibilants hiss ominously throughout the quatrain.

The last six quatrains are one long and complicated sentence. In the second stanza the head speaks, saying it feels "as if to the vertebrae / Shadows were spreading" (*comme aux vertèbres / S'éployer des ténèbres*). The shadows could be those of the knife or of the spurting blood since they all spread "in one shudder / In unison" (*Toutes dans un frisson / A l'unisson*). They could be death itself. In the third quatrain the scythe or knife in its descent causes the head to rise up in "Solitary vigil" (*Solitaire vigie*), while in the fourth this rupture is described as *franche,* clean, frank, straightforward, forthright, clear, unequivocal, since it "cuts / The former dissensions" (*tranche / Les anciens désaccords*) between the intelligence as represented by the head and the physical needs as represented by the body. The dissensions are "former" because now dead.

In the fifth quatrain the head "drunken with fasting" (*de jeûnes ivre*), stubbornly follows "in some haggard leap / Its pure glance" (*En quelque bond hagard / Son pur regard*). The "pure glance" recalls the "clear glance" of Hérodiade but the nuance of difference between pure and clear is important. The look is "Up there where the eternal / Cold" (*Là-haut où la froidure / Eternelle*) cannot bear being surpassed by the glaciers, those of the nurse in the overture and those of the frozen water in the mirror of Hérodiade.

The final quatrain begins with "But according to a baptism" (*Mais selon un baptême*), reminding us that this is the head of John the Baptist speaking. The "incandescent" sun of the introduction has become the "illuminated" head of the conclusion, "Illuminated by the same / Principle" (*Illuminée au même / Principe*) or destiny that chose John, that is, martyrdom. Death by decapitation becomes a second baptism, the true and final baptism that ensures eternal salvation. Thus the head as it falls "Bows in salutation" (*Penche un salut*), the word *salut* meaning both salutation and salvation.

The story of Hérodiade ends with the death and redemption of John the Baptist. After his disappearance the historical and symbolic Hérodiade is no longer interesting. Her momentary descent into crime made possible the eternal deliverance of John. That was her destiny.

Chapter Five
The Secret Terror of the Flesh

In the midst of writing the glacial "Hérodiade" Mallarmé began the composition of its companion piece and opposite, the warm and sensuous *L'Après-Midi d'un Faune*. The definitive version, published separately with illustrations by Manet in 1876, differs radically from the first version of 1865. As indicated in chapter 1, Mallarmé intended his monologue for the theater but Constant Coquelin and his Théâtre Français did not find it acceptable. In its final form the poem was also refused for publication by the editor of the third *Parnasse Contemporain*. As fate would have it, this initial failure became one of Mallarmé's most popular and enduring poems.

L'Après-Midi d'un Faune carries the subtitle "Eglogue" or short pastoral poem. Mallarmé also called it "an heroic interlude."[1] The dialogue of "Hérodiade" has become a monologue in which the faun ruminates to himself on a dream he has had, a vision he has witnessed, or a reality he has experienced. He himself is never sure which it is.

The 110 alexandrines are broken into uneven stanzas of less than one line to thirty-one lines. For the first time Mallarmé uses three different sizes of type. In contrast to the faun's present meditations, interspersed passages in italics describe what the faun thinks must have happened. In addition, two words are in capitals, the verb CONTEZ in the imperative and the single word SOUVENIRS. The poem is thus the recounting of the faun's memories on two levels so that the effect is almost as much that of a dialogue as "Hérodiade."[2]

The theme of the poem is expressed in the first ten syllables. The faun begins by saying that he wishes he could make these nymphs endure forever, these nymphs whose rosiness (*incarnat léger*) hovers in the drowsy air. But did he love a dream? His doubt, which results from his sleepy state (*amas de nuit ancienne*), has many subtle ramifications. Mallarmé uses the word *rameau*, branch of a tree, and these branches prove in the faun's waking to be "the true / Woods themselves" (*les vrais / Bois mêmes*). Even though the branches of his dream exist in reality, the possibility remains that he was "all alone" (*bien seul*) and that he offered himself as a victory something that was nothing more than *la faute idéale de roses. Faute* can mean fault or error, but also lack or absence. His triumph may have been nothing more than a rosy illusion, no more substantial than the already mentioned *incarnat léger,* an illusion that is a lack or absence, ideal because dreamed. As a result, the faun must think about it all and when he says *Réfléchissons,* he draws the reader into his meditations.

These women about whom he is thinking—and here Mallarmé uses the verb *gloser,* which most frequently signifies commenting closely on a text—may be nothing more than a creation of his own "fabulous senses" (*de tes sens fabuleux*), with *fabuleux* meaning both extraordinary and fable-made. The faun now remembers that there were two nymphs. One, the more chaste and thus more innocent, had cold blue eyes from which illusions poured forth "like a spring in tears" (*comme une source en pleurs*). The other, full of sighs (*tout soupirs*), was like a gentle breeze on a warm day wafted through the faun's fleece. But no, that could not be true since the fresh morning breeze, even if it tried, could not prevail against the suffocating stillness, and there was no sound of water except that of his flute which sprinkled the woods with music (*Au bosquet arrosé d'accords*). The only wind other than that which issued forth from the pipes of his flute and which was quickly dispersed "in an arid rain" (*dans une pluie aride*), arid because it was not actually water, was "The visible and serene artificial breath / Of inspiration" (*Le visible et serein souffle artificiel / De l'inspiration*) seen on the motionless horizon and which quickly rose again to heaven whence it had come.

After a pause, indicated by a change of stanza, the faun addresses himself to these "Sicilian shores of a calm marsh" (*O bords siciliens d'un calme marécage*) where he disported himself like a busy ray of the sun and which now lies "Silent under the sparkling light" (*Tacite sous les fleurs d'étincelles*), asking them to tell him what happened. The first passage in italics follows, revealing that here he cut two reeds necessary to fashion his flute, reeds "tamed / By talent" (*domptés / Par le talent*), his talent both for making and playing the flute. Suddenly he saw an animal whiteness undulating on the glaucous gold of distant verdures. At the first note of his flute a flight of swans, or rather of naiads, took off or plunged into the water.

The faun's thoughts are interrupted as he succumbs to inertia induced by the burning heat. Mallarmé uses the word *fauve,* as he had in "Hérodiade," to indicate both the savagery of the heat and the tawny color of the summer air. The faun is unable to determine how these nymphs could have scampered off together, nymphs too much desired by him as he was tuning his pipes (*Trop d'hymen souhaité, de qui cherche le* la). Will he awaken to his first fervor, his original desire, to find himself standing straight and alone in an ancient flood of light as ingenuous as a lily among lilies? Like many another poet, Mallarmé uses the rose to symbolize the female, while he uses the lily to indicate the male. The phallic overtones are inescapable here.

The faun searches his breast for some telltale mark of an amorous encounter with the nymphs. Other than "this sweet nothing" (*ce doux rien*), which is the soft kiss of the faithless, his chest is "virgin of proof" (*vierge de preuve*) except for "a mysterious / Bite, due to some august tooth" (*une morsure / Mystérieuse, due à quelque auguste dent*). Does it mark him as a chosen one? In any event, in some mysterious (*arcane*) way the twin-piped flute he is playing under the azure sky was chosen as a confidant. The flute, diverting to its own purposes all the difficulty involved in playing it (*détournant à soi le trouble de la joue*), dreams, in a long solo, deluding the surroundings (*nous amusions / La beauté d'alentour*) by confusing the reality of what one sees with the imaginativeness of what one hears (*notre chant crédule*). The faun will attempt to create "A sonorous, vain and monotonous line" (*Une sonore, vaine et monotone ligne*) of music that will rise as high as, partake of the superior essence of, love. The sound and the sentiment have for their source the sight (*songe ordinaire*) of the back or flank of the nymphs that the faun followed with his half-closed eyes while playing the flute.

Suddenly the faun tires of his flute, calling it an "instrument of flights" (*instrument des fuites*) since it caused the nymphs to flee, a "malignant / Syrinx" (*maligne / Syrinx*), evil because it caused him to lose the object of his desire, Syrinx because she was a nymph of Acadia who was changed into a reed to escape the pursuing Pan. The latter fashioned his flute from the reed and gave to it the name of the nymph. The faun throws down his flute, telling it to attempt to grow again like a reed while waiting his return. Proud of the sounds he can make (*de ma rumeur fier*), the faun has discarded the flute for the sound of his voice. After attempting to create or re-create the nymphs musically, he will attempt it verbally. By means of "idolotrous paintings" (*idolâtres peintures*) he will attempt to lift the veils of mystery surrounding the nymphs. Here in the first line of the mathematical second half of the poem Mallarmé uses the word *ombre* in speaking of the nymphs, a word that establishes a relationship between the shadow that was Hérodiade and the nymphs, and that leads us directly to the conclusion of the poem. In the same way, the faun had banished his regret by the ruse of drinking wine (*bannir un regret par ma feinte écarté*) and then blowing up the empty grape skins and squinting through them at the summer sun all day long. When he says that he has sucked the clarity of the grapes (*des raisins j'ai sucé la clarté*), he means that he has both devoured their fruity pulp and juice and derived from them the heightened vision that supposedly attends the drinking of too much wine. He also means that his vision caused by the wine was similar to his present vision of the nymphs, induced by the drowsy heat.

After having addressed himself to the Sicilian shores and then his flute, the faun now speaks directly to the nymphs and begins the third and concluding section. He uses the verb *regonflons,* which recalls the blowing up of the grapes. This time, however, he wants to blow up, expand, make live again his memories. Just as the blowing up of the grape skin is only an illusion that seems to make the fruit whole again, so the blowing up of memories cannot render the illusory nymph real again.

In italics he remembers peering through the reeds at the "immortal / Neck" (*encolure / Immortelle*) of the nymphs who are cooling themselves in the water while the faun gives forth a cry of rage at not being able to possess them then and there. The water and hair images of "Hérodiade" return as the faun sees "the splendid bath of hair disappear / In shimmerings and shiverings" (*le splendide bain de cheveux disparaît / Dans les clartés et les frissons*), as Professor MacIntyre so aptly translated *les clartés et les frissons.*[3] The use of *clartés* with reference to the water recalls its use eleven lines earlier with reference to the wine of the grapes. The shower of water sparkling in the sun like precious stones (*pierreries*) recalls the jewels of Hérodiade.

The faun hastens over to the nymphs to find them all gone except two, asleep at his feet in each other's arms. The arms are described as *seuls* because they only apparently unite the two nymphs and *hasardeux* because they are only casually linked together in sleep. Although they are both nymphs and both asleep and seem to be joined together, they suffer the fate of all living things to be one and alone (*ce mal d'être deux*) and forever separated from others, exiled within themselves, just as the faun is separated from the nymphs in illusion as well as in reality. He carries them off without disentangling them to a little thicket of roses that are being dried of their perfume by the sun. In like manner their frolic will wear itself out as the day consumes itself (*notre ébat au jour consumé*).

The thicket is described as "hated by the frivolous shade" (*haï par l'ombrage frivole*). Professor Cohn indicates that "haï: is the blackness of shadow contrasted with the bright sun" and calls attention to a similar use in "Hérodiade": *le sinistre ciel ait les regards haïs / De Vénus.*[4] Such an interpretation seems somewhat misleading since it is not *haï* that is the blackness of shadow but the thicket that is "in the full sunlight (and therefore detested by the shadows of the forest)" as Professor Fowlie puts it.[5] Another critic suggests that the thicket is "steeped in sunlight, the wandering, fickle shade having left it."[6] *L'ombrage frivole* might be translated as the moving, flickering, unstable shadow. Nor does the use of haï here seem parallel to that in the earlier poem. There it is *haïs / De Vénus* and here it is *haï par l'ombrage*. While the prepositions *de* and *par* are interchangeable in certain instances, Hérodiade seems to be speaking first of a sky that is sinister, playing on the two meanings of the word, sinister as an adjective and fire as a noun, and second, a sky that is sinister because in it shines the light (*les regards*) of Venus, hated because it is the star of the love goddess, the light of love, the emotion that frightens Hérodiade.

The next seven lines are in roman type and in them the faun reveals the complex psychology involved in what had appeared to be to this point only physical desire. In a burst of masochism the faun maintains that what he really likes is the "virgins' wrath" (*courroux des vierges*), their resistance, their attempts to flee, the "wild / Delight of the sacred naked burden" (*délice / Farouche du sacré fardeau nu*), sacred because both virginal and divine, which seeks to avoid the kisses of his burning lips. The verb *tressaille* means to thrill to, to shiver, to shudder, to tremble. Thus the comparison, "as a shaft of lightning / Quivers!" (*comme un éclair / Tressaille!*), could refer to his "wild delight," to the quivering of the bodies, to the rapid movement of his lips, and to the electrical effect the kisses have as they drink in "the secret terror of the flesh" (*la frayeur secrète de la chair*). With this expression the faun demonstrates that his basic attitude toward the realities of life and love and physical desire is not so different from that of Hérodiade. What is desired is frightening, frightening because desired. What is genuinely frightening is the realization of desire, the revelation of his illusion as reality. In this vision of reality his kisses travel from the feet of the heartless (*l'inhumaine*) nymph to the heart of the timid one who is at the same time being abandoned by her innocence (*Que délaisse à la fois une innocence*), "humid / With foolish tears or less sad vapors" (*humide / De larmes folles ou de moins tristes vapeurs).* Such vapors could only be seminal fluids but in the faun's vision they are as amorphous as vapors.

After this realistic description of what might have happened the faun reverts to his thoughts in italics and analyzes his "crime," the reason for his failure. He was eager to conquer his fears, which were *Traîtresses* because what was feared was also desired, because they might prove his undoing. His problem was that the nymphs were two, so that he had to divide his attention. While kissing the more forward of the nymphs he had to hold lightly (*Par un doigt simple*) onto the smaller, more naive one in the hopes of arousing her also. But just as he was attempting this difficult maneuver his arms were relaxed for a moment by his own climax (*par de vagues trépas*), more than ample time for his forever ungrateful prey to slip from his grasp with no thought for the orgasm that still held him in its thrall (*du sanglot dont j'étais encore ivre*).

In his defeat the faun affects a sour-grapes attitude (*Tant pis!*). In the future there will be others whose tresses will get entangled with the horns on his forehead and who will lead him to happiness. His passion, to which he speaks and which he describes, is always purple and already ripe, like a pomegranate ready to explode and murmuring with bees. His blood and that of his passion, caught up by the object of his desire (*épris de qui le va saisir*), suffices for the swarm of demands desire might make on it (*Coule pour tout l'essaim éternel du désir*). But day is almost over, the day of his encounter with the nymphs. The woods at this hour are taking on golden tints from the last rays of the sun and the ashen color of dying day, a veritable feast in the extinguished leaves. Etna itself is lighted by the lowering rays, Etna that was visited by Venus, the goddess of love, just as the faun had been visited by desire. She comes only when the volcano sleeps or its flame has expired. After the explosion the silence of the sleeping volcano is thunderous (*Quand tonne un somme triste*). The sleep is sad because desire has passed, passion has been satisfied. The faun is convinced that he has held the very queen of love in his arms.

For what he has done there will be an "inevitable punishment" (*O sûr châtiment*). Or perhaps the only true punishment is the lassitude that follows such an adventure. In any event his soul and his body are at last overcome by the silence of noon, the noon in which he dreams of what may have happened to him the previous afternoon. He must sleep, and sleep itself will be a forgetting of his blasphemous act (*dormir en l'oubli du blasphème*), lying on the thirsty sand with his mouth open to the sun that is *efficace* because it has the power to mature the grapes for the wine that will slake his thirst.

As he falls into drowsy sleep the faun bids farewell to this couple, the nymphs with whom the poem opened. In his slumber he will find the shadow they have become, he will know their true nature, which is that of illusion, a vision that can only be realized in a dream. Were the nymphs real or a figment of his imagination? At certain moments dream and reality cannot be separated, they are in fact one, and their fusion is an act of creation resulting in the poem the faun has just completed.

Different as they are, "Hérodiade" and *L'Après-Midi d'un Faune* have much in common. More important than any recapitulation of events they may recount, both poems are a state of mind. Hérodiade seems to be looking forward with fear to what the future will bring, the few *pierreries* that will be Mallarmé's poems. The faun seems to be looking back on what has just happened to him, but in the final line he projects himself into the future when he says *je vais voir*. The shadow which the nymphs may become is no less substance than substance itself, since without shadow there is no substance. The poem may be the shadow that gives contour to the substance of life, without which there would be no life. Until re-created in the imagination, there is no lasting life.

Form and content cannot be separated but the beauty with which Mallarmé expresses himself in *L'Après-Midi d'un Faune* has seldom been equalled in French literature. He has completely dislocated the alexandrine and ruptured French syntax to the point where they are almost unrecognizable. Yet such violence results in myraid, suffused possibilities of meaning, and ambiguity that is the very ambiguity of what may or may not have happened to the faun, an ambiguity which is the faun's state of mind. The beauty of the rhymes, the choice of vocabulary, the music of the lines, make the poem an unforgettable poetic experience. To have lived the faun's adventures is to have relived a scene that perhaps never took place and that is all the same fundamental to the human endeavor.

Chapter Six
The Hyperbole of Pure Poetry

Any commentator on the poems Mallarmé wrote during the last thirty-odd years of his life—that is, roughly after the composition of the first version of *L'Après-Midi d'un Faune*—is presented with two problems: choice or quantity and order. In addition to the forty-five poems in verse generally included in this section of the complete works, Mallarmé published twelve poems in prose that must be taken into consideration. The more than 470 occasional pieces of from two to seventy lines need not occupy us here, although the serious student will want to consult them in order to get a complete picture of Mallarmé's poetic production. Space must be dedicated, however, to his last great experiment, *Un Coup de Dés*.

The commentator always seems to have chosen to talk about those poems that are perfectly clear to any reader and to have ignored those poems which give the most difficulty. Because of space, I have therefore arbitrarily chosen thirty-one of the last forty-five poems, omitting among the "Feuillets d'album" the poem of that name, "Remémoration d'amis belges," and the sonnet "O si chère de loin et proche . . . ," in addition to the two "Rondels," the eight "Chansons bas," and the "Billet à Whistler." Something, after all, should be left for the reader's delectation.

The question of order of presentation is much more difficult to resolve. The exact chronology of composition is almost impossible to establish since Mallarmé frequently reworked his poems over a period of twenty years, ending with something that barely resembles the original. The date of publication is almost never much help because years may have elapsed between composition and appearance in print. And of course a few poems were never published during the poet's lifetime. I have therefore followed the order of the Pléiade Edition which is *roughly* that of Mallarmé himself. It is only vaguely chronological and progresses from the simpler to the more complex in a general way. We could do worse, however, than to let the poet himself be our guide.

The Music of Silence

Although the sonnet "La chevelure vol d'une flamme . . ." (Hair, flight of flame . . .") was not published until 1887, Mallarmé chose to place it immediately after *L'Après-Midi d'un Faune*. In it he followed the Shakespearean form of three quatrains plus a distich, one of a few such examples among his numerous sonnets. The poem illustrates very well Thibaudet's expression, the "hyperbole of pure poetry,"[1] for at first reading it seems to make no sense whatsoever. After several readings the already mentioned "internal mirage of words" creates some sort of "cabalistic sensation" and an impression formulates itself in the reader's mind.

The basic image is that of hair compared to a flame. We have already witnessed Mallarmé's frequent use of the hair symbol, culminating in the extended metaphors of "Hérodiade." Nor is it his last reference to hair. Baudelaire before him had underlined the sensual quality of hair and while Mallarmé often insists on its liquid quality, as in "the splendid bath of hair" of *L'Après-Midi d'un Faune,* he employs here the quick-moving flame, repeated in the second quatrain as fire, in the third as fires, and in a circular movement, as torch in the last word of the sonnet.

The pulsation of the flame, the darting of desire, results from the contrast between words like *vol* and *déployer* and *Se pose* and *mourir, soupirer* and *ignition, mouvant, fulgurante,* and *semer.* The sparkling reflection of the diadem of the first quatrain is echoed by the gold and jewel of the second, the star and fires or jewels on the finger (*astre ni feux au doigt)* of the third, and the rubies of the distich. The comparison of the forehead to an "antique hearth" (*ancien foyer),* the center of the household because the seat of fire, is continued by the "ever interior fire" (*du feu toujours intérieur*) of the second quatrain while the forehead itself has become in the third the whole head (*chef*) which in turn becomes the "guardian torch" (*tutélaire torche*) of the distich. The echo of *joyau* as well as *rieur* of line eight in the *joyeuse* of the last line emphasizes the element of doubt so important to desire.

The hair as it is combed or shaken out is like the flight of a flame in its evocation of extreme desire. The word *Occident* indicates the West and suggests that the hair is the color of the golden rays of the setting sun, according to Professor Cohn.[2] Just as fire dilates and diminishes and as desire expands and contracts, the hair in its flight unfolds itself and comes to rest like a diadem. Just as the diadem crowns the head, so the hair crowns the forehead (*le front couronné*). The forehead, however, has no real gold other than the hair. Professor Cohn also suggests that *soupirer* is an imperative (p. 147). According to such a reading the observer hopes to himself that "this living cloud" (*cette vive nue*) of hair, which was originally the only kindler "of the ever interior fire," will continue to spark desire in the jewel which is the eye. Such a provocative glance may of course be genuine or only mocking. The presence of a tender hero with naked desire in his eyes would be a defamation where such beauty is concerned (*Une nudité de héros tendre diffame*).

The point of view resembles that of Hérodiade who was sufficient unto herself. Such beauty does not have to move a finger (*ne mouvant astre ni feux au doigt*), does not need the artificial brilliance of rings of gold and precious stones. By the simplest means (*Rien qu'à simplifier*), this woman, flashing with light (*fulgurante*), can by a shake of the head sow the ruby red gleams of desire at the same time as she grazes doubt (*De semer de rubis le doute qu'elle écorche*). That is, her hair has now become "a joyous and guardian torch" (*une joyeuse et tutélaire torche*) and with its light she illuminates desire but also creates a doubt in the beholder's mind about her seriousness.

The vision is that of a beautiful woman who simply by combing or shaking her radiant hair arouses desire in the observer. Half the pleasure results from the fact that one is never sure whether she is being sincere or coquettish. The rhyme in -*ème* of the first quatrain is echoed by that in -*ame* of the third. The rapid movement from the one to the other with the repeated harsh sounds of *c* and *t*, and the final rhyme of *le doute qu'elle écorche* and *tutélaire torche*, reinforce the feeling of doubt while transforming the hair of the beginning into a glorious torch at the end.

The little masterpiece "Sainte" provides in its simplicity a striking contrast to the preceding poem. The first version was composed in 1865 while Mallarmé was still working on *L'Après-Midi d'un Faune*. The final version appeared in 1883. This chaste portrait of a saint with its ethereal and ineffable beauty remains one of Mallarmé's most charming creations.

Within the limited framework of four quatrains of octosyllables Mallarmé manages to suggest an astonishing amount. The opening phrase reminds us of the window-mirror images in "Les Fenêtres" and "Ouverture ancienne." It may suggest that the woman is merely seated at the window or that her portrait is actually part of a stained glass window. The present participles repeated at the rhyme combined with the simple verb *Est* in its surprising position as the first word of the second quatrain render the picture present in the senses both of here and now. The use of *Le santal vieux* in the first quatrain and *le vieux santal* in the last creates a circular movement echoed by *Le livre vieux* of the second quatrain repeated as *le vieux livre* in the last. The first quatrain is linked to the second by the similarity of construction: the second lines begin with *Le santal vieux* and *Le livre vieux* both of which are followed by a relative clause; the third lines both begin with the preposition *de;* the fourth lines both begin with *Jadis* to emphasize the antiquity of the vision.

The musical instruments of the first quatrain indicate that this is a portrait of the patron saint of music, Saint Cecilia, although by the use of the word *Sainte* as title Mallarmé suggests all women chaste and holy. The window harbors or contains (*recélant*) the sweet smelling sandalwood of the viol, which is so old it is losing its gilt. The use of *étincelant* suggests the glitter of the instruments themselves and the sparkle of the music they made.

The first quatrain describes the setting while the second reveals the saint herself. *Le livre vieux* which she has open in front of her reminds us of *le cher grimoire* of the nurse in "Ouverture ancienne" and of her *vieux livre ou noir* in "Hérodiade." The use of *ruisselant* echoes that of *étincelant* and suggests both the music which streams across the written pages and the sound of the flowing music at vespers and compline.

The opening expression of the third quatrain, *A ce vitrage*, repeats that of the first quatrain, *A la fenêtre*. While the first window harbored or contained, this window, like that of a monstrance, is designed to reveal. As if visited by divine inspiration the window has been brushed by a harp formed by an angel in its evening flight specifically for the delicate fingers of the saint. Having put aside her viol and songbook, she plays "the instrumental plumage" (*le plumage instrumental*) and in so doing is the "Musician of silence" (*Musicienne du silence*).

An ontology can be constructed around this idea of the musician of silence. Mallarmé was preoccupied by the silence between the spoken words and the white space surrounding the printed words. At a certain juncture he seems to be attempting to make poetry out of silence or silence into poetry. As the conclusion of the poem, however, the expression captures the stillness of the picture, of the stained glass itself. The music is suggested by the rhymes. The ending in *-dore* of the first quatrain is echoed by the *-soir* of the third. The liquid *l*'s of *l'Ange* of the third are heard again in the *-antal* and *-lance* of the final quatrain. These nasals recall those of the first two stanzas like the reverberations of harp strings. The ephemeral beauty of such a poem can be expressed only in the words of the poem itself.

"Toast funèbre" ("Funereal Toast") is a poem that stands midway between the simplicity of "Sainte" and the poems that preceded it and the complexity of "Prose pour des Esseintes" and the poems that followed it. The great Parnassian poet Théophile Gautier died in 1872. A year later more than eighty poets published their tributes to the departed writer. Among them was Mallarmé's "Toast funèbre" in which he expresses his admiration for the older man. In a letter to François Coppée Mallarmé wrote: "Beginning with 'Oh thou who . . .' and finishing with a masculine rhyme, I want to sing in rhymed couplets one of the glorious qualities of Gautier: the mysterious gift of seeing with the eyes (take out mysterious). I shall sing the *seer* who, placed in this world, looked at it, something no one does."[3] With its fifty-six lines the poem is among Mallarmé's longer works, certainly the longest of the numerous tributes he dedicated to famous men.

The contradictory title reveals the two sentiments Mallarmé wants to develop in his poem; homage to the immortal genius with his toast and lament for the death of the mortal man. The poem is sometimes published in five stanzas of one, fourteen, sixteen, sixteen, and nine lines, sometimes in four of one, fourteen, sixteen, and twenty-five. The opening is representative of Mallarmé's best and in its concision states the theme of the poem: "Oh of our happiness, thou, the fatal emblem!" (*O de notre bonheur, toi, le fatal emblème!*). An emblem is both a symbolic figure with a motto and an attribute that represents a group. Gautier in death has become a symbolic figure with his poetry as his motto. As an attribute he is representative of the poet among poets, the poet among men, and the man among men. With his poetic genius he is the symbol of the happiness of other poets and because of what his creations have to offer he is the symbol of the happiness of all men. At the same time, as a dead poet he is a symbol of the destiny of all men.

Mallarmé calls his toast "lunatic" (*Salut de la démence*), his libation "exceptionally pale" (*libation blême*), his cup "empty" (*ma coupe vide*), first, because there is no eternal life (*magique espoir du corridor*), secondly, because there is no toast worthy of immortal genius. On the cup which he raises there is a writhing monster sculpted in gold (*où souffre un monstre d'or*). The apparition he is evoking will not suffice, will not materialize, since he knows that he himself has laid to rest the mortal remains. One of the human rites is to witness the death of those

around us (*Le rite est pour les mains d'éteindre le flambeau*) and one would
be mistaken if he did not think that the tomb encloses all there is of
man, even this chosen one (*élu pour notre fête*), chosen by genius and
because of his genius. Precisely because he was a genius and a poet,
something of "the burning glory of his trade" (*la gloire ardente du métier*)
clung to him right up to his death (*Jusqu'à l'heure commune et vile de la
cendre*), "common and vile" because shared by all men. Even the setting
sun is proud to illuminate the window panes of his tomb (*Par le carreau
qu'allume un soir fier d'y descendre*), encountering as it does there the light
of his "burning glory" which in turn "Returns towards the fires of the
pure mortal sun" (*Retourne vers les feux du pur soleil mortel*), that is, shares
with the sun its brilliance, its purity, and its cyclical, rising and setting, waxing and waning (*mortel*) nature. We are reminded of the glass
of "Les Fenêtres" that may be art or may be mysticism. We are also
reminded of the window of the monstrance that was brushed by the
wing of an angel in its evening flight in "Sainte."

The third section of the poem begins with a great triple apostrophe
to Gautier: "Magnificent, total and solitary" (*Magnifique, total et solitaire*), which will be echoed eight lines later by "proud, blind and
mute" (*fier, aveugle et muet*). The former describes the living poet, the
latter the dead. In the face of such a man "The false pride of ordinary
men trembles to reveal itself" (*tel / Tremble de s'exhaler le faux orgueil des
hommes*). As mortal men (*Cette foule hagarde*) we are nothing more than
the physical being of the ghost we shall become, "the sad opacity of
our future specters" (*La triste opacité de nos spectres futurs*). Mallarmé
scorned both the meaningless outward signs of mourning (*le blason des
deuils épars sur de vains murs*) and "the lucid horror of tears" (*l'horreur
lucide d'une larme*), with translucent referring both to the tear that is
clear like water and to the horror that is clearheaded because clear-
seeing. At the moment Mallarmé was doing that, some passerby, or
someone who had passed beyond, Gautier that is, was transforming
himself "Into the virginal hero of the posthumous waiting" (*En le vierge
héros de l'attente posthume*). The dead man is deaf even to the verses of
the poet. These verses are sacred because dedicated to Gautier and cannot alarm him precisely because he is dead, "proud, blind and dumb,"
the guest of his own shroud (*Hôte de son linceul vague*). In his death the
hero is virginal because new to the experience of the beyond and he
must wait for the posthumous fame that will be his. Although the poet
uses many words in his profession he is now haunted by all that he did
not say, the "Vast gulf borne amidst the mass of mist / By the irascible

wind of words he did not speak" (*Vaste gouffre apporté dans l'amas de la brume / Par l'irascible vent des mots qu'il n'a pas dits*). *Gouffre*, *amas*, and *brume* lead to the nothingness (*Le Néant*) that engulfs him. The nothingness into which he has gone asks "this Man recently abolished," dead (*cet Homme, aboli de jadis*), that is, Gautier, symbolic of all men: "What was Earth to you other than memories of horizons?" (*Souvenirs d'horizons, qu'est-ce, ô toi, que la Terre?*) What was life other than memories of places? The question has become for the dead man nothing more than a dream howled at him by the nothingness. As a dead man the clarity of his voice has changed and the endless space does nothing but play with his reply: "I don't know!"

In the fourth section of the poem Mallarmé returns to the idea he expressed in his already quoted letter, that of Gautier as seer. The poet is now called "The Master" (*Le Maître*) and it was he who "with his keen eye" (*par un oeil profond*) was able as he walked the earth to "Appease the disquieting miracle of Eden," of this earth of ours (*Apaisé de l'éden l'inquiète merveille*). By his voice alone (*dans sa seule voix*) he created "the mystery of a name" (*le mystère d'un nom*) because it is the poet who creates by naming, the Rose and the Lily for example. His voice is "the final shudder" (*le frisson final*) of the whole disquieting miracle that causes the world to exist, just as God created Eden.

Mallarmé poses the question, "Is there nothing of this destiny which endures?" (*Est-il de ce destin rien qui demeure, non?*). He then addresses himself to those listening to his toast, saying that they should forget this "somber belief" (*croyance sombre*) because "Splendid eternal genius has no shadow" (*Le splendide génie éternel n'a pas d'ombre*), never fades. Mallarmé, attentive to the desire of his listeners to perpetuate the memory of Gautier (*de votre désir soucieux*), would like to see the one survive who died only yesterday (*A qui s'évanouit, hier*). The best way the living can do honor to the dead is to continue to do that for which we are best suited, thus "ideal," in "the gardens of this star," this earth (*dans le devoir / Idéal que nous font les jardins de cet astre*). We do it "in honor of the tranquil disaster" (*pour l'honneur du tranquille désastre*), in honor of the poet's death, which tranquilizes all. The works of the poet are, after all, words and we find the earlier *frisson final* echoed in the beautiful line "A solemn agitation through the air / Of words" (*Une agitation solennelle par l'air / De paroles*), that is, because his words are immortal they will continue to agitate the air. His description of the rose becomes "purple drunkenness" (*pourpre ivre*) and of the lily "great clear calyx" (*grand calice clair*). The eye of the opening line of this section now becomes a "diaphanous gaze" (*regard diaphane*), which gave the flowers their name and was as necessary to them as "water and light" (*pluie et diamant*). His gaze also partakes of the life-giving properties of the rain and the purity and brilliance and sparkle of the diamond. Because he has named them by his gaze the flowers will never fade (*ces fleurs dont nulle ne se fane*). Because he has named them they stand out amidst all that surrounds them (*Isole parmi l'heure et le rayon du jour*).

In the final movement the poet's works, these gardens, "our true groves" (*nos vrais bosquets*), constitute his real immortality. The *nos* takes us back in a circular movement to the *notre* of the opening *de notre bonheur*. The poet's task is to write. Thus idle daydreaming must be banished from his sojourn on earth (*le poète pur a pour geste humble et large / De l'interdire au rêve, ennemi de sa charge*). If he has not done so, then the morning after the death of Gautier (*le matin de son altier repos*), this "ancient death" (*mort ancienne*), which is for Gautier as it is for all men a closing of the eyes, "sacred" because of what they have accomplished, and a silencing of the mouth, his "solid sepulcher" (*sépulcre solide*) will be no more than "a tributary ornament on the cemetery path" (*de l'allée ornement tributaire*) "Wherein lies all that which is harmful" to his reputation (*où gît tout ce qui nuit*), all that which is truly mortal. The eyes that no longer open and the mouth that no longer speaks, of the fourth from the last line, are repeated in reverse order in the closing line by "Both the avaricious silence and the massive night" (*Et l'avare silence et la massive nuit*). The sibilant *s*'s and the sharp *i*'s of the last two lines emphasize the anguish and horror of what is being said. But we know that in Gautier's tomb lie only his mortal remains and that his works are immortal.

The poem seems somehow very "talky" for Mallarmé and not just because of its exceptional length. He asks one rhetorical question too many, while expressions like *un lieu de porphyre, le beau monument,* and *son repos altier* seem stilted. The section on the Master as namer and thus creator of flowers and all things, while an interesting idea, seems unnecessarily drawn out. Baudelaire's poet "Who hovers over life, and understands without effort / The language of the flowers and all mute things" (*Qui plane sur la vie, et comprend sans effort / Le language des fleurs et des choses muettes*), is more convincing in his brevity. Rimbaud's "flower which told me its name" (*une fleur qui me dit son nom*) expresses something of the same idea much more directly. On the other hand, expressions like *Nous sommes / La triste opacité de nos spectres futurs* and

Une agitation solennelle par l'air reveal Mallarmé at his best. "Toast funèbre" remains a great tribute by one great poet to another.

The Era of Authority

Like "Toast funèbre" "Prose pour des Esseintes" ("Prose for des Esseintes") has fifty-six lines but is shorter since the lines are octosyllables rather than alexandrines. It is also the last poem in verse of such length that Mallarmé wrote. He may have conceived the poem earlier, but the publication of Joris-Karl Huysmans's novel *A Rebours* in 1884 gave the poem its full title and occasioned its appearance in 1885. Huysmans's hero, des Esseintes, a super-aesthete typical of the Decadent period, devotes six or seven pages at the end of chapter 14 to the works of Mallarmé in poetry and prose, including those which had appeared in the *Parnasses* of 1866 and 1871 as well as "Toast funèbre," *L'Après-Midi d'un Faune,* and the poems in prose. His remarks are highly flattering but they also constitute an early, sensitive, and revealing evaluation of Mallarmé's technique and style. Des Esseintes's "ardent aspirations towards an ideal" and "feverish desire for the unknown"[4] strongly resemble the artistic aspirations and desires of Mallarmé. As a result of Huysmans's remarks about Mallarmé the poet's fame spread much more widely. By way of acknowledgment of this encomium Mallarmé published his "Prose" whose title may hark back to the subtitle "Prose des fous" of "Mysticis umbraculis" to suggest the ecclesiastical use of the term as indicated in chapter 2. He may have been replying to the prose of Huysmans's novel by the prose of every poet which is poetry. In his modesty he may have been suggesting that compared to his conception of the ideal poem this one is merely prose. In any event, and like so many of his other poems, "Prose" offers an *art poétique* and is, almost all critics agree, among Mallarmé's most difficult.

The fourteen quatrains of the poem can be divided into three sections: the first two stanzas as introduction, the following ten as development, and the final two as conclusion. In addition, they separate into symmetrical groups of 2, 3, 2, 2, 3, 2. The opening exclamation *Hyperbole!* suggests that all great art in its quintessence is hyperbole that arises triumphantly from the only source of creation, memory. All that is really remembered is that which is contained in books, symbolized today by the ancient *grimoire* of Hérodiade's nurse and the faun. Such books were so precious they were bound in iron to discourage theft. Mallarmé's daring use of the long five-syllabled adverb *Triom-*

phalement in the eight-syllable line is in itself poetic hyperbole. If the first quatrain indicates the source of poetry, the second reveals the means by which the poet transforms memory into art. The strong verb *installer* with its overtones of the solemn and dignified conferral of an honor and the more physical meaning of setting up or putting in place, indicates the effort necessary on the part of the poet to create. Inspiration alone does not suffice. It takes all the poet's knowledge, *science* in the French sense as well as the art or skill of the English sense, to produce a poem with the music of a hymn that will apeal to sensitive souls (*L'hymne des coeurs spirituels*). Any genius involved is a necessary compound of knowledge and patience. The works brought into existence will be an *Atlas* in the sense of collections of maps to orient the mind, geographies of the inorganic; *herbiers* in the sense of collections of dried plants, studies of the organic; and *rituels* in the sense of books that enumerate the ceremonies that must be observed in administering the sacraments, that is, the traditional forms and techniques of poetry itself that must be followed. *Rituels* thus echoes the *installer* of the first line.

In the third quatrain, the first stanza of the development, Mallarmé switches from the first person singular to the plural. The total realization of poetry requires two people, the poet and his reader. Poetry unread is like music unplayed, and Mallarmé insists they were two (*Nous fûmes deux, je le maintiens*). He calls this person sister and when we remember the *coeurs spirituels* for whom his poetry is intended we think of the French expression *âme soeur*, kindred spirit. The attraction of the female element, however, is not eliminated by the use of the word. Baudelaire speaks to his beloved in "L'Invitation au voyage" as *Mon enfant, ma soeur*. Mallarmé in the conclusion to his poem also calls her *enfant*. Just as Gautier in "Toast funèbre" was a true poet because of his vision, so these two were looking around (*Nous promenions notre visage*). In so doing, the poet compares the many charms of his companion to those of the landscape.

The next two quatrains tell what they saw, define the landscape, and are one long sentence of enormous complexity. "The era of authority" (*L'ère d'autorité*), any age or any group that claims to know what is because it is, is troubled when someone, for no apparent reason (*sans nul motif*), maintains that this "sunny southland," *midi* meaning here both the sun and the south, this landscape of the previous stanza, exists, is understood unconsciously, fathomed by the unconscious of both the poet and his companion (*ce midi que notre double / Inconscience appro-*

fondit). The latter claim that "its site, the earth of a hundred iris" (*sol de cent iris, son site*), and the iris certainly know if it has existed (*Ils savent s'il a bien été*), "Carries no name which is quoted / By the gold of the Summer trumpet" (*Ne porte pas de nom que cite / L'or de la trompette d'Eté*), has no name and thus no existence revealed by the blinding light of day.

In the next two stanzas the isolated site of the preceding quatrain becomes an island, the true site of creation. The air charges it with sight, not visions (*De vue et non de visions*), profound insight into the genuine nature of things, not a fantasy about what they may be. Again, just as the poet Gautier in "Toast funèbre" gave true being to flowers by his gaze, so in this garden "Every flower showed itself off more broadly," more freely, bigger than life (*Toute fleur s'étalait plus large*), "without our talking about it," without our having to mention it (*Sans que nous en devisions*). Each flower seemed so immense that it took on its own translucent contour (*se para / D'un lucide contour*), which created around it a lacuna, an empty space which separated it from the rest of the garden (*lacune / Qui des jardins la sépara*), just as every true creation of art separates itself from everything around it and becomes itself and nothing else. The effect is the same as that of the line *Isole parmi l'heure et le rayon du jour* of "Toast funèbre." The use of the five-syllable adverb *Ordinairement* at the beginning of the second line recalls the *Triomphalement* of the second line of the first stanza. Here the adverb is used in the sense of "as if it were the usual thing to do," the thing always done by these exceptional blooms.

These works are the "Glory of the long desire" (*Gloire du long désir*), the fruition of the patience of the second stanza. The poet is exalted to see his ideas, this family of iridaceous flowers, spring forth in this new form, this new life, serve this new purpose (*Surgir à ce nouveau devoir*). Mallarmé was guilty of a neologism since he coined the word *iridées* from the example of *orchidée*. It gave him a rhyme so rich, *désir, Idées— des iridées,* that no less than eight elements correspond, but it also cost him a great deal in the ridicule of those who were not interested in attempting to understand his poetry. In the fifth stanza he used the iris as an example of the flower that has been created. In the tenth quatrain he mentions another specific flower, the lily, which is, as we have seen, one of his favorites. In the last quatrain he mentions the gladiolus, also of the iridaceous family. The reaction of his companion, "this sister," is, however, quite different. Because she is sensible and although she is tender she goes no further than a smile (*Ne porta son regard plus loin / Que sourire*), the enigmatic smile on which the poet has spent so much of his attention in an attempt to understand it (*comme à l'entendre / J'occupe mon antique soin*). The expression *mon antique soin* will find its echo two stanzas later in *mon jeune étonnement* which, like its predecessor, completes the quatrain.

The next three quatrains are again one long sentence and bring the development to a close. In them Mallarmé addresses himself to the carpers (*l'Esprit de litige*), those who do not want to understand his poetry or any poetry. Such carpers should know, once the poem is written (*A cette heure où nous nous taisons*), that the stem of the multiple lilies (*de lis multiples la tige*), the idea with its possible multiple connotations, the work of art with its multiple meanings, has become too big for mere reason (*Grandissait trop pour nos raisons*). It is not as they would have it (*Et non comme pleure la rive*), that this country did not exist (*Que ce pays n'exista pas*). Their monotonous game is a lie (*son jeu monotone ment*), since the poet in his youth discovered to his astonishment all the abundance of nature at his command (*l'ampleur arrive / Parmi mon jeune étonnement*), attested to by the heaven and earth through which he has walked (*D'ouïr tout le ciel et la carte / Sans fin attestés sur mes pas*), "By the very wave that ebbs away" (*Par le flot même qui s'écarte*). *Rive* and *flot* remind us that this land of creation is an island, separated from the mainland of consciousness and reason.

In the two quatrains of the conclusion the companion, the sister, the infant, abandons her smile of the ninth stanza (*L'enfant abdique son extase*), and now that she has been initiated into poetry by the ground they have covered together in their promenade (*Et docte déjà par chemins*), she pronounces only the name *Anastase!* This word, which in its origins means to stand out, this strange name with its Byzantine overtones, is beautiful enough to have been "Born for eternal parchments" (*Né pour d'éternels parchemins*), to be worthy of everlasting poetry. In the words *par chemins—parchemins* Mallarmé manages to rhyme seven elements. The gaping sepulcher laughs at the idea that anyone or anything should think it can be avoided in whatever climate, no matter how imaginary (*Avant qu'un sépulcre ne rie / Sans aucun climat*). *Climat* recalls the country of stanza 12 and the island of stanza 6 as well as the site of stanza 5, the southland of stanza 4, and the landscape of stanza 3, all synonyms for the source of creation, the ancestor, the forebear of all art (*son aïeul*). *De porter ce nom* recalls the *Ne porte pas de nom* of the fifth quatrain. The name has now been found and spoken: *Pulchérie!* It carries with it the overtones of the Latin word for beauty, *pulcheria,* and recalls Mallarmé's remark quoted in chapter 1: "There is only Beauty;—and it has only one perfect expression—Poetry." *Pulchérie* represents the absolute, ideal beauty for which the poet searches but which may be "Hidden by the too large gladiolus" (*Caché par le trop grand glaïeul*), by the vision the poet thinks he has rather than the insight he must have in order to create a poem and a great work of art. Mallarmé thus gives us in "Prose" a complete *art poétique*. He describes the source of poetry and analyzes the means by which the poet transforms memory into art. According to him creation is much more a matter of hard work than inspiration although he does delineate the peculiar sensitivity necessary for creation. He warns the poet of the inevitable detractors, those who cannot or will not understand what he is trying to do. Acceptance and comprehension do not come immediately to the artist and he in turn must take care not to lose himself in his own fantasies. Mallarmé couches this somewhat mundane statement of the artist's eternal task in terms that make it seem at each reading a surprisingly new and fresh discovery. The rhymes are at times almost suffocatingly rich, particularly in view of the short line. "Prose" has not to date yielded all its treasures and will continue for decades to provide a great source for study and pleasure.

The Subtle Lie

Mallarmé wrote eighteen short occasional pieces that he called "Eventails" ("Fans"). The important poems with that name were written for the three women in his life, his wife, his daughter, and Méry Laurent. All three "Eventails" demonstrate very well how Mallarmé transformed the object into poetry.

The first is called "Eventail de Madame Mallarmé" and is in the form of a Shakespearean sonnet but with a line of seven syllables, a rarity in Mallarmé's works. Mallarmé was always interested in feminine fashions and we should remember that he published eight issues of his own magazine, *La Dernière Mode,* from September through December 1874. The "Eventail" of Madame Mallarmé was written in red ink on a fan of silvery paper decorated with white daisies,[5] and first published in 1891.

In the first two lines the poet seems to be describing the language of the fan, which is "Nothing more than a beating in the skies" (*Rien qu'un battement aux cieux*). Never far from the subject of poetry, however, Mallarmé reveals that it is the future line of poetry as it disengages itself from the poet's mind, which is, at this moment where language is concerned, nothing more than a flutter or palpitation in the air. The expression *logis très précieux* to describe the head, or mind, or imagination recalls the forehead of "La chevelure vol d'une flamme . . ." described as *ancien foyer*. The *logis* can also be the hand of Madame Mallarmé. The movements of the fan anticipate the rhythm of the poetic lines the fan inspires.

In the second quatrain the fan becomes a "Wing swooping low" (*Aile tout bas*), a courier, a messenger, provided (*si c'est lui*) it truly is the fan of Madame Mallarmé since she and it are the source of inspiration for the poet. The beloved wife is a limpid mirror that reveals the artist to himself and encourages him in his task.

The parenthesis of the third quatrain reveals that the movement of the fan has dislodged some ashes from Mallarmé's eternal cigarette. That these ashes will settle on the mirror disturbs the poet because it means work for the wife. In the distich the poet hopes that the fan will always appear in the ever busy hands of his wife. *Sans paresse* can indicate that her hands are always busy as they manipulate the fan. It can also indicate that as a housewife she is never idle. The sonnet thus becomes a slight but charming tribute to the dutiful wife.

The "Autre Eventail de Mademoiselle Mallarmé" was composed and published in 1884. The poem reveals the evolution of Mallarmé's conception of poetry during the twenty years that separate it from "Las de l'amer repos . . ." of 1864. There the symbolism was descriptive with a blue line for a lake and three green eyelashes as reeds. Here the subject itself speaks directly to Mademoiselle Mallarmé in five quatrains of octosyllables, calling her "Dreamer." If the fan is to continue to plunge "Into the pure delight" (*pour que je plonge / Au pur délice*) which is the refreshing breath of air it creates, but without going anywhere, with no true direction (*sans chemin*), then she must keep the fan in her hand. As in the "Eventail de Madame Mallarmé" the fan is a wing but one that will never fly, thus the subtle lie (*par un subtil mensonge*).

The movements of the fan create for her "A twilight coolness" (*Une fraîcheur de crépuscule*) by means of a blow that is actually the prisoner of her hand (*le coup prisonnier*). The arc shape of the fan is like a little horizon which is delicately pushed back by the movement. The fan can also hide, and as it moves it may hide the real horizon from Mademoiselle Mallarmé.

If the fan can be described as a wing that does not fly, the breath of air it arouses can be compared to a kiss. The fricative *v*'s and *f*'s and the sibilant *s*'s of *Vertige! voici que frisonne / L'espace* reproduce onomatopoetically the vertigo, the shivering of space as the fan pulsates, creating a breeze like a caress, a kiss destined for no one and thus can neither gush forth nor calm itself. Even *jaillir* and *s'apaiser* describe their meaning by their sound.

All of the folds of the fan have been folded into one "unanimous fold" (*unanime pli*). Mademoiselle Mallarmé coquettishly holds the folded fan at the corner of her smiling mouth, which hides her laughter (*un rire enseveli*). The personality and temperament of this playful maiden is a "savage paradise" (*le paradis farouche*) as she flirts with her fan.

In the last stanza the folded fan has become the scepter of the princess of a faraway land with its "rose-colored shores / Motionless over golden evenings" (*des rivages roses / Stagnants sur les soirs d'or*). The poetic conceit of the rhyme *ce l'est—bracelet* and its meaning, "that's it," add a slightly humorous touch to this romantic picture of the young girl who is resting "This closed white flight" (*Ce blanc vol fermé*) on the gold of her bracelet. Certainly in this brief but beautiful little poem Mallarmé succeeds in describing "not the thing, but the effect it produces."

Mallarmé wrote the "Eventail" for Méry Laurent in 1890 in white ink on a fan of gilt paper decorated with roses.[6] Although a sonnet like the first "Eventail," it is a regular one and in octosyllables like the second. Of the three it is perhaps the least interesting. In any event, Mallarmé never published it during his lifetime. In the first quatrain "frigid roses" (*De frigides roses*), all living alike because all printed on the same paper of the same fan and thus making the same movements, will with their white calyx (*Avec un blanc calice*) interrupt with their breeze the breath of Méry, which has been refreshed by their movement (*Votre souffle devenu givre*).

By beating too hard they might dislodge a tuft, a lock of her hair. If they did, her coldness might flower drunkenly into laughter (*Cette frigidité se fond / En du rire de fleurir ivre*). The *frigides* of the first stanza thus becomes *frigidité* that may say something about the relationship between Mallarmé and Méry Laurent. In addition to the sharp *i*'s of the rhymes in *-ivre,* the sixteen syllables of the two lines just quoted contained six *i*'s, adding to the frigid effect. There is no need to go as far as Richard in hunting for sexual overtones in the word *touffe,*[7] although they certainly may be there.

The conclusion of the two tercets is that a good fan, with its movements that seem to break up the sky into pieces, is much more suitable than a vial. The expression *A jeter le ciel en détail* reminds us of the lines *Dont le coup prisonnier recule / L'horizon délicatement* of "Autre Eventail." The fan needs no stopper like the perfume bottle and does not run the risk of losing or of spoiling "The aroma emanating from Méry" (*L'arôme émané de Méry*). In short, a frivolous poem on a frivolous subject written for a somewhat frivolous woman.

Mallarmé wrote the sonnet "Dame sans trop d'ardeur . . ." ("Lady without too much ardor . . .") late in 1887 as a New Year's Day gift for Méry Laurent. He might almost have named it "Eventail" since a comparison with a fan is found in the final tercet. The poem, which was not published until 1896, describes very accurately the unusual friendship between these two unusual people.

The first line contains a play on words since *ardeur* comes from the Latin verb meaning to burn. It would then read "Lady without too much fieriness at the same time enflaming," meaning that she is a woman who can without much effort inspire a burning friendship. The contrast is between the excesses of passion and the rewards of friendship. The sentiment, the passion, is a rose that can be cruel but can also be torn and weary of the exterior show of emotion (*lasse / Même du blanc habit de pourpre*). When this happens, the sentiment withdraws into itself in an attempt to return to its original, pure state, to realize its own true nature (*Pour ouïr dans sa chair pleurer le diamant*).

The diamond's tear becomes the drop of dew on the rose but it also becomes the tears of a quarrel (*ces crises de rosée*). Although the wind of jealousy may bring about some separation in space, the stormy skies pass (*Ni brise quoique, avec, le ciel orageux passe / Jalouse d'apporter je ne sais quel espace*), leaving one with the realization that such sentiments feed on memories shared, on time past (*Au simple jour le jour très vrai du sentiment*).

The days become years and with their passage the spontaneous grace of Méry is born anew each year (*chaque année / Dont sur ton front renaît la grâce spontanée*). This special grace suffices to arouse the feelings of the poet (*Suffise selon quelque apparence et pour moi*), just as a fan is surprised that it can with its small but fresh breeze arouse the little emotion necessary to keep alive a friendship (*Comme un éventail frais dans la chambre s'étonne / A raviver du peu qu'il faut ici d'émoi*). The relationship itself is described as "our natural, monotonous friendship" (*notre native amitié monotone*), natural because almost innate, native to both, and monotonous because calm and unchanging. This sonnet with its fresh expression of an ancient sentiment is distinctly superior to the "Eventail" Mallarmé wrote for Méry two years later.

Mallarmé wrote three little sonnets in Shakespearean form under the title of "Petit Air," all with seven-syllable lines. The first, published in 1894, brings together several of Mallarmé's often employed symbols: the swan, the setting sun, whiteness, water. In the first quatrain Mallarmé sets the scene and creates the atmosphere that is summed up by the long adverb *langoureusement* of the third stanza. The solitude of this place without swan or quay mirrors its own desuetude in the reflecting waters (*Sans le cygne ni le quai | Mire sa désuétude*). He had been looking at the sky (*Au regard que j'abdiquai*), so high it could not be touched (*Haute à ne la pas toucher*), which was painted in the gaudy golds of sunset (*Dont maint ciel se bariole | Avec les ors de coucher*).

But at that moment his companion lets drop languorously her white shift like a white bird coasting on the water. The liquid *l*'s and the long adverb of the first two lines echo this languid movement: *Mais langoureusement longe | Comme de blanc linge ôté*. She plunges into the water and in a marvelous transformation becomes both the wave and her own naked jubilation (*Dans l'onde toi devenue | Ta jubilation nue*). The peace and purity and calm happiness of this little poem are ineffable in their beauty.

"Petit Air II" was not published during Mallarmé's lifetime but it was scheduled to be included in the edition of the *Poésies* he was working on at his death. It recounts with anguish the fate of the poet who aimed too high and thus was never understood. Again Mallarmé begins the short line with a great adverb *Indomptablement*, underlining how the hope of the poet rushes forth uncontrollably at the same time as his voice, stranger to this earth (*Voix étrangère au bosquet*), bursts forth and is lost (*Eclater là-haut perdu*). It is not followed by any echo since it is like the sound of a bird never before heard (*L'oiseau qu'on n'ouït jamais | Une autre fois dans la vie*). The sob of the poet, this haggard musician (*Le hagard musicien*), will expire in doubt (*Cela dans le doute expire*) if it really came from his breast and not that of another (*Si de mon sein pas du sien*). The play of *sein–sien* here recalls the *longe–linge* of the preceding poem. Torn to pieces, his voice, his sob will fall on some unknown path and remain forever unnoticed (*Déchiré va-t-il entier | Rester sur quelque sentier!*). Mallarmé never expressed better, more succinctly, and with such quiet desperation the fate of the poet whose ideals prove to be impossibly high.

The third "Petit Air," subtitled "Guerrier," dates from 1895. In it Mallarmé recounts ironically the effect on him at seeing a military uniform. He does not mind except he cannot keep quiet about it (*Ce me va hormis l'y taire*), as long as he does not have to be a part of it: *Ce me va hors militaire*. He is waiting for the invasion of the soldier's swagger stick, which is still unused (*Avec le vierge courroux*). The expression could also refer to the poet who in his waiting is not sure just what irritates him about the stick held in the white gloves of these footsloggers (*Au gant blanc des tourlourous*).

The stick, which may be polished (*Nue*) or rough (*d'écorce tenace*), was not intended for beating up the Teuton (*Pas pour battre le Teuton*) but for another menace that will make the poet stop talking, cut short this wild nettle or outbreak of sympathy (*De trancher ras cette ortie / Folle de la sympathie*). Almost in spite of himself the poet is impressed by a uniform and talks so much about it that everyone would be pleased if he would be quiet.

The Ancient Dream

The four poems included under the title "Autres Sonnets" constitute by their subjects and their difficulty a great contrast to the preceding "Little Airs." They are all in great alexandrines that roll forth broadly and sonorously and all are excellent examples of the "hyperbole of pure poetry." The first, "Quand l'ombre menaça . . ." ("When the shadow menaced . . ."), which was published in 1883, recounts again the fate of genius, the creator, the artist, the poet, and man. Just at the moment when the shadow of death menaced the ancient dream of the poet with its fatal law (*Quand l'ombre menaça de sa fatale loi*), a dream that was both his desire and the fruit of all those sedentary hours (*Tel vieux Rêve, désir et mal de mes vertèbres*), a dream that would be "Afflicted at dying beneath the funereal ceilings" (*Affligé de périr sous les plafonds funèbres*), just at that moment the dream "folded its undoubted wing" within him (*Il a ployé son aile indubitable en moi*), undoubted because even at this juncture the poet retains his faith in himself and his genius.

The "funereal ceilings" become those of a luxurious hall of ebony whereon are sculpted well-known garlands that were intended to seduce a king and that writhe in their agony (*Luxe, ô salle d'ébène où, pour séduire un roi / Se tordent dans leur mort des guirlandes célèbres*). They are nothing more than a pride to which the shadows give the lie (*Vous n'êtes qu'un orgueil menti par les ténèbres*) in the eyes of the solitary poet who is dazzled by his own faith (*Aux yeux du solitaire ébloui de sa foi*). For many critics these "funereal ceilings" are the sky itself with its "well-known garlands" of moving, dying stars whose reality is hidden by the vast distances from the solitary observer who nevertheless retains his faith that they do exist and are there.

In his faith the poet knows that "into the vast distances of this night, the Earth / Throws the unwonted mystery with great brilliance" (*au lointain de cette nuit, la Terre / Jette d'un éclat l'insolite mystère*) under the weight of "the hideous centuries" (*les siècles hideux*), which with the advance of human knowledge and progress "hide it less" (*qui l'obscurcissent moins*).

The great void of the heavens, this space that is always "equal to itself whether it expands or contracts" (*L'espace à soi pareil qu'il s'accroisse ou se nie*), "Revolves in this boredom," which is boredom because always the same and endless, "vile fires," the stars themselves, vile because as far as man knows they are dead. These "well-known garlands" are witnesses (*Roule dans cet ennui des feux vils pour témoins*) "That the genius of a festive star has been kindled" (*Que s'est d'un astre en fête allumé le génie*). No matter how vast the distances and how impressive the stars, they are nothing without the consciousness that observes and interprets them. No matter how great the universe, the mind of man, his genius, makes of this earth "a festive star." Few poets have stated so positively and so beautifully their ultimate faith in mankind.

The second sonnet, "Le vierge, le vivace et le bel aujourd'hui" ("The virginal, living, and beautiful today"), which was first published in 1885, shares with the fourth an unusual rhyme scheme. All of the rhymes of the second are in *i* while the fourth is called "the sonnet in -*yx*" because one of its two rhymes takes that form. The second sonnet is frequently anthologized because it is not so difficult to interpret and because of its beauty and perfection. Almost a fourth of all the syllables contain the bright, clear sound of *i* or the glide *i*, thus heightening the effect of this cold, snowy, icy, sparkling, winter scene in white.

Mallarmé sets that scene in the first quatrain. The time is today, which, because it is "virginal, living, and beautiful," is a day that lets us see with blinding clarity (*Va-t-il nous déchirer avec un coup d'aile ivre*) beneath the frozen lake of forgetfulness (*Ce lac dur oublié*) "The transparent glacier of flights which have not fled" (*Le transparent glacier des vols qui n'ont pas fui!*), the risks never run, the ideas never tried, the attempts never realized, the flights of imagination never accomplished.

By the use of *aile* and *vol* Mallarmé prepares the reader for the bird introduced into the scene in the second stanza. The bird is of course the swan, "A swan of other times" (*Un cygne d'autrefois*). *Autrefois* in the first line of the second quatrain contrasts strongly with the *aujourd'hui* of the first line of the first quatrain while the verb *se souvient* develops the idea of *Ce dur lac oublié*. The magnificent bird is attempting to free itself but without hope since he failed to sing of the living land (*Pour n'avoir pas chanté la région où vivre*) "When the boredom of sterile winter shone" (*Quand du stérile hiver a resplendi l'ennui*). Winter with its monotonous white is boring and because nothing grows it is sterile, but it is resplendent in its sparkling mantle. The songs unsung of the second quatrain recall the flights untried of the first.

In the first tercet the swan, caught in the frozen lake, shakes its neck in agony (*Tout son col secouera cette blanche agonie*). Even the agony of the white bird in the white snow appears white. The first two lines can also read: the swan will shake off this white agony that is the wintry landscape over which it must fly but which it denies precisely because it can fly (*Par l'espace infligée à l'oiseau qui le nie*). That agony it can avoid but not the horror of being caught in the frozen ground.

The opening word of the concluding tercet, phantom, is the "Swan" of the last word. The swan is like a phantom that, because of its pure whiteness, seems destined for such a landscape (*Fantôme qu'à ce lieu son pur éclat assigne*). The agonizing movement of the first tercet becomes total stillness in the second. The swan accepts its fate with contempt, "It remains motionless at the cold thought of scorn" (*Il s'immobilise au songe froid de mépris*), the only attitude the swan can wear "amidst its useless exile" (*Que vêt parmi l'exil inutile le Cygne*). The flight never took off, the song was never sung, the swan is captive in its useless exile. The poet will never realize his ideal and can accept his own miserable creations only with the contempt they deserve. The numerous hissing sibilants and troubling fricatives heighten the effect of the bright *i*'s to culminate in a final line that, with its rhythm capturing the sad idea being expressed, remains one of the joys of French literature.

The first version of the third sonnet, "Victorieusement fui le suicide beau" ("Victoriously fled the beautiful suicide"), was written probably in 1885 but differs radically from the final version, which was, with a couple of minor exceptions, that of the 1887 edition of the *Poésies*. It is among Mallarmé's more difficult poems, but it is also among the more rewarding.

We are now accustomed to Mallarmé's use of the long adverb, frequently at the beginning of the line, as we again find it here in the six-syllable *Victorieusement*. Such emphasis heightens the feeling of victory over the attractions of self-destruction, "beautiful suicide": "Torch of fame, blood through foam, gold, tempest" (*Tison de gloire, sang par écume, or, tempête!*). In a subtle way all of these attributes can apply to the "vanished sky" (*ciel évanoui*) of the first tercet. The poet has avoided self-destruction while the sun has participated in its daily suicide like a "Torch of glory" that in setting turns the foamy clouds blood-red, covers them with gold, creates the effect of a storm that has not actually taken place, just as the suicide did not take place. The poet can laugh at his narrow escape if the purple cloth, the deep and royal color just after the sun has set, is being prepared only for his absent tomb, absent because avoided, not now needed (*O rire si là-bas une pourpre s'apprête / A ne tendre que mon absent tombeau*).

In the second quatrain it is midnight and the poet asks if "of all that brilliance not even a shred / Loiters" (*de tout cet éclat pas même le lambeau / S'attarde*), again mingling the metaphor of the colors of the sky with cloth. Only the shadows are keeping the poet and his companion company (*l'ombre qui nous fête*). For light, all that is left is a "head's presumptuous treasure" (*Excepté qu'un trésor présomptueux de tête*), presumptuous because it dares to equal the sun in brilliance, which "Pours its caressed nonchalance without a torch" (*Verse son caressé nonchaloir sans flambeau*). *Flambeau* echoes the earlier *Tison* and indicates that this head, caressed both by the light, the poet, and the comb, nonchalantly gives off light without need of a torch. The figure of the head of hair as a torch recalls the *tutélaire torche* of the conclusion of "La chevelure vol d'une flamme. . . ."

The head is, of course, that of his companion and, yes, it is always a delight (*La tienne si toujours le délice*). Professor Cohn suggests that *si* is the affirmative answer to the negative question, *pas même le lambeau*, of the preceding stanza.[8] Mallarmé repeats the expression "yours / Yes" (*la tienne / Oui*) and maintains that it "alone retains from the vanished sky / A little of the childish triumph" (*seule qui du ciel évanoui retienne / Un peu de puérile triomphe*). The triumph is childish when one compares a shining head of hair to the sun itself, but childish also because the companion will be called infant in the final tercet just as she had been in "Prose pour des Esseintes." We also note the double *La tienne–la tienne.*

In the last stanza the companion who is crowned in light (*en t'en coiffant / Avec clarté*) lays her head on the cushions "Like the warrior helmet of an infant empress" (*Comme un casque guerrier d'impératrice en-fant*). The use of *impératrice* recalls the *royal* of the first stanza and reminds us that Mallarmé always finds in the woman the child as well as the princess. Rays of light glance off the helmet of hair like roses and in their glint they give contour to her face and a rosy tint to her complexion (*Dont pour te figurer il tomberait des roses*).

To the grave question of suicide posed by Mallarmé at the beginning of the poem, he has answered that, although the momentary triumph over death may be childish and thus temporary, the simple pleasures of life, the beauty of the loved one's hair, for example, render suicide foolish and useless. To give one's self up to death is to surrender to an absolute. The poet may have to kill himself in his attempt to attain the absolute that is his ideal. The most he can do is to be content with second best, his creations, and take the pleasures of living where he finds them.

The last sonnet of this group, the one in *-yx* that begins "Ses purs ongles . . ." ("Her pure fingernails . . ."), was written perhaps as early as 1868 but the version we know is that of the 1887 *Poésies*, which differs widely from its earlier form. This is the poem of which Mallarmé was speaking when he wrote to his friend Cazalis of "an internal mirage of words" that produces "a rather cabalistic sensation." In the same letter of 1868 Mallarmé put the sonnet in other words that are still his own:

. . . a window open at night, the two shutters fastened back, a room with no one in it, in spite of the air of stability created by the shutters fastened back, and in a night compounded of absence and questioning, without furniture, except for the plausible outline of vague consoles, a warlike and agonizing frame, of a mirror hung in the background, with its stellar and incomprehensible reflection, of the Great Bear, which alone links to the sky this lodging abandoned by the world.[9]

The description is of course of the earlier version but it can help us with the later version of this difficult and perhaps somewhat overcrowded sonnet.

Mallarmé set himself the complicated task of inverting the gender of the rhymes between the quatrains and the tercets: the masculine *-yx* of the quatrains becomes the feminine *-ixe* in the tercets while the feminine *-ore* of the quatrains becomes the masculine *-or* of the tercets.

Such manipulations should not intrude on the poem. If they do, they rapidly degenerate into the most facile of poetic games.

The time is midnight and again out of the darkness light will come, recalling "Victorieusement fui le suicide beau." Anguish is personified as a lamp-bearer (*lampadophore*) sustaining "Many a vespertine dream burned by the Phoenix" (*Maint rêve vespéral brûlé par le Phénix*), the miraculous bird of the Egyptian religion fabled to be consumed by its own act and to rise in youthful freshness from the ashes. As in the "Ouverture ancienne" we witness Mallarmé's use of synecdoche; the part for the whole, the fingernail for the finger and even the hand. There it was *De sibylles offrant leur ongle vieil aux Mages*. Here it is *Ses purs ongles très haut dédiant leur onyx*. As I mentioned then, *onyx* comes from the Greek word for *ongle*. Thus when Anguish holds up her hands, her fingernails can be seen because of their onyxlike properties. They give off a faint light against the dark of midnight. In the circular movement we now associate with Mallarmé's poems, the last line will also be filled with twinkling light.

In the empty room, of which Mallarmé spoke in his letter, there is "no funerary urn" to receive the ashes of the burned-out dreams of Anguish (*Que ne recueille pas de cinéraire amphore*). The opening line of the second stanza, "On the credenzas, in the empty salon" (*Sur les crédences, au salon vide*), can refer both to the funerary urn of the preceding quatrain and to the *ptyx* that follows. The word *ptyx* means "shell" in Greek. Thus in this empty salon there is no shell, "Abolished bibelot of sonorous inanity" (*Aboli bibelot d'inanité sonore*). The many *b*'s and *l*'s of *Aboli bibelot* are ironic, slightly humorous even, while the empty shell is a sonorous inanity because the sound of the sea one is supposed to hear is an illusion. There is no shell because "the Master has gone to dip up tears in the Styx" with it (*Car le Maître est allé puiser des pleurs au Styx*). The Styx was the river of Hades whose waters rendered one invulnerable. Thus the poet would render himself invulnerable by the tears he has wept for the burned-out dreams of the first stanza. The shell is "the only object of which Nothingness is proud" (*Avec ce seul objet dont le Néant s'honore*) because it is empty, filled with nothing, and yet apparently gives off a sound coming from that very nothingness.

In the two tercets Mallarmé completes his description of the empty room. The line "But near the vacant window to the north" (*Mais proche la croisée au nord vacante*) has several interesting overtones. The reader

finds out why this must be a window on the north only in the last line
of the poem while *la croisée* means "window," but comes from the effect
created by the wooden strips separating the panes. They are in the form
of an X and of course the rhymes are in -*yx*. Thus the idea echoes the
sound. At that window, a bit of "gold / Agonizes according perhaps to
the decor" (*un or / Agonise selon peut-être le décor*), that is, a ray of light
is shining on one of the sculptured gilt details of the ornate decoration
in the room, perhaps on the sculptured frame of the mirror mentioned
in the last tercet. *Un or / Agonise* recalls "Toast funèbre" with its cup
où souffre un monstre d'or. The monsters here are unicorns, the fabled
animals of antiquity, which are attacking a nymph (*Des licornes ruant
du fer contre une nixe*). As the light flickers over the gilt sculpture, the
animals seem to move, the unicorns seem to be kicking up fire. The
naked nymph is dead because she is only a bit of sculpture or painting
reflected in the mirror. The mirror itself is described as "forgetfulness
enclosed by the frame" (*l'oubli fermé par le cadre*), forgetful because once
the subject of the mirror has moved away, the mirror "forgets" it, no
longer reflects it. Remembering that the nixe is a water sprite, we also
remember Hérodiade's mirror, *Eau froide par l'ennui dans ton cadre gelée,*
wherein she, like the "Master" of the present poem, learned the use-
lessness of her dreams, *J'ai de mon rêve épars connu la nudité*. We are also
reminded of *Ce lac dur oublié* of "Le vierge, le vivace et le bel aujour-
d'hui." At this point Mallarmé makes another of those transitions from
mirror to window to sky that we saw in "Ouverture ancienne," wherein
the inside becomes outside and vice versa, wherein the near at hand
becomes far away and the far away near. In the mirror we see the twinkling of a septet, a musical term used to refer to the seven stars of the
Big Dipper, Ursa Major, a northern constellation. Their twinkling is
echoed by the six sibilant *s*'s of *se fixe / De scintillations sitôt de septuor.*
In one magnificent movement the microcosm of the abandoned room
becomes the macrocosm of the universe, the burned-out hopes of the
first stanza, like the Phoenix, rise again, aspire to the stars, realize
themselves in the perfect work of art.

The beauty of the conclusion does a great deal to relieve the poem
of its earlier preciosity. The personification of Anguish, the use of the
beautiful but somewhat recherché *lampadophore,* the mention of the
Phoenix, the Styx, the unicorns, and the nixe, the capitalizing of Master and Nothingness, crowd the two quatrains and spill over into the
tercets. The last two stanzas, however, reveal Mallarmé at his best.

Again he states the aspirations of the poet in a calm but anguished cry that is the hallmark of his genius.

In the poems to be taken up in the next chapter, several of which are tributes to great men, we hear this same cry of hope mingled with despair.

Chapter Seven
Sumptuous Allegories of the Void

Unlike the tributes dutifully written by great and not so great poets upon the death of famous men and so often soon and better forgotten, the "tombs" and homages of Mallarmé are among his greatest creations. After the "Toast funèbre" to Gautier of 1873 he wrote seven, which I shall consider here, in addition to the little sonnet he wrote in 1893, as a toast to his fellow poets. The last eight poems are sonnets on various subjects. Among them are to be found some of Mallarmé's most famous and most difficult poems, "sumptuous allegories of the void" as Mallarmé thought of titling a book.[1]

Tombs and Temples

Among the earlier and less complicated poems is one written in memory of a woman now thought to have been Ettie Yapp, the English wife of Mallarmé's good friend Henri Cazalis. The poem carries the date of All Souls' Day, 2 November 1877, and begins *"Sur les bois oubliés . . ."* ("'Over the forgotten woods . . .'"). The poem is in quotation marks, indicating that the soul of the departed is speaking to the loved one left behind. We are now accustomed to Mallarmé's wintry decor and to the implications of his use of *oubliés*. The dead wife calls her husband the "solitary captive of the threshold" of the tomb (*ô captif solitaire du seuil*), solitary because left alone and captive of the threshold because still among the living. She alone inhabits the sepulcher constructed for two, and because it is winter there are no flowers to cover it. Mallarmé expresses this last idea with marvelous indirection: the sepulcher "is encumbered only with the lack of heavy bouquets" (*du manque seul des lourds bouquets s'encombre*).

We are also accustomed by now to the hour of midnight in Mallarmé's poetry. It has stuck "its vain number" (*son vain nombre*), vain because the husband has not even heard it. On this anniversary of her death he is thinking about her so hard that he is unable to sleep (*Une veille t'exalte à ne pas fermer l'oeil*). He is hoping that her shadow will come in the light of the last torch to occupy the chair where she formerly sat (*Avant que dans les bras de l'ancien fauteuil / Le suprême tison n'ait éclairé mon Ombre*). We remember the *Tison de gloire* of "Victorieusement fui le suicide beau" and its connection with death.

In the first tercet the dead wife expresses an unusual idea: "he who hopes to be visited by the dead" (*Qui veut souvent avoir la Visite*) should not put too many flowers on the tomb (*ne doit / Par trop de fleurs charger la pierre*) since it must be raised by a dead hand (*que mon doigt / Soulève avec l'ennui d'une force défunte*).

In the final tercet she reveals that she is trembling, eager to sit again before this happy fire (*Ame au si clair foyer tremblante de m'asseoir*). All that is necessary to bring her back is that her husband murmur her name throughout the evening (*Pour revivre il suffit qu'à tes lèvres j'emprunte / Le souffle de mon nom murmuré tout un soir*). The idea is that she will borrow the breath of life used to murmur her name in order to appear among the living. That breath must of course be the breath of the loved one left behind. The sonnet remains an eloquent expression of love as well as a sad and beautiful sigh of regret at the inevitability of death.

In 1875 a monument was erected in Baltimore to Edgar Allan Poe who had died a quarter of a century earlier. To celebrate the event a memorial volume was published there in 1877 containing, among other tributes, Mallarmé's "Le Tombeau d'Edgar Poe" which had been written the year before. Critics agree that it is among Mallarmé's greatest poems and one of the most important of the last twenty-five years of the nineteenth century.

The first line is one of the most frequently quoted in French literature of the last hundred years: "As into Himself eternity finally changes him" (*Tel qu'en Lui-même enfin l'éternité le change*). That is, the poet becomes his true self only after the physical body is gone and fads and fashions have had their day, leaving the great poet imperturbably and forever himself. Each new generation interprets him anew, revealing another aspect of his eternal genius. Until such time the Poet, alone and with the naked sword of his works (*Le Poète suscite avec un glaive nu*), arouses his century, which is frightened not to have known that death triumphed in that strange voice (*Son siècle épouvanté de n'avoir pas connu / Que la mort triomphait dans cette voix étrange!*). The poet may not have been understood while he was living, but death is not for him a

defeat. It is rather his death that will prove him to be the great poet
he is.

The use of *glaive nu* in this poem recalls the lines from an earlier
poem, "Le Guignon": *un ange très puissant / Debout à l'horizon dans le nu
de son glaive.* The horizon and the century are frontiers, the one in
space, the other in time. Mallarmé sees the poet as a valiant warrior
who must attack both.

The second quatrain contains an equally famous line, this time having to do with the task of the poet rather than his fate. If he is a truly
great poet he will "Give a purer meaning to the words of the tribe"
(*Donner un sens plus pur aux mots de la tribu*) through his poetry. The
first word of the quatrain, *Eux,* although it is the usual form for the
third person plural pronoun subject separated from its verb, nevertheless takes on the somewhat pejorative tone of all those of the century,
the contemporaries of Poe, who were frightened because they did not
understand his voice. To their ears what the angel was saying was "like
the vile start of a hydra" (*Eux, comme un vil sursaut d'hydre oyant jadis
l'ange*). It can also mean that their reaction to what the poet said was
"like the vile start of a hydra." The archaic form *oyant* emphasizes the
full temporal implications of *jadis.* The use of the hydra is appropriate,
particularly in view of the *bu* and *flot* of the last two lines. Because
they did not understand, they "Proclaimed aloud that this magic had
been drunk / In the dishonored wave of some black mixture" (*Procla-
mèrent très haut le sortilège bu / Dans le flot sans honneur de quelque mélange
noir*), that the true source of Poe's haunted and haunting poetry was
alcohol and drunkenness. The somber word *noir* will be repeated by
noirs in the last line of the poem.

In the first tercet Mallarmé fears that this tribute will be unaccept-
able to heaven, the ideal, the eternal, as well as to earth, the here, the
now, the real (*Du sol et de la nue hostiles, ô grief!*), if the idea he and his
companions have of Poe, with all that they know of his greatness, does
not succeed in sculpting a bas-relief in words that will decorate his
dazzling tomb (*Si notre idée avec ne sculpte un bas-relief / Dont la tombe de
Poe éblouissante s'orne*). The tomb is dazzling primarily because it is Poe's
and only secondly because it is in itself beautiful.

The first line of the last tercet is also much quoted. On the literal
level "Calm block fallen here below from some obscure disaster" (*Calme
bloc ici-bas chu d'un désastre obscur*) can refer to the granite block of the
tomb itself, calm because a tomb and at rest—which seems to have
been dislodged from its mountainside by some grave upheaval. But it

can also designate the poet, who like an aerolite has landed on this earth after some starry collision or conflagration. Mallarmé's final hope is "That this granite at least put a limit forever / To the dark flights of Blasphemy scattered in the future" (*Que ce granit du moins montre à jamais sa borne / Aux noirs vols du Blasphème épars dans le futur*). The *à jamais* and *dans le futur* of the last two lines recall the eternity of the opening line of the poem. If the monument and the memorial volume succeed, then Poe will have begun his voyage through eternity to become in the minds of men the great poet he is. The sordid biographical details will have been forgotten and only the genius will be remembered.

In 1892, twenty-five years after Baudelaire's death, a group of French poets decided to raise a monument of some kind to him and to publish a special issue of the review *La Plume* consecrated to him, to be republished in book form. Mallarmé's "Le Tombeau de Charles Baudelaire" appeared in the magazine in 1895, along with tributes from twenty-eight other poets.

The works of Baudelaire are his temple and his tomb. Buried in time like a temple buried in sand (*Le temple enseveli*) they divulge "through the sepulchral / Sewer mouth" (*par la bouche / Sépulchral d'égout*), sepulchral because belonging to a tomb, their "mud and rubies," their "Spleen and Ideal" as Professor Davies put it,[2] the extremes of Baudelaire's poetry. That they come from a sewer is not surprising, given Baudelaire's penchant for the city, the nature of many of his subjects, and the title of his major work, *Les Fleurs du mal*. Mallarmé again uses a long adverb to begin a line, *Abominablement,* and what issues is "some idol, Anubis" (*quelque idole Anubis*), the jackal-faced god of the dead in Egyptian religion. Death is a major preoccupation in Baudelaire's works, and Mallarmé was acquainted with Egyptian mythology through his friend the Egyptologist, Eugène Lefébure. We have already noted his reference to the Phoenix in "Ses purs ongles. . . ." The muzzle of the gem-encrusted Anubis is twisted in a fierce and frightening snarl (*Tout le museau flambé comme un aboi farouche*), according to Professor Davies.[3] According to Professor Cohn the *flambé* refers to burning sewer gas in keeping with the second line of the poem.[4] Both are possible. All readers are impressed by the number of *b*'s encountered in the poem recalling the *b* of Baudelaire.

In spite of the various lights mentioned, the second quatrain remains somewhat obscure, or at least lends itself to multiple interpretations. The introductory *Ou* (Or else) indicates that it will provide another symbol of the works of Baudelaire. Mallarmé uses the relatively recent invention of gaslight, a typical appurtenance of the city that he mentions frequently in his writings. The advantage of gas was that it needed no troublesome wick (*Ou que le gaz récent torde la mèche louche*). Gas has replaced the wick just as the recent appreciation and understanding of Baudelaire has replaced the squinting, one-eyed, shifty view of the earlier poet's time. *Louche* comes from the Latin *luxus* meaning "one-eyed," and thus in modern French, "equivocal, suspect." As a noun it means that which lacks clarity. Even so (*on le sait*), the intellectual enlightenment of the time should have been sufficient to wipe away, eliminate the insults endured (*Essuyeuse on le sait des opprobres subis*) by Baudelaire. The gas "lights up wildly an immortal pubis" (*Il allume hagard un immortel pubis*). The pubis is one of the three bones of either half of the pelvis. Thus Baudelaire's works, like the gaslight, illuminate the eternal problem of sex whose movement as revealed by the streetlight would seem to indicate that it sleeps out, is always on the prowl (*Dont le vol selon le réverbère découche*). The last line could also be read to mean that the streetlamp reveals the furtive movements of sex that occur most frequently at night.

Death in the form of Anubis, and sex in the form of the pubis become the symbols of Baudelaire's poetry. In the first tercet Mallarmé asks himself "What dried foliage of these cities without night" (*Quel feuillage séché dans les cités sans soir / Votif*) could possibly suffice as a votive to Baudelaire? The foliage could be dried because it is subjected to all the unhealthy conditions of city life while the city with its streetlamps is without night. Or the dried foliage could be the withered flowers already on the tombs in the cemeteries that are cities without evening because perpetually dark with the night of the tomb. The next problem is to identify the pronoun *elle* (*pourra bénir comme elle*). Usually in French such pronouns refer to the first preceding noun of the same number and gender. Here, however, poetic license allows it to refer to an expression that follows in the last tercet, *Celle son Ombre même*. Any tribute placed on Baudelaire's tomb would be in vain since it cannot match his greatness (*se rasseoir / Contre le marbre vainement de Baudelaire*). The only tribute worthy of Baudelaire is his own works which are his Shadow, the spirit of his thought and ideas, the soul of his creations, still veiled in some obscurity (*Au voile qui la ceint*) and although absent, in the sense that Baudelaire is absent in death, still alive with an energy and a power of its own (*absente avec frissons*). The soul, the shadow of his works, is "a guardian poison" (*un poison tutélaire*), a poison so strong it will kill if taken in too large a dose but that is salutary if taken in the right amount. The shadow is a poisonous gas, recalling the gas of the second quatrain, which must be breathed even though we die from it (*Toujours à respirer si nous en périssons*). Baudelaire's works are an experience that must be lived through. After reading them we are forever changed, a part of us inevitably dies, but we are led on to a more profound comprehension of life itself. Mallarmé pays tribute to the true genius of Baudelaire although this "Tombeau" is perhaps the least satisfying of those he wrote.[5]

The little sonnet entitled "Salut," which Mallarmé intended as an epigraph for the *Poésies,* was written in 1893, the same year as "Le Tombeau de Charles Baudelaire," and recited by Mallarmé at a banquet given by the review *La Plume.* The "virginal verse" he is reciting— virginal because never before heard—has only one purpose, to act as a toast that is also symbolized by the cup he holds up (*Rien, cette écume, vierge vers / A ne désigner que la coupe*). The poetry is no more substantial than the foam of the toast, but the foam brings to mind the faraway sea wherein a troupe of sirens disport themselves (*Telle loin se noie une troupe / De sirènes mainte à l'envers*). The poetry of the toast should also be as attractive as the song of the sirens.

The sea becomes the sea of life through which we all sail (*Nous naviguons, ô mes amis / Divers*). Mallarmé, at his age, is at the stern of the ship (*moi déjà sur la poupe*) while his younger poet friends are in the sumptuous bow, sumptuous because of the beauty of their creations (*Vous l'avant fastueux*), which sails triumphantly through the stormy, wintry sea (*qui coupe / Le flot de foudres et d'hivers*).

Mallarmé is drunk with the pleasure and honor accorded him of proposing the toast (*Une ivresse belle m'engage*). He is so drunk he does not fear the pitching of the boat (*Sans craindre même son tangage*), the peril of such an undertaking in front of such an eminent group. He is so drunk he no longer fears that his poetry may be as uneven as the pitching of a boat.

No matter what the risks, the solitude in which we must live and create, the submerged reefs upon which we may founder, the guiding star of our ideals that may lead us astray (*Solitude, récif, étoile*), we all must make the same voyage in life (*A n'importe ce qui valut / Le blanc souci de notre toile*). By running such risks poets and artists become the "Phares" of Baudelaire's poem, the guiding lights, the beacons for all mankind. With the reef and the star Mallarmé has brought together the high and the low, the faraway and near at hand, and with solitude he describes the poet's fate as well as the basic human condition. This little sonnet in octosyllables is another of Mallarmé's gems.

Verlaine died on 8 January 1896. To celebrate the first anniversary of his death Mallarmé wrote a "Tombeau" which was published in the January 1897 issue of *La Revue Blanche*. In the three "tombs" Mallarmé contrasts in some way the material and the immaterial. In that of Poe the *Calme bloc* stood against *le flot sans honneur*. In that of Baudelaire *le marbre* contrasted with *son Ombre*. In that of Verlaine *Le noir roc* of the first quatrain is played off against *la bise* of the first and *Cet immatériel deuil* of the second. No matter how much "The angry black rock" of the temperament and works and reputation of Verlaine is buffeted by the wintry wind (*Le noir roc courroucé que la bise le roule*), it will not be stopped in its course even by those pious hands (*Ne s'arrêtera ni sous de pieuses mains*), which are interested only in feeling out its resemblance to all human ills, which are interested only in verifying the weaknesses of the human man (*Tâtant sa ressemblance avec les maux humains*), as if in order to consecrate with them some ill-fated mold, as if the funeral mask thus molded to reveal all the defects of his human failings could reveal the whole man, the genius behind the human mask (*Comme pour en bénir quelque funeste moule*). Mallarmé uses *bénir* here in the sense of "to consecrate" as he had in the poem to Baudelaire.

Opposed to the mourners who are interested only in celebrating the human failings of the dead poet, there are always those whose "immaterial mourning" is like the cooing of the ringdove, the symbol of grief (*Ici presque toujours si le ramier roucoule*). Such meaningless, ill-considered grief only succeeds in hiding under "many / Nubile folds" (*Cet immatériel deuil opprime de maints / Nubiles plis*) the future star of Verlaine's genius. *Nubiles* means "marriageable." Professor Davies interprets it as marriageable in the sense of being ready for, being old enough, for marriage. Thus the folds are ready to drop to reveal Verlaine's genius.[6] Professor Cohn underlines the connection between *nubile* and *nue*, thus establishing the cloudy effect of the folds. He also demonstrates that the word points toward the future marriage of the poet and the crowd when the latter has come to appreciate the genius of the former.[7] The folds can also be marriageable among themselves, that is, in such a similar state that they all become one big fold that hides Verlaine's star. The important transformation is that of *Le noir roc courroucé* into *l'astre mûri*. Just as with Poe, *Tel qu'en Lui-même enfin l'éternité le change,* so with Verlaine. When his star has matured in the future (*l'astre mûri des lendemains*), when his genius has come to be accepted, then its "gleam will silver the crowd," ordinary men will benefit from his creations (*Dont un scintillement argentera la foule*).

Mallarmé asks the question, "Who is hunting for the real Verlaine by following his solitary movements which are, after all, only an exterior manifestation of our vagabond?" (*Qui cherche, parcourant le solitaire bond / Tantôt extérieur de notre vagabond—Verlaine?*). As with Gautier in his tomb, we know that the physical Verlaine "is hidden amidst the grass" (*Il est caché parmi l'herbe, Verlaine*). Mallarmé again uses the same word to begin and end a line, *Verlaine–Verlaine*. The repetition is particularly effective here, given the soft beauty of Verlaine's name with its overtones of green and wool and the soft beauty of many of his poems with their reiterated vowels.

In the final tercet Mallarmé suggests that the living genius Verlaine knew perfectly well the essential relationship between life and death, that life is in one sense only a living death. His lips were naively, naturally in agreement (*A ne surprendre que naïvement d'accord*) with death and were not surprised to find it nothing more than "A much maligned shallow brook" (*Un peu profond ruisseau calomnié*). His lips knew about the waters of death without ever having drunk of them (*La lèvre sans y boire*), nor will his breath be dried up by death, nor will Verlaine's singing end with his death (*ou tarir son haleine*). The word *ruisseau* also means gutter so that an ambiguous effect is created. The reader remembers *le flot sans honneur de quelque mélange noir* of the tribute to Poe. Mallarmé in this brief sonnet has written a glowing tribute to a poet whose talent and temperament differed radically from his own, but whose genius he appreciated at its true and full worth.

Homages and Honors

Mallarmé reserved the title "Tombeau" for his tributes to poets. For musicians and painters he used the word *Hommage*. In 1885 he published an article entitled "Richard Wagner, Rêverie d'un poète français" without, as he himself wrote, "ever having heard any Wagner."[8] In the same letter he described his study as "half article, half poem in prose" and since Mallarmé was a poet and not a musician he was more interested in Wagner's theories than in his music. I have discussed in chapter 1 how the poet was attracted to Wagner's ideal of the synthesis of all the arts, described by Mallarmé as the "Monster-Who-Cannot-Be."[9] Mallarmé, while granting that Wagner had effected the marriage

of "the personal drama and the ideal music," "the fusion of these disparate forms of pleasure" (p. 543), nevertheless had reservations about
Wagner's ideal as an unattainable absolute. The poet could think only
of the word, which came first in the theater, with music as a relatively
recent addition. With the poet the word always comes first.

Some of the preoccupations of the article are reflected in the "Hommage" Mallarmé wrote for Wagner, in 1885, just two years after Wagner's death. In the first quatrain Mallarmé describes the state of the
theater after Wagner's death. There "The already funereal silence"
reigns (*Le silence déjà funèbre*), already although it is only two years. The
silence is signified by the watered silk draped over the unused furniture
(*d'une moire / Dispose plus qu'un pli seul sur le mobilier*). Mallarmé again
uses *pli* to indicate that something is being hidden, as he had in the
poem on Verlaine. The silence has been precipitated by "the settling
of the principal pillar" (*Que doit un tassement du principal pilier / Précip-
iter*), the death of Wagner, at the same time as "the lack of memory"
(*avec le manque de mémoire*). For the moment Wagner himself may be
forgotten but in the meantime the actors have forgotten their lines,
the theater has forgotten its sources, and the public has forgotten the
theater. Where words should ring out there is only silence.

The same thing has happened to books. The old book that was the
source of "Our so ancient triumphant frolic" (*Notre si vieil ébat triomphal
du grimoire*) is now nothing more than hieroglyphs by which thousands
give themselves a familiar and vulgar shudder (*Hiéroglyphes dont s'exalte
le milier / A propager de l'aile un frisson familier!*). We note Mallarmé's
use of *grimoire*, referred to so many times before, and of *aile* to symbolize the page of the book. We remember also the *frisson* brought
about by the *aile* of the fan. If this is the use to which books are being
put, then they are good only for storing in a closet (*Enfouissez-le-moi
dans une armoire*).

With the use of *parvis* in the first tercet we return to the theater of
the first quatrain and to the origin of the theater itself, the church
porch. A new god of great clarities has sprung up "From the original
smiling din" (*Du souriant fracas originel*) of the early theater. This new
god is Wagner and he is, of course, hated (*haï*) by the old theater, even
though its stage would seem to have been born specifically for the
representation of his clarities (*un parvis né pour leur simulacre*).

In the final tercet the words of Wagner are not just words on a page,
as in the book of the second quatrain, but trumpets that sound on high
the words of gold that lie fainting because unspoken on the pages

(*Trompettes tout haut d'or pâmé sur les vélins*). Wagner took as his source many of the ancient German myths that until his time had been only illuminated manuscripts. As a god he radiates a sacrament, a blessing with the sound of his music (*Le dieu Richard Wagner irradiant un sacre*), a beauty that is "Ill, silent" (*Mal tu*) when restricted to the ink on the page. The ink, when compared to the trumpets of Wagner, gives off only "sybilline sobs" (*par l'encre même en sanglots sibyllins*). Thus does Mallarmé pay tribute to a great musician. He has fewer reservations about Wagner's musical accomplishments in his sonnet than he does about his musical theories in his article. Nevertheless, the sonnet is so ambiguous that several interpretations can be made of it, at least some of which are not totally flattering to Wagner.

The second "Hommage" was first published in 1895 in *La Plume*, in the issue devoted to the muralist Pierre Puvis de Chavannes. As if to differentiate this tribute to a living artist from those for the dead which are in alexandrines, Mallarmé composed the sonnet in lines of seven syllables. For the first time in many poems both dawn and azure make their appearance, but here they are muted as in the paintings of the artist. *Azur* even rhymes with *obscur*. Mallarmé again recounts the struggle of the artist for recognition, concluding with his eventual victory if he is a true artist. Just as the two quatrains of "Sainte" were connected by the first word, the verb *Est*, of the first line of the second quatrain, so the first word, the verb *A*, of the second quatrain of this "Hommage" connects the two quatrains. Here, however, the subject is the first noun of the first line so that the sentence reads "Every Dawn . . . Has its shepherd." This dawn, the dawn of recognition, is described as numb and deaf: "Every Dawn even though too numb / To clench a dark fist" (*Toute Aurore même gourde / A crisper un poing obscur*) "Against the trumpets of azure" (*Contre des clairons d'azur*), "Blown as they are by this deaf one" (*Embouchés par cette sourde*). That is, every dawn even though it seems too weak to be able to chase away the shadows of night, nevertheless announces, trumpets the coming of another day of which she is the source.

Even such a dawn has its "shepherd with his drinking gourd / And his staff" (*le pâtre avec la gourde / Jointe au bâton*), which is "striking hard / Just in front of his footsteps" (*frappant dur / Le long de son pas futur*) "Until the ample spring wells up" (*Tant que la source ample sourde*) for him and his flock.

Puvis de Chavannes thus lives in advance of his times, leading the flock of his followers (*Par avance ainsi tu vis*), solitary like the shepherd and as every artist must be, but never alone. By unusual spacing Mallarmé accentuates the idea that no matter how solitary the great artist is, he is never truly alone because there are those who will understand him.

As the shepherd leads his flock to water, so the artist leads his time to drink (*De conduire le temps boire*) at the living, true, godlike source (*A la nymphe sans linceul*). The nymph was a goddess of rivers and fountains among other aspects of nature, here revealed as living because she has no shroud. This source of inspiration and creation will be revealed to the men of the artist's time and of all times by the Glory, the greatness that is his (*Que lui découvre ta Gloire*). Although Puvis de Chavannes's neoclassical style is not much appreciated by the taste of today, Mallarmé's little sonnet remains a touching tribute to the genius of every great painter.

Mallarmé's seventh and final tribute, a sonnet in the Shakespearean form, carries no title other than its first line, "Au seul souci de voyager" ("To the sole concern of voyaging"). Long thought not to have been published during Mallarmé's lifetime, a scholar revealed in 1947 that the poem had appeared in April 1898. Mallarmé died in September of that year.[10] The sonnet was included in a volume celebrating the four-hundredth anniversary of the voyage of Vasco da Gama around the Cape of Good Hope to India. Mallarmé addresses the Portuguese navigator as he would any artist in search of the unknown. As the artist experiments for the sake of finding something new, so the explorer travels for "the sole concern of voyaging / Beyond an India splendid and uneasy" (*Outre une Inde splendide et trouble*). Mallarmé asks that "This salutation be the messenger / Of time" (*Ce salut soit le messager / Du temps*), across the four hundred years of time since Vasco's voyage, across all time as a message of good hope, the "cape which your ship rounds" (*cap que ta poupe double*). Vasco's trip was a journey not only in space but also in time and thus has a message for all times.

"On some spar plunging / Low with the caravel" (*sur quelque vergue bas / Plongeante avec la caravelle*) there was "A bird of new tidings" (*Un oiseau d'annonce nouvelle*) that "Foamed in its flutterings" (*Écumait toujours en ébats*) just as the great ship foamed in the restless sea.

The bird announced monotonously over and over again (*Qui criait monotonement*) "Without the helm's being altered" (*Sans que la barre ne varie*) "A useless bearing" (*Un inutile gisement*). The three lines contain several ambiguities. *Barre* can mean "helm" or "tiller," but it can also mean "bar" in the sense of a sand bar, thus an ever-present danger. *Gisement* can mean "bearing" or "direction" of a ship but it can also mean "bed" in the sense of a vein or lode of precious metal or stones. In addition it can mean "landfall."[11] Given the last line of the quatrain, "Night, despair and precious stones" (*Nuit, désespoir et pierrerie*), all the readings of *gisement* are possible. The bird's message foretells that every voyage is a voyage through the night of the unknown with, on the one hand, despair as a companion and, on the other, hope of discovery. Some critics compare *Nuit, désespoir et pierrerie* to the *Solitude, récif, étoile* of "Salut." One critic insists that it is a recapitulation of "Une Inde (Nuit) splendide (pierrerie) et trouble (désespoir)."[12]

All of these things are reflected by the song of the bird (*Par son chant reflété*) "to the / Smile of the pale Vasco" (*jusqu'au / Sourire du pâle Vasco*). Vasco with his great white beard appears pale in his portrait. After weeks and months at sea his hope must have been pale. In spite of the portents of the bird he smiles and sails on into the unknown and to discovery. Artists and all men would do well to emulate him.

An Unparalleled Feast

The last eight sonnets of Mallarmé constitute the quintessence of his poetry. Their density and concision surpass everything written before and since in French literature. The point of such poetry is, as one critic put it, "not to be understood but to cause to understand."[13] Their fragile beauty stems from the poetic precision of their composition, the unexpected variety of their content, and the mysterious magic of their message. For him who will give himself up to them they are, according to Mallarmé's biographer, "an unparalleled feast."[14]

The first of these sonnets, "Toute l'âme résumée" ("All the soul summed up"), appeared in 1895. On the one hand it offers a semiserious *art poétique*, while on the other it seems to dismiss poetry humorously as a hoax, a *fumisterie* as the French would call it. The first two quatrains develop the image of smoke rings slowly drawn from the cigar (*Quand lente nous l'expirons*), which evolve one into the other (*Dans plusieurs ronds de fumée / Abolis en autres ronds*). We note the use of one of Mallarmé's favorite words, *Abolis*, always in a special sense. To produce such smoke rings takes great care (*quelque cigare / Brûlant savamment*) and while doing so one must not forget the inevitable ash as it "separates itself / From its clear kiss of fire" (*se sépare / De son clair baiser de feu*). The point of the first two quatrains is that the whole soul is summed up in these unsubstantial, immaterial, ever-evolving, vague, and rapidly disappearing smoke rings.

The comparison with literature comes in the third quatrain. "Thus the chorus of romances / Flies to the lip" (*Ainsi le choeur des romances / A la lèvre vole-t-il*). The words and music of romantic songs come to mind and lip so easily because they are made of nothing more substantial than smoke rings. To be successful with such songs and such poetry one must exclude "The real because base" (*Exclus-en si tu commences / Le réel parce que vil*). The distich states unequivocally, "The too-precise meaning erases / Your vague literature" (*Le sens trop précis rature / Ta vague littérature*). Excessive precision in literature leaves no room for the imagination, restricts whatever sensations might be produced, reduces the implicit to the explicit, and robs poetry of its power of suggestion. The older and more experienced Mallarmé is speaking here with a hint of irony in his voice. In his reply to Jules Huret's inquiry on literary evolution four years earlier in 1891, Mallarmé was not joking when he wrote: "*To name* an object is to suppress three-fourths of the enjoyment of the poem which is derived from divining little by little: *to suggest* it, that is the dream. It is the perfect use of this mystery which constitutes the symbol: to evoke an object little by little in order to reveal a mood, or, inversely, to choose an object and elicit from it a mood, by means of a series of decodings."[15] Mallarmé had long practiced what he preached and would continue to do so through his last poem. With its line of seven syllables "Toute l'âme résumée" is also an illustration of Verlaine's "Art poétique" of 1882 in which he admonishes: "prefer the Uneven / More vague and more soluble in the air" (*préfère l'Impair / Plus vague et plus soluble dans l'air*) in order to arrive at "the gray song / Where the Imprecise joins the Precise" (*la chanson grise / ·Où l'Indécis au Précis se joint*). His exhortation, "Let your poetic line be the thing flown away" (*Que ton vers soit la chose envolée*) conjures Mallarmé's smoke rings and one understands Mallarmé's "Tombeau" for Verlaine somewhat better. "Toute l'âme résumée" is a half-serious, half-humorous admonition to younger poets to remember that poetry can be, should be, and perhaps always is no more substantial than its own soul symbolized by smoke rings wafted gently on the breeze.

The next three sonnets are often called a triptych because they were published together in *La Revue Indépendante* of January 1887. One critic suggests that their first version dates from as early as 1866.[16] The preoccupations do seem to be those of the period of "Hérodiade" and

"Sainte," the ancient empty room with its tattered trophies, the sepulcher, the absent bed, the mandola, the musician, the window. A certain temporal progression can be observed from the *soir* of the first to *la veillée* of the second to *la vitre blême* of the third. They share the same decor and atmosphere and each has one capitalized word: *Orgueil, Chimère,* and *Jeu.* The tone is that of despair relieved only by the faintest gleam of hope, which is sensed rather than stated.

The first line of the first sonnet, "Tout Orgueil fume-t-il du soir" ("Does every pride of evening smoke"), by its construction and its verb, reminds the reader of the later "Toute l'âme résumée," but its sense is much more somber. Is there no enduring pride? Does the pride one might take in one's accomplishments in the evening of life smoke like a "Torch snuffed out by a sudden movement" (*Torche dans un branle étouffée*)? Cannot "the immortal puff of wind," the breath of life (*Sans que l'immortelle bouffée*) "defer the abandonment" (*Ne puisse à l'abandon surseoir!*), put off the moment of extinction?

The second quatrain sets the scene in "The ancient chamber of the heir / Of many a rich but fallen trophy" (*La chambre ancienne de l'hoir / De maint riche mais chu trophée*). Just as the torch has gone out so the room "Would not even be heated / If he arrived by the corridor" (*Ne serait même pas chauffée / S'il survenait par le couloir*). *Survenait* carries with it some idea of surprise so that if the heir did come his arrival would be unexpected.

The tercets describe the one piece of furniture visible in the room, "the flashing console" (*la fulgurante console*) of the last line. Its presence reminds us of Mallarmé's already quoted description of the empty room of "Ses purs ongles . . ." with its "vague consoles" and of *les crédences, au salon vide.* Taking the second tercet first, the heavy marble top of the console seems to be isolated (*Sous un marbre lourd qu'elle isole*) by the light reflected from the console in this room where "No other fire is lighted" (*Ne s'allume pas d'autre feu*).

The heavy marble of the final tercet suggests the image of the sepulcher of the first. Every tomb is a disavowal, a repudiation of life (*Le sépulcre de désaveu*). No one wishes to die, and we are all by the "Necessary pangs of the past" (*Affres du passé nécessaires*), the memories and events and sufferings of our past life, "Clutching as with talons" (*Agrippant comme avec des serres*) the rim of the tomb. Exegetes have suggested that the claws, as in so many of Mallarmé's poems, are sculpted details of the decor. The *passé* of the first tercet recalls the *ancienne* of the second quatrain while *désaveu* echoes *l'abandon* of the first. The *pas d'autre feu* of the next to the last line returns us to the *Torche . . . étouffée* of the second line. In the gloom the only hope is the faint glow of a sepulchral console, small solace for our manly Pride.

The second sonnet of the triptych, "Surgi de la croupe et du bond" ("Having risen up from the rump and the bound"), presents the same decor of the dark and empty room as the first, but here the pessimism is unrelieved except by hope symbolized by the absent rose. This time attention is focused on the neck of a vase, ignored, unknown, neglected, which is interrupted since it does not extend into the natural continuation of a stem and a flower (*Le col ignoré s'interrompt*). In addition, the neck is described as "Having risen up from the rump and the bound / Of an ephemeral glassware" (*Surgi de la croupe et du bond / D'une verrerie éphémère*). At what point does the neck of a vase cease being vase and become neck? Mallarmé describes beautifully the upward movement of the well-proportioned vase in which the neck starts at the bottom or rump of the vase and by a subtle but sudden movement becomes the neck. The glassware is ephemeral because fragile, breakable, and since it holds no rose it does not "fill with flowers the bitter vigil" (*Sans fleurir la veillée amère*).

I should like to suggest that the vigil is that of the sylph sculpted on the cold ceiling of the second quatrain (*Moi, sylphe de ce froid plafond!*). The sylph was the spirit or genie of the air in Celtic mythology of the Middle Ages, which explains its position on the ceiling in the sonnet. The Swiss alchemist Paracelsus conceived of the sylph as mortal but soulless. As sculpture the sylph is mortal, subject to destruction, but soulless. Thus its ceiling is cold. The sylph is observing the vase which has become for it a sort of cup, the source of life, at which neither of its parents drank (*Je crois bien que deux bouches n'ont / Bu, ni son amant ni ma mère*). These two mouths have never drunk at the same Chimera (*Jamais à la même Chimère*). The vase may be decorated with a chimera, an animal half-goat, half-lion, with a dragon's tail, just as the cup in "Toast funèbre" had its golden monster and the cup in "Salut" had its sirens. With its capital, and given the import of the rest of the quatrain, Chimera carries at the same time the idea of vain imagination and the hybrid animal act of procreation. Generalized, it becomes every act of creation, whether that of the living being the sylph would like to become or the poem that may or may not be born with a soul, the spark of life.

This pure vase, pure because empty, holds no other drink than that of inexhaustible widowhood, of eternal sterility (*Le pur vase d'aucun breuvage / Que l'inexhaustible veuvage).* Because of its condition it "Agonizes." If there is any light in this room perhaps the vase seems to move in the flashing gleam, to agonize as did the gold in "Ses purs ongles. . . ."

It "Agonizes but does not consent, / . . . / To breathe forth anything" (*Agonise mais ne consent, / . . . / A rien expirer*). Such an expiration of breath would be a "Naive and most funereal kiss" (*Naïf baiser des plus funèbres!*), naive because natural but funereal because to give birth to is to subject to death. Both meanings of *expirer,* to breathe out and to die, hover over the final tercet. The vase refuses "to breathe forth anything announcing / A rose in the shadows" (*A rien expirer annonçant / Une rose dans les ténèbres*). In "Tout Orgueil fume-t-il du soir" we were left with the glimmer of a material hope in the form of the glittering console. In the conclusion of "Victorieusement fui le suicide beau" the fall of roses was conditional but positive. Here nothing hints at the rose except our own knowledge and memory of it, like our nostalgia for the ideal flower "absent from every bouquet."[17] The hope of great artistic creation is dim, "A rose in the shadows."

In the last sonnet, "Une dentelle s'abolit" ("A lace disappears"), the creative act becomes the ultimate, the "supreme Game" (*Jeu suprême*). Hope here is no more than the suggestion of dawn at "the pale window" (*la vitre blême*). After the console and the empty vase, the central image becomes a white lace curtain that seems to disappear in the dubious rays of the rising sun (*Dans le doute du Jeu suprême*), with dawn as the supreme act of creation, or re-creation. The curtain in its fluttering half-opens "To reveal like a blasphemy / Only the eternal absence of a bed" (*A n'entr'ouvrir comme un blasphème / Qu'absence éternelle de lit*). Again the room is empty, this time even of the essential site of procreation, the bed.

The second quatrain is another description of the curtain, this time as "This unanimous white conflict / Of a garland with the same" (*Cet unanime blanc conflit / D'une guirlande avec la même*). The garlands are the garlands of lace on the curtain while its conflict is its fluttering, its movement. Because it is all white and "Fled against a pale window" (*Enfui contre la vitre blême*), like white on white, it is "unanimous." It "Floats more than it buries" (*Flotte plus qu'il n'ensevelit*), it moves more than it hides, since there is not even a bed in the room.

In opposition to the doubt and blasphemy, absence and conflict of the quatrains, the tercets are introduced by the conjunction "But" (*Mais*), allowing an alternative. The possibility is to be found "within him who gilds himself with dreams" (*chez qui du rêve se dore*), the poet who takes time, dares to use his imagination. Within him "Sadly sleeps a mandola / With its hollow musical void" (*Tristement dort une mandore / Au creux néant musicien*). In addition to the internal rhyme *dore—dort—dore*, Mallarmé repeats the same word in one line by means of a pun, *-ment dort—mandore*. The tercet is a marvel of condensation. Within every poet willing to dream there sleeps a musical instrument like the mandola, hollow and empty, but from which music can emanate.

All of this would take place "near some window" (*vers quelque fenêtre*). We have seen Mallarmé's many uses of the word window but perhaps the presence of *la vitre blême* in the second quatrain calls to mind first the line from "Les Fenêtres":—*Que la vitre soit l'art, soit la mysticité— / A renaître.* Whether the window is art or mysticism, it plays an important role in Mallarmé's concept of poetic creation. "By means of no stomach but its own" (*Selon nul ventre que le sien*), that is, of the mandola, "Like a son, one might have been born" (*Filial, on aurait pu naître*). The sterile white curtain that hides and the absent bed of the quatrains are contrasted with the window, which is an opening, which looks out, which allows one to see through, and the silent mandola which still retains its potential for making music, creating poetry. The poet is father to the poem but only through his poems does the writer become a poet, thus "Like a son," the impersonal and generalized "one" (*on*) "might have been born." The most hope one can draw from the triptych is this "might have been" and the verb *naître* which brings it to a close. One has the impression that Mallarmé, while saying in three sonnets that it cannot be done, has done it. The message is relatively simple and straightforward, but the anguished voice and tortured syntax, the somber setting and hopeless tone, create a dramatic tension that is eternal and ever-present in any life struggle. For Mallarmé the creation of poetry was the life struggle.

The sonnet "Quelle soie aux baumes de temps" ("What silk with balms of time") first appeared in 1885, two years before the triptych. As in "Surgi de la croupe et du bond" the word *Chimère* is capitalized while *Gloires* is in the plural but capitalized as in the "Hommage" to Puvis de Chavannes. *Chimère* is in the second line, *Gloires* in the last. The development proceeds from the one to the other with silk and hair as the primary attributes. Other objects with which we are already familiar in Mallarmé's poetry include the mirror and the diamond as well as the verbs *expirer* and *étouffer*.

The poet asks the question, "What antique silk / . . . / Is worth the twisted and native cloud" of your hair (*Quelle soie aux baumes de temps / . . . / Vaut la torse et native nue*)? Time has acted as a balm on the silk, which is embroidered with a writhing chimera (*Où la Chimère s'exténue*). The comparison of the hair to a cloud recalls "La chevelure vol d'une flamme . . ." where it is described as *cette vive nue*. The movement of the hair, "beyond your mirror" (*hors de ton miroir*), recalls the same poem. As the woman combs her hair the motion seems to add a third dimension to the mirror.

The silk and hair of the first quatrain become the flags of the second. Although they are worn and used, full of holes, the flags are flying to celebrate some holiday, a victory (*Les trous de drapeaux méditants / S'exaltent dans notre avenue*). That is the scene outside. Inside, the poet has "your naked hair / In which to bury my contented eyes" (*Moi, j'ai ta chevelure nue / Pour enfouir mes yeux contents*).

In the tercets the poet must choose between personal pleasure and professional achievement, between private and public life, between the symbols of the hair and the flag. The sacrifice must be total but the final choice remains ambiguous. The poet cannot simply bury his eyes in the hair of his beloved, thus the resounding "No!" (*Non!*). As he says, "The mouth will not be sure / Of tasting anything in its bite" (*La bouche ne sera sûre / De rien goûter à sa morsure*) unless he is willing to go the whole way. The *morsure* recalls the love bite, the *morsure / Mystérieuse* of *L'Après-Midi d'un Faune*. Professor Cohn points out the pun, *morsure—mort sûre*, which is consistent with the ambiguity of *expirer*.[18] The "princely lover" (*ton princier amant*) also recalls the *héros tendre* of "La chevelure vol d'une flamme. . . ."

The lover will not succeed if he does not cause to expire "like a diamond" (*comme un diamant*) "In the considerable tuft" (*Dans la considérable touffe*) that is the abundant hair of the beloved, "The cry of Glories which he is stifling" (*Le cri des Gloires qu'il étouffe*). The lines can be read literally as the sexual act. While obvious, such an interpretation seems secondary to Mallarmé's purpose. As in "Surgi de la croupe et du bond," the ambiguity of *expirer* in the next to the last line provides the key to the conclusion. On the one hand, it can be interpreted to mean that the lover will succeed only if he causes the cry of Glories to exhale, to breathe out like a diamond, pure, brilliant, and perfect in form, in her abundant hair. This cry is the voice to be heard in his poems that will assure his reputation and that he is at present stifling in his love of woman. That is, through love and in spite of love, he must produce his poems. On the other hand, he will succeed in love only if he gives himself to it completely, only if he forgets all about poetry and future glory, only if he causes the cry of Glories to die, as a diamond deprived of light loses its brilliance, in the beloved's abundant hair. In the poem Mallarmé does not choose, but in life four years after this poem, he wrote a lingering farewell to Méry Laurent.

The sonnet "M'introduire dans ton histoire" ("To introduce myself into your story") appeared in 1886, one year after "Quelle soie aux baumes de temps." Proust's narrator quoted the second quatrain of "Le vierge, le vivace et le bel aujourd'hui" as well as both tercets of this sonnet in the narrator's farewell letter to Albertine in *Albertine disparue*. T. S. Eliot acknowledged the second line of the first tercet, *Tonnerre et rubis aux moyeux*, as the source for two lines, "Garlic and sapphires in the mud / Clot the bedded axle-tree," in "Burnt Norton," the first of his *Four Quartets*. The flashing figures of speech in this erotic and ambiguous little love poem bring Rimbaud to mind.

The first two lines read, "If I were to introduce myself into your story [the story of your life], / It would be as a frightened hero" (*M'introduire dans ton histoire / C'est en héros effarouché*). This is not the "princely lover" of "Quelle soie aux baumes de temps," but more nearly the "tender hero" of "La chevelure vol d'une flamme . . . ," particularly when we note that the present hero is frightened "If he has touched with his naked heel / Some grassy plot of territory" (*S'il a du talon nu touché / Quelque gazon de territoire*). In "La chevelure" it is *Une nudité de héros tendre [qui] diffame*. In *L'Après-Midi d'un Faune* it was the visit of the *talons ingénus* of the love goddess Venus that caused the eruption. The hero here is frightened because he has touched in his nakedness and with his heel, his Achilles' heel perhaps, his weakest point, some forbidden grassy territory. The exegetes have taken great pleasure in deciphering all the hidden and not so hidden erotic suggestions in this quatrain and in many instances they certainly are right.

Without going that far we can see that the grassy territory of the first quatrain has become glaciers in the second. What the narrator at first simply brushed against must now be assaulted like a glacier (*A des glaciers attentatoire*). We remember *l'eau perfide des glaciers* of "Le Pitre châtié," *le glacier / Farouche* of the "Ouverture ancienne," the cold glaciers of "Cantique de Saint Jean," and *Le transparent glacier des vols qui n'ont pas fui* of "Le vierge, le vivace et le bel aujourd'hui." The grassy plot has become a cold and forbidding glacier. As a result the narrator does not know what naive, innocent sin the heroine might have permitted (*Je ne sais le naïf péché / Que tu n'auras pas empêché*) "To laugh aloud its victory" (*De rire très haut sa victoire*). Now that she has changed her mind he is not sure what little intimacies she might have allowed him. For such a frightened hero any intimacy would have been a victory to enjoy and brag about.

He is happy for what she has already permitted him (*Dis si je ne suis pas joyeux*), so happy his joy erupts like the Etna of Venus, explodes into a vision of the setting sun. He is happy "To see in the air which this fire pierces" (*De voir en l'air que ce feu troue*) "the wheel / Of my only evening chariot" (*la roue / Du seul vespéral de mes chars*). The use of fire and vesperal recalls the *Maint rêve vespéral brûlé par le Phénix* of "Ses purs ongles . . ." while the *royaumes épars* recall the *rêve épars* of "Hérodiade." The flashing wheel has "Thunder and rubies at the axles" (*Tonnerre et rubis aux moyeux*) and seems to be taking with it "scattered kingdoms" that appear to be dying in the purple of twilight (*Avec des royaumes épars / Comme mourir pourpre*). We remember *l'exploit / De semer de rubis* of "La chevelure" and the *égout bavant boue et rubis* of "Le Tombeau de Charles Baudelaire," so that the wheel in this poem seems to be showering sparks like rubies. The setting of the sun is a spectacle sufficiently magnificent to symbolize the frightened hero's small victory and because it is setting it also implies the calm and peace after effort and accomplishment, after joy and achievement, after sexual satisfaction, if you will. *Mourir pourpre* recalls *une pourpre s'apprête / A ne tendre royal que mon absent tombeau* of "Victorieusement fui le suicide beau," suggesting the calm of death after the experience. The ascending–descending, increasing–decreasing tension of the poem is reinforced by the lack of punctuation that allows no respite until the end. In this poem Mallarmé comes closer to a direct expression of eroticism than in any poem since "Une négresse. . . ." Nevertheless, he couches it in such ambiguous terms that only the prude could be shocked by the timorous yet glorious adventures of this "frightened hero."

The sonnet "A la nue accablante tu" ("Silenced to the overpowering cloud") dates from 1895 and like "M'introduire dans ton histoire" has no punctuation except for the two commas isolating *écume* in the second quatrain. In the first quatrain Mallarmé sets the scene, this time a stormy, rocky seascape. The reader does not discover what has been silenced until the second quatrain, but he discovers by what it has been silenced in the fourth line, "By a trumpet without virtue," the alarm which was never sounded, thus without strength, useless (*Par une trompe sans vertu*). Mallarmé contrasts, as we have seen so often, the high and the low. Here the news of whatever has happened has been "Silenced to the overpowering cloud" (*A la nue accablante tu*), to the "Shoal of basalt and of lava" (*Basse de basalte et de laves*), "Even to the slavish echoes" (*A même les échos esclaves*) of the waves beating on the rocks. The menacing, overpowering cloud recalls the line from "Las de l'amer repos . . . ," *Un clair croissant perdu par une blanche nue*, as well as one from "Le Tombeau d'Edgar Poe," *Du sol et de la nue hostiles, ô grief*, and the expression *la torse et native nue* of "Quelle soie. . . ." The *Basse* recalls the *récif* of "Salut," and the *barre* of "Au seul souci de voyager," the ever-present, hidden danger. Basalt is a dark-gray-to-black igneous rock while lava is also created by fire, giving the impression of a cold, burned-out world. The waves are the slaves of time and tide and prisoners of their own shores, their echoes resounding relentlessly.

The second quatrain is in the form of a question about "What sepulchral shipwreck" (*Quel sépulchral naufrage*) may have taken place, sepulchral because of the lives that may have been lost. The only witness who knows whether or not there was a shipwreck is the foam, but all it does is drool at the place where it might have happened (*tu / Le sais, écume, mais y baves*). The shipwreck is described as having "Abolished the stripped mast" (*Abolit le mât dévêtu*). We remember Mallarmé's many uses of *abolir* in the sense of to kill, while the mast has been divested of its sails but precisely because it is the mast it is "The highest one among the pieces of wreckage" (*Suprême une entre les épaves*).

The tercets continue the questioning attitude of the second quatrain by asking if it might be something else that was drowned. "Or is it that for furious lack / Of some high perdition" (*Ou cela que furibond faute / De quelque perdition haute*) something very ordinary took place. Will the whole vain abyss, vain because empty, outspread to receive all wrecks (*Tout l'abîme éployé*), have avariciously drowned (*Avarement aura noyé*) in the white hair of foam that drags across its surface (*Dans le si blanc cheveu qui traîne*) "The infant flank of a siren" (*Le flanc enfant d'une sirène*)? In spite of appearances, was there after all no shipwreck? Was the sea so avaricious that it was celebrating only the drowning of a siren? We remember the line from "Salut," *Telle loin se noie une troupe / De sirènes*. The siren, that enticing, dangerous creature with her alluring song, belongs to the sea, half divinity, half human, half woman, half bird, associated with death and represented as carrying off souls. Was what was thought to be great, true tragedy only this insignificant incident at sea? Or is the child (*Le flanc enfant*) father to the man and was inspiration, the soul of poetry, being drowned in the bottomless abyss? The water-hair image of *le si blanc cheveu qui traîne* takes us back to all the doubts and questions of Hérodiade. There would seem to be no hope left in the poetry of Mallarmé and yet the hope is to be found perhaps in the posing of the question. In the asking, poetry is created, the only answer to the yawning void.

Mallarmé chose to close his volume of *Poésies* with the sonnet in alexandrines, "Mes bouquins refermés . . ." ("My books closed . . ."), published in 1887 with the triptych. The closed book is consistent with the images of the empty room, the empty vase, and the silent mandola of the triptych. The poet has closed his books on the name of Paphos, the ancient city of Cyprus, famous for its temple to Aphrodite, goddess of love, thought to have been founded by the Amazons (*Mes bouquins refermés sur le nom de Paphos*). It amuses him to choose as the subject of his ruminations a ruin, something gone and almost forgotten, and by his genius, his imagination alone (*Il m'amuse d'élire avec le seul génie / Une ruine*). Because the city no longer exists, only by imagination can it be brought to life. This city by the sea is "blessed by a thousand foams / Beneath the hyacinth, far off, of its triumphant days" (*par mille écumes bénie / Sous l'hyacinthe, au loin, de ses jours triomphaux*). The time, space, and beauty of ancient Greece are magically and majestically evoked. This ruin stands on shores washed by the endless waves of the sea and of time, under the hyacinth. *Hyacinthe* is the early form of the modern French *jacinthe,* so that the flower may be implied. It is also the color blue-red, the color of the clear sunny skies of Greece. Noulet indicates that the *hyacinthe* was a ceremonial cloth, blue-red in color,[19] which would have been worn on days of triumph. Whichever it is, it is all *au loin,* far away in time and distance just as the triumphant days of Paphos have long since passed.

In the second quatrain the poet expresses his contempt for the reality that might deny the vision of the first. "Let the cold run with its sickle silences" (*Coure le froid avec ses silences de faux*), let the cold light of winter and reason mow down with its scythe of silent disdain the dream of the poet. He will not howl, lament over it in some empty funeral song (*Je n'y hululerai pas de vide nénie*), the *nénies* being Greek funeral chants used here in the singular by poetic license, "If this very white struggle denies / To every site the honor of the false landscape" (*Si ce très blanc ébat au ras de sol dénie / A tout site l'honneur du paysage faux*). The very white struggle at ground level is the winter snow that would smother any summery vision and deny it the honor of an imaginary landscape.

In the tercets the poet answers this threat. His hunger, which feasts on no fruit here, finds in this knowing lack an equal savor (*Ma faim qui d'aucuns fruits ici ne se régale / Trouve en leur docte manque une saveur égale*). Although the poet is not fulfilling his appetite with real fruit, he can find an equal pleasure in the absence of the fruit which is presence by means of the poetic vision. All this, even "Though one of them bursts with human and perfuming flesh" (*Qu'un éclate de chair humain et parfumant!*). The fruit has become a human breast that leads to the final image of the poem.

With his foot on an andiron in the form of an heraldic monster, the wivern, a two-legged winged creature with a dragon's head, the poet gazes into the fire that love stirs (*Le pied sur quelque guivre où notre amour tisonne*). This love is not physical love but the love of the imaginary expressed by the poet in the first quatrain. He "thinks longer, perhaps desperately / Of the other, the burned breast of an ancient Amazon" (*Je pense plus longtemps peut-être éperdument / A l'autre, au sein brûlé d'une antique amazone*). He is thinking of the other breast, the missing one, because the Amazons were reputed to have burned off one breast to facilitate the shooting of arrows. With the final word, Amazon, we are brought back to the Paphos of the first line. In this uncomplicated poem Mallarmé has restated his faith in poetic vision, the necessity of imagination and its power. The beauty of the poem stems in part from its perfect architecture, in part from allusion and in part from illusion. The references to long ago are sustained by descriptions of unsurpassed but past splendor. The threat to such a vision is accepted calmly and without fear, for Mallarmé's faith in the power of poetry to conjure the absent and the unreal is unshakable.

To make something of nothing, to create out of nothingness, is the province of the poet. At the same time he transforms words into poetry, he transmutes life into art. While art is a product of life, it transcends the living and makes of life something more than living. As Professor Strauss wrote, Mallarmé's sumptuous allegories of the void "transmute the void into a glorious lie, but a lie that has more poetic reality than the void, because it also has metaphysical reality."[20] To experience Mallarmé's poetry is to experience something more than life, something less than death, to know the realm where man's imagination and vision can lead him if he has the patience and the dream.

Chapter Eight

The Mysterious Seal of Modernity

Poetic Prose

Mallarmé wrote and published the twelve poems in prose at various times and in many places between 1864 and 1887. He finally collected them under the title *Pages* and published them in 1891. He republished them along with other works in *Divagations* in 1897. Baudelaire and Aloysius Bertrand with his "Gaspard de la nuit" did much to give new life to the ancient form of poetic prose. Rimbaud made something quite different of it in both *Les Illuminations* and *Une Saison en enfer*, as did Lautréamont in his *Chants de Maldoror*. As a result, French poets have continued to compose poems in prose to the present time. Mallarmé's contributions were, as usual, not numerous but unique.

Like his early poems in verse, Mallarmé's first poems in prose reveal the great influence of Baudelaire. Some are even autobiographical, which is unusual in Mallarmé's canon. "Le Phénomène futur" ("The Future Phenomenon") probably dates from about 1864, the year Mallarmé began "Hérodiade," because the relationship between the two so disparate poems is quite evident. It begins with a description of the setting sun, reflected in many of Mallarmé's poems in verse. Streetlamps are mentioned also. But more interesting is the sideshow tent of the "Showman of things Past" for he has inside a "Woman of other times," miraculously kept alive, who can only be Hérodiade. Her hair is "an ecstasy of gold" while that of Hérodiade is *de l'or*. Her breasts rise as if "filled with an eternal milk." Hérodiade speaks of her nurse's milk, *ton lait bu jadis*.

The conclusion Mallarmé draws from this early vision is consistent with the poetic theory he illustrated with almost all of his works. Some of the observers remain indifferent to what they have seen because they do not have the strength to understand. Others are moved to tears but are resigned to their powerlessness to do anything about it. Poets, however, will rush to their lamps, their brains "drunk for a moment with a confused glory." They are haunted not only by the beauty of what they saw but also "by the Rhythm." They forget that they exist "in an epoch which has outlived beauty." Mallarmé with his "Hérodiade" was certainly a "Showman of things Past," of a "Woman of other times," who knew that his creation would be understood by few people, misunderstood by most. His faith in poetic vision as stated here in 1864 was the same as that of "Mes bouquins refermés . . ." with which he terminated his *Poésies*.

"Plainte d'automne" ("Autumn Lament") was first published in 1864. Mallarmé speaks of the effect on his life of the death of his sister Maria. He learned to love solitude with only his Baudelairean cat for companion and "everything that was summed up in the word: 'fall'"; that is, the last long days of summer before autumn, the hour before the sun finally sets, "the agonizing poetry of the last moments of Rome." While reading a poem and stroking his cat, suddenly he heard a barrel organ sing "languishingly and melancholically" beneath his window in the path of poplars where Maria last passed. The barrel organ is the instrument of the sad. The piano sparkles, the violin gives off light, but the barrel organ "in the sunset of memory" caused him to dream. Its "joyously vulgar air" made him weep as would a romantic ballade. He did not go to the window to throw money because he did not want to disturb himself and because he feared he would find that the barrel organ was not playing all by itself. The melancholy voluptuousness of the poem with its mixture of sight, sounds, and touch recalls Baudelaire. The use of the long adverbs is repeated in some of Mallarmé's briefest and most poetic works.

The very title, "Frisson d'hiver" ("Winter Shiver"), also of 1864, recalls Baudelaire, as well as many of Mallarmé's poems in verse. This poem is a veritable inventory of much of the bric-a-brac in Mallarmé's living room that was to find its way into his poems in verse. We do not see any clocks in those poems but we do hear many tollings of midnight. The Saxony porcelain clock is always slow and, humorously enough, chimes thirteen times. Its decoration of flowers and gods suggests many of the details described in the poems in verse.

A haunting leitmotiv of spiders' webs runs through the poem. Spiders and webs make us think of Poe and Baudelaire before Mallarmé, but they are first described as "unusual shadows" that "hang at the worn out window." *Ombres* and *vitres usées*, which become *grandes croi-*

sées, are very much a part of Mallarmé's vocabulary in his poems in verse.

The next object is the Venetian mirror and, like Hérodiade's, it is "a cold fountain" bordered with tarnished gilt wiverns, the same fabulous animals we saw in "Mes bouquins refermés. . . ." He is sure that "more than one woman has bathed in this water the sin of her beauty," recalling Hérodiade and her watery mirror. Humorously, however, the mirror often says nasty things to him.

As in many of the poems in verse, the light of the fire plays over the details of the room: the old cupboard with its sad wood, the faded curtains, the tapestry of the chairs with their worn paint, the ancient pictures on the walls. Even the waxbills or Java sparrows and the blue bird are beginning to fade with time.

The remainder of the poem is autobiographical. The poet speaks of his wife, saying that he can live with her precisely because she loves old things. It was she who wanted him to use the phrase "the grace of faded things" in one of his poems. The expression recalls the *roses fanées* and the *modes surannées* of Baudelaire's "Spleen LXXVI," and, like Baudelaire, Mallarmé in this poem calls his wife both sister and child, so important in the interpretation of "Prose pour des Esseintes," for example.

He asks her to close her old German almanac so he can talk to her for hours, not of the fields that no longer exist, nor of the empty streets, but of their furniture. She knows the furniture only too well, so he must ask her, "Are you distracted?" The spiders' webs, which he at first noticed as simply hanging there, tremble in the middle of the poem and shiver at the end, high in the great casements. In spite of debts to Poe and Baudelaire this poem in prose offers much that is Mallarméan.

"Le Démon de l'analogie" ("The Demon of Analogy") probably dates from 1864 also, although it was not published until ten years later. This meditation tells us a great deal about Mallarmé's sensitivity to words, about how anyone, but above all the writer, can become obsessed by an apparently unremembered and absurd word or phrase because of its sound, its rhythm, and finally its meaning. At first, as he was leaving his apartment, all he heard was the sound of "a wing gliding over the strings of an instrument," which recalls the harp brushed by the angel's wing in "Sainte." Soon a voice replaced the instrument, pronouncing the phrase "The Penultimate is dead" (*La Pénultième est*

morte), but with a pause after penultimate as if it were the last word in
the poetic line.

After walking a bit farther, the narrator recognized the sound of the
syllable *nul* as being that of the taut string of a musical instrument
just visited by glorious Memory "with its wing or a palm leaf." The
phrase continued to repeat itself until it took on a life of its own.
Finally, the narrator repeated it himself. He was perfectly aware that
penultimate signifies the next to the last syllable of a word. Such a
facile explanation was only a torment. He repeated the phrase over and
over to himself in the hope of exorcising it, when suddenly he saw
himself reflected in the glass of a store window. There he found old
stringed instruments hanging on the wall and beneath them yellowed
palm leaves and, in the shadows, wings of ancient birds. He fled, a
"person probably condemned to wear the mourning of the inexplicable
Penultimate." Certainly the narrator was pursued by the demon of the
analogy between what he had been thinking and what he actually saw.
The exegetes have had a good time with this poem in prose primarily
because *nul* means, of course, "no, no one, none, no man," and as an
adjective, "worthless." Although Mallarmé never simply plays nor
plays simply with words, the poem would seem to be the somewhat
humorous relation of an hallucination.

"Pauvre Enfant pâle" ("Poor Pale Child") was first published in
1864. This touching portrait of a ragamuffin singing in the streets for
money never received would seem to be by François Coppée, if it were
not for what Mallarmé sees in the child. He sees the future criminal
and remarks that crime is not difficult; all it takes is courage after the
desire. Mallarmé also feels guilt at the role he plays in the fate of this
unknown child. It would all seem predestined: "we shall see you in the
newspapers. Oh! poor little head!"

"La Pipe" ("The Pipe") dates from 1864 and was first published in
1875. The poet puts aside his summer cigarettes to take up his pipe
for a long winter evening's work. Instead of work, the pipe brought
back the London of his unhappy days with Maria, a London with its
"dear fogs" that have a smell all their own when they penetrate his
somber room with its leather furniture and lean cat; the big fire in the
fireplace; the red-armed maid; the sound of coal being dumped; the
two raps of the postman at the door. Looking out the windows, which
are so important in Mallarmé's poems in verse, he sees the sea and as
in "Brise marine," the steamer, this time the one that carried his poor
Maria back and forth. Around her neck she wears "the terrible hand-

kerchief which one waves while saying good-bye forever." The phrase recalls *l'adieu suprême des mouchoirs,* also in "Brise marine." As evocative as many of the poems in prose are, one can feel that the poems in verse gained a great deal when these autobiographical details were relegated to prose.

"Un Spectacle interrompu" ("An Interrupted Spectacle") was first published in 1875. Its style and technique differentiate it from the seven, including "Réminiscence," which were first written in 1864 and the four which followed it, ten years later, between 1885 and 1887. The central idea recalls "Le Phénomène futur," but the poet purposely sets out to distinguish the vision he experienced from the reality the crowd witnessed. Reality is, after all, only "an artifice for fixing the average intellect amid the mirages of a fact." The poet wants to see "if there isn't after all, in the ideal, a necessary, obvious, simple aspect, which may serve as a type."

What the poet saw as a spectacle was the classic fairy tale, "The Beast and the Genius," in which a bear was used. His description of the stage is almost surrealistic: "from evasive pallors of muslin taking refuge on twenty pedestals in the style of Baghdad architecture, there came a smile and open arms to the sad clumsiness of the bear." The description of the actor recalls many of the heroes of Mallarmé's poems in verse: "the hero, evoker and protector of these sylphs, a clown, in his lofty silver nakedness." By a gesture, by opening his fist in the air, the puppet, whom Mallarmé later calls the mime, induced the bear to rise up and put one paw on his shoulder and to rest his other paw on the actor's arm, almost as if they were going to dance. The audience is breathless at this unusual and fearsome spectacle. In this unnatural position the bear becomes "an inferior, squat, kindly man, standing on two straddled hairy legs." In contrast the man becomes his "brilliant and supernatural brother." While standing there the bear asks the trainer to be kind enough to explain to him what this stage means. He who works to make the actor free is "still covered with the shapeless habitation of the caves." By their embrace they seal their pact. The poet had witnessed "one of the dramas of astral history." Many of Mallarmé's poems in verse seem to be dramas of astral history. Suddenly the crowd vanished, and, just as in "Le Tombeau de Charles Baudelaire," that "modern dispenser of ecstasy, alone, with the impartiality of an elementary thing, the gaslight, in the heights of the hall, continued a luminous noise of expectation."

The charm was broken by a piece of raw meat thrown to the bear.

Following his instincts, he dropped to all fours and went to eat his prey. Everyone breathed a sigh of relief and the curtain was lowered. The others saw only a bear standing on its hind legs while the poet was serene. His "way of seeing, after all, had been superior, and even the true way." Mallarmé may have doubted his own ability to create but he never doubted the power of poetic vision.

"Réminiscence" ("Reminiscence") dates from 1864 and was first published in 1867. The form we know differs widely from the original "L'Orphelin" of 1864. One of the significant lines of the earlier version is a bald statement of Mallarmé's preoccupation with and concept of white: "the ravished lilies, the snow, the feather of swans, the stars, and all the whitenesses sacred to poets."[1] In the later version it becomes "already the snow of the summits, the lily or other whiteness constituent of wings within." Otherwise, the poem in prose recounts simply and sadly the meeting of an orphan with the children of the wonderful world of the circus, much before "the holy hour of the footlights." The circular movement we have noted so often in the poems in verse is evident here. In the opening line the orphan's eye is "empty of family." In the conclusion, he is more than ever and "all at once disappointed not to have parents." One of the children is wearing "a night cap cut like Dante's hood," which recalls the night caps and the Dante of the humorous "Sonnet" of 1862 or 1863 on the birth of the poet. Not only do the circus children lead a marvelously vagabond life and eat "a superior repast," "a chaste meal," of soft cheese on a slice of bread, the cheese being the source of all the poetic whiteness, but they also can do surprising pirouettes and tell funny stories about their parents. The parade takes off, leaving the orphan to his lonely fate. Some of the anguish of the poem must have stemmed from Mallarmé's own situation, more or less abandoned as he was by his father after his mother had died when he was five. The irony is, of course, that circus children are generally thought of as abused and abandoned, but in the eyes of the orphan their life is a magic one.

The last four poems in prose, dating from 1885 to 1887, in their complexity and density resemble much more the great Mallarmé of the late poems. "La Déclaration foraine" ("The Strolling Declaration") dates from about 1887, the year of its publication, and is the only one in which the poem in verse encounters the poem in prose for within the declaration "La chevelure vol d'une flamme . . ." is quoted in its entirety. As a matter of fact, the poem is the declaration. The poet and a lady friend were taking a carriage ride in the suburbs during Mallarmé's eternal sunset. At this moment when all should have been calm and quiet, "the ordinary strident laughter of things and their triumphant brassiness" left one painfully aware of "the obsession with existence." At that moment they passed a fair, and his companion, called significantly "the child," asked to stop. The idea of mingling with the crowd was distasteful, but he agreed. In the "bizarre and purple twilight" with its "incendiary cloud," they observed a "poignant human spectacle."

Among the attractions of the fair the poet and his companion came across an empty stand. She suddenly asked the old attendant to sound the drum for a performance while she climbed on the stage and waited for the crowd to gather. With a glance at her hair, "a hair where smokes, then lights up like garden displays, the pallor of her crepe hat," the poet realized his duty, recited his poem "Une chevelure vol d'une flamme . . ." and announced to the crowd that his companion had no need of theatrical accessories to communicate her charm. In the silence that followed several agreed and some even clapped. At the exit of the fair they saw "a childish soldier still waiting in white gloves" who recalls the *gant blanc des tourlourous* in "Petit Air (Guerrier)."

The poet's companion thanked him for his chivalrous gesture, his declaration that he would not have been able to make in the isolation of their carriage. The poem was forced out of him, as if by a "brutal blow in the stomach," caused by these people to whom "one must declare something even if it is daydreams." The poet feared that his friend might not have noticed his compliments to her if he had not used the Shakespearean sonnet in which the last two lines rhyme. "Perhaps!" was the most reassuring answer the poet received for his gallant efforts in this charming poem in prose.

"Le Nénuphar blanc" ("The White Water Lily") was published in 1885. In it we find Mallarmé in his yawl on the Seine hunting for water blossoms and reconnoitering the site of the property of the friend of a friend to whom he should pay his respects. Having lost himself in his rowing, he suddenly noticed that the boat had stopped and he had to ask himself what was happening and where he was. He had run aground on a clump of reeds. Looking around, he found that the greenery hid the arch of a bridge connecting the lawns of the woman to whom he was supposed to speak.

Any woman who would choose such a place for a retreat would certainly be to his taste. Like Hérodiade, she would have made "of this crystal her interior mirror." When she came there, "the chill silvery

vapor of the willows was soon only the limpidity of her glance." He
already felt the beginnings of the poet's enslavement to this "feminine
possibility" when suddenly he heard an imperceptible noise.
The footsteps ceased. In a second, he has conjured the ideal woman.
Should he use chance as an excuse for an introduction? Here they are,
together but separated. There are so many things he could say, "so
many idle discourses in comparison with the one he was making in
order not to be heard." What to do? Pluck "one of these closed magical
water lilies" which "enclose in their hollow whiteness a nothing made
of untouched dreams, of happiness which will not take place?" Rowing
backwards silently, he avoids having to throw at her feet "the transparent likeness of the abduction of my ideal flower," avoids meeting
her whether she be Meditative, Proud, Wild, or Gay. He is carrying
off his imaginary trophy "like a noble swan's egg, from which no flight
will ever spring," a phrase that recalls the swan and the *vols qui n'ont
pas fui* of "Le vierge, le vivace et le bel aujourd'hui." His trophy "is
swollen with nothing except the exquisite emptiness of self" which all
women love to pursue along their garden paths. The haunting beauty
of this might-have-been encounter with which the actual encounter
could never compare is another illustration of Mallarmé's faith and belief in the poetic vision that not only creates something that never was
but also something that can never be. By its promise it moves the
world.

"L'Ecclésiastique" ("The Ecclesiastic") was published in 1886 in
Turin. Mallarmé notes how spring causes flowers and animals to do
things they would do at no other season. How much more interesting
it would be to observe the effect of "the climatic moment" on "the
behavior of individuals made for spirituality." Mallarmé had just had
the opportunity to do so while strolling in an unfrequented part of the
Bois de Boulogne. He has seen an ecclesiastic with his three-cornered
hat and silver-buckled shoes "responding to the solicitations of the
grass." Mallarmé sneaked away carefully without looking back so that
the ecclesiastic would never know that he had been observed rolling in
the grass. Under the influence of spring the ecclesiastic "had come to
recognize by an immediate, clear, violent, positive contact with Nature, stripped of all intellectual curiosity, the general well-being."
Such a contact with the world would seem to resemble that of the poet.
In any event, the passerby's recompense is that in his dreams he can
complete the image, marked as it is "by the mysterious seal of mod-

ernity, at once baroque and beautiful." No more brief but accurate description has been given of Mallarmé's own poetry.

"La Gloire" is a word used frequently by Mallarmé in his poems in verse, and a word difficult to translate into English. Glory, fame, honor, reputation are all included. In the poem in prose of that name, which was first published in 1886 by Verlaine in his series *Les Hommes d'aujourd'hui*, Mallarmé describes his encounter with true glory, irrefragable, undeniable fame. He had taken the train to the forest of Fontainebleau, which was "in its time of apotheosis." There all was in "some extraordinary state of illusion" in "this exceptional, stately October" filled with "bitter and luminous sobs." Mallarmé would be "the royal intruder" in "this diurnal vigil of immortal trunks" "where torches [the flame-colored trees of autumn] consume, in a proud watch, all previous dreams." There, in the purple clouds of sunset, Mallarmé waited until the train was reduced to "a childish chimera" to enter alone into this true glory. In its density and beauty "La Gloire" seems about to become a poem in verse. The vocabulary is very close to that of the later poems and reveals Mallarmé's "immediate, clear, violent, positive contact with Nature," which distinguishes his greatest works.

Therefore, the Catastrophe

On 14 November 1869 Mallarmé wrote in a letter from Avignon to his friend Cazalis, "I'll tell you just a word about my work which I'll bring to you next summer: it's a story, by means of which I hope to overcome the old monster of Powerlessness. . . . If it is written (the story), I am cured."[2] If the story was *Igitur* (*Therefore*), and we have every reason to believe it was since Mallarmé read fragments of *Igitur* to Mendès and Villiers on their vist to Avignon during the summer of 1870, then Mallarmé was never cured because the story was never finished and never published by him. The only logical conclusion to *Igitur* came thirty years later with the publication of *Un Coup de Dés* and the death of Mallarmé himself.

A reading of the 194 letters extant written by Mallarmé from 1862 to 1871 reveals all the pain, boredom, and discouragement he suffered in exile in Tournon, Besançon, and Avignon. How much of it was truly physical and how much actually psychological is difficult to ascertain a hundred years later. More important for us are the changes his conception of "the Work" underwent during those years and the important role *Igitur* played in this development.

A detailed analysis of Mallarmé's evolution in those ten years, aside from the abbreviated one I gave in the introduction, is beyond the scope of this book. I might note, however, that in July 1866 Mallarmé felt that he had at last found the key to his future work and that it would be in five volumes and necessitate twenty years to complete. By May 1867 the work was to consist of three poems in verse of an unprecedented purity, of which "Hérodiade" would be the overture, and four poems in prose "on the spiritual conception of Nothingness" (p. 242), which would take ten years to complete. By September of the same year Mallarmé felt that he had understood "the intimate correlation of Poetry with the Universe, and, in order that it be pure, conceived the idea of taking it out of the Dream and out of Chance and of juxtaposing it with the conception of the Universe" (p. 259). To achieve this end would necessitate two books, "one a totally absolute 'Beauty,' the other personal, the 'Sumptuous Allegories of the Void,'" with no mention of how long they would take to write. By April 1868 Mallarmé was suffering excessively, both physically and mentally. It was then he wrote "for two years I have committed the sin of seeing the Dream in its ideal nudity . . . having arrived at the horrible vision of a pure work, I have almost lost the meaning and the sense of the most familiar words" (p. 270). Not until July 1869 do we hear a note of hope and that comes with the first mention of *Igitur* (p. 305). By November we have the statement of faith in the story quoted above.

Igitur as we know it consists of twelve prose fragments that vary in length from a short paragraph to a bit more than seven pages. Mallarmé had requested that all his papers be destroyed at his death, but his family could not bring itself to this destruction. Mallarmé's son-in-law, Dr. Edmond Bonniot, published the fragments in 1925. We do not know why, aside from its actual and obvious meaning, Mallarmé chose the Latin adverb *igitur* for his title. The Bible has been suggested as a source but only a biblical concordance could tell us how many *therefore's* are in that volume. The subtitle, *La Folie d'Elbehnon (The Folly of Elbehnon)*, is of no help either. Scholars, with their many different and contradictory conjectures, have not been able to decide on the source or significance of the name Elbehnon. *Igitur,* even though fragmentary and unfinished, is, like everything Mallarmé created, a poetic experience.

Dr. Bonniot, after much study, arrived at what seems a logical order for the fragments. According to him there is an Introduction and an Argument followed by five titled sections of development, "Le Minuit" ("Midnight"), "Il quitte la chambre et se perd dans les escaliers" ("He leaves the room and gets lost on the stairway"), "Vie d'Igitur" ("Life of Igitur"), "Le Coup de dés" ("The Throw of the Dice"), and "Il se couche au tombeau" ("He lies down in the tomb"). Dr. Bonniot has grouped under the title "Scolies" ("grammatical or critical notes on ancient authors") four versions of the section titled "Il quitte la chambre," one of which carries the title "Touches" ("Essays" or "Attempts"), three of which are simply indicated as Gamma, Delta, and Epsilon, plus a final section entitled "Malgré la défense de sa mère, allant jouer dans les tombeaux" ("Despite the interdiction of his mother, going to play in the tombs"). As arranged by Dr. Bonniot the fragments do present a sort of beginning, middle, and end, and although they are obviously only in the most elementary form, their style is of an astonishing density, managing to suggest a great deal more than is actually stated. Their very incompleteness renders them mysteriously tantalizing while their obvious connection with *Un Coup de Dés* makes them enormously important for Mallarmé students.

Without in the least intending to imply that Mallarmé was an existentialist *avant la lettre,* I should like to use an existentialist approach in analyzing *Igitur.* The work is addressed not to the feelings or the emotions but as Mallarmé himself said in epigraph, "to the Intelligence of the reader."[3] *Igitur* is an exploration of the human consciousness, an investigation of the nature, essential properties, and relations of being. As such it constitutes a sort of poetic ontology. The story is an analysis of perception, a description of phenomena as they present themselves to the consciousness. As such it is a sort of symbolic phenomenology. Igitur descends into "the human mind" or spirit, into "the depths of things," as the "absolute" he is as a being (p. 37). In so doing he discovers a great deal that anticipates Sartre's *Being and Nothingness.*

In the "Ancienne étude" ("Old Study") that Dr. Bonniot has styled an Introduction, we are presented with the phenomena of sound, light, and shadow, the symbols of the candle and the book. The concepts of the absolute, immortality, and time are introduced. Mallarmé elaborates at length on these phenomena, symbols, and concepts in the subsequent sections of the story.

Igitur is an abstraction of his race, the total consciousness of his race, as anyone is theoretically at any given moment the total consciousness of all his forebears. In addition, he is an "*I*-projected absolute" (p. 38),

"projected outside of time" (p. 52). Because of these special attributes
he is able to explore for the moment the true meaning of being and
time. In "this state of conscious anguish" (p. 69) Igitur, aware that he
is the product of tradition, attempts to go beyond tradition. If an
ancestor was careful "to be reflected in a proper self," Igitur attempts
to be reflected "in his own self" (p. 45). In his heightened awareness
he arrives at "the consciousness of self" (p. 46). Going one step further
he arrives at the "perception of self" (p. 49), "the notion of himself"
(p. 68), comes face to face with the *I* who is another, the consciousness
of self as a conscious being. He has, as Sartre would put it, arrived at
the concept of being-for-itself, conscious, human being.

The consciousness of being-for-itself brings with it the awareness of
a radically different type of being, being-in-itself, the unconscious
being of things. All the trappings in *Igitur*—the furniture, the tapes-
tries, the heavy draperies—take on a being of their own that depends,
paradoxically, upon the consciousness Igitur has of that being. They
seem to move, to shiver and shake, and come to rest only when Igitur
is no longer conscious of them. He calls it "the candle of being, by
which all has been" (p. 38). On the other hand, the certainty of the
existence of being-for-itself is contingent upon the existence of being-
in-itself. Igitur says that "the certainty is reflected in the evidence" (p.
46)—we know we exist by the evidence presented to consciousness in
the form of senorial phenomena.

Being-for-itself is distinguished from being-in-itself by its memory,
its consciousness of time, past, present, and future. As Igitur puts it,
"I have always lived with my soul fixed on the clock" (p. 51). He would
impute to things "their mystery, the unknown, their memory, their
silence," but he knows that these are all "human faculties and impressions" (p. 53). In the "chamber of time" (p. 40) the light and the book
of the Introduction become for consciousness "the opaline clarity of its
knowledge" and "the volume of its nights, now closed" (p. 46). The
past and the future converge upon the present, which is Igitur. Mallarmé puts it this way: "The past composed of his race which weighs
on him in his sense of the finite . . . and his expectation of the fulfill-
ment of the future, form pure time, or boredom, rendered unstable by
the illness of ideality" (p. 52), the nostalgia for the ideal. All we have
is the present, and in that sense the present is eternal. Igitur says, "The
pure shadow of the past and the future, having reached a pinnacle in
me, dominates perfectly and finishes, outside them" (p. 46). "The ex-
plored lie of infinity" stretches before and behind him (p. 47). The

infinity of the past is a lie because it has been lived but is forever dead. The infinity of the future is a lie because it is unknown, has not yet been lived, cannot be lived as future, and brings with it death, which will extend forever into infinity. Although we are our past only in the sense of no longer being it, and our future only in the sense of not yet being it, all being is a projection into the future. As Igitur puts it, his race, whose time weighed so heavily it has fallen into the past, was full of chance and thus lived only for its future (p. 57). All finite human being is an anachronism in view of infinity just as Igitur is the "supreme incarnation of this face,—who feels in him, thanks to the absurd, the existence of the Absolute." The book and the candle are again used by Mallarmé. In order to achieve this sense of the absolute he has "forgotten the human word in the old book, and the thought in the luminary, the one announcing this negation of chance, the other illuminating this dream in which he finds himself" (p. 57), that is, the dream that is being.

Along with the consciousness of existence comes the awareness of its opposite, "the existence of Nothingness" (p. 76). This was Mallarmé's dizzying and frightening discovery. Although as the opposite of being, nothingness can only be nonbeing, it nevertheless exists and plays an important role in being. Although the constellations and the sea are two types of infinite being, they "are separated from Infinity" and "remaining, in exteriority" to the human consciousness, are "reciprocal voids" (p. 39). On the one hand being-for-itself lives in constant fear of discovering that it does not exist. On the other hand it envies the uncaring, unfeeling, unthinking existence of being-in-itself and wants more than anything to realize its "desire for an escape" (p. 47), to achieve the impossible combination of being-in-itself-for-itself, the perfect awareness of self free of all contingency. Igitur terms it "Tombs—ashes (neither feeling nor spirit), neutrality" (p. 37). Such an absolute would be God. According to Sartre, however, there is no God and we are left with being-for-itself, a consciousness that is nothingness since it exists only by means of what it is not, by means of exterior being-in-itself, which it can never be except in death and which it will inevitably become. In this sense Igitur can say, "I was destined to end in Infinity" (p. 38).

Mallarmé localizes, materializes if you wish, this abstraction by having it take place in a tomb in a chateau as midnight sounds. Mallarmé manipulates the mirror in many ways but his final realization is that even if we know that we exist by means of our reflection in the mirror, the reflection has no being and is another sort of nothingness by which we exist. As Igitur puts it, "Time has not disappeared through a mirror" (p. 39). We also know we exist by means of sound, the ticking of the clock that symbolizes the passing of time, the beating of the heart that tells us that we are alive and that time is passing, the flapping of a bird's wings that symbolizes the sounds of the world while acting as an omen. All of these sounds become the same sound in a frightening way in Mallarmé's story, the "sound of the closing of the sepulchral door" (p. 45).

In the face of this inevitability Mallarmé offers the act, the throw of the dice, the opportunity for chance. The chance, in one throw of the dice, is either won or lost, but since we never know which it will be, affirmation and negation have no meaning. Chance contains the absurd, with somewhat the connotations Sartre would give it, but according to Igitur chance only implies the absurd in a latent state and thus prevents it from being. All of this theoretically permits Infinity to be, since there are an infinite number of throws of the dice. But, as Mallarmé puts it, "the Act is accomplished" (p. 55). We must accept all its consequences and realize that with the act "Infinity is finally *fixed*" (p. 56).

In the end Igitur, having cast the dice, closes the book, blows out the candle, allowing chance to operate for the last time, and, after crossing his arms, lies down on the ashes of his ancestors. He finds "the act useless" since "there is and there isn't any chance." The act "reduces chance to *Infinity*" (p. 58) by the endless throws of the dice, while one throw suffices to end everything. His ancestors had arrived at the chateau, "the chateau of purity" (p. 59), of emptiness, sterility, of all that is not done, as the result of a shipwreck, the accident, the chance that exists for all being.

Igitur drinks "the drop of nothingness"—that is, consciousness, "which the sea lacks" (p. 59)—and reposes on the ashes of his ancestors. The nothingness of the vial is the infinity of his race, which will come to nothingness in him, the last of the race. As being-for-itself Igitur was "the substance of Nothingness" (p. 64). He can say for Mallarmé: "the difficulty of living which I suffer is frightful: at the depths of this perverse and unconscious confusion of things which isolates its absolute—it feels the absence of the self, represented by Nothingness in substance" (pp. 75–76). The throw of the dice that Igitur had made at midnight yielded, of course, a twelve.

With this descent of Igitur into the tomb came the resurrection of Mallarmé. One can understand why he was unable to go any further with the story. He had pushed thought to its ultimate, witnessed nothingness, and said all that he could say for the moment. He was also, I fear, writing himself into a dialectical corner and knew it. After thirty years more of experience he would again have something to say on the subject, but in a very different way. In any event, by March 1871 Mallarmé was able to write that his work was no longer a myth. It would consist of a volume of stories, undoubtedly as a result of *Igitur,* which were still in the dream stage, a volume of poetry, and a volume of criticism, strictly literary, which would take all of his mornings for twenty years to write.[4] We actually have only the unfinished fragments of *Igitur,* which might be called a story, as well as the poems in prose, which could conceivably fit the category; one volume of *Poésies;* a few literary portraits of varied length and quality; and the final poem, *Un Coup de Dés.*

The Loaded Dice

Un Coup de Dés was Mallarmé's boldest poetic experiment, and like James Joyce's *Finnegans Wake* it is something of a magnificent failure. Typographically it was the predecessor of the experiments of Apollinaire, the surrealists, the dadaists, Michel Butor among the New Novelists, and many another poet and writer, French and otherwise, of the twentieth century. Unfortunately, its slender intellectual content cannot support the elaborate metaphysical structures the exegetes seem so eager to build on it. In addition, poetry cannot be read exactly like music so that Mallarmé's harmonic intentions get lost in the typographical inventions. But its aesthetic beauty, visual as well as auditory, cannot be denied.

The best introduction to *Un Coup de Dés* and the clearest description of the author's intentions in writing the poem are to be found in Mallarmé's own brief preface he provided for the 1897 edition. He intended the poem to be printed in several sizes and kinds of typeface, to be published on eleven double pages, and to be read from left to right and from top to bottom across both verso and recto. He scattered the various typefaces over the two pages to produce visual effects, to form ideograms, pictorial representations of the subject of the poem surrounded by a great deal of white space. In addition, the ideas expressed by the various type sizes are not confined to any one page but intermingle and are intended to produce a harmonic effect, verbal as well as conceptual. Thus the primary statement in the boldest type, UN COUP DE DES JAMAIS N'ABOLIRA LE HASARD ("A throw of the dice will never abolish chance"), appears on Pages 1, 2, 5, and 9, with Page indicating Mallarmé's double page. A second idea, *Quand bien même lancé dans des circonstances éternelles du fond d'un naufrage* ("Even when cast in eternal circumstances from the depths of a shipwreck"), is expressed entirely on Page 2 and sets the scene of the poem. The idea is continued on Pages 3 and 4 with *Soit le Maître,* which because of its type size is related to *naufrage* ("shipwreck be it the Master"), equating the shipwreck and the Master. The *comme si* ("as if") on Page 6 is repeated by the *si* of Page 8 and results in the expression *Si c'était le Nombre, ce serait* ("If it were the Number, it would be"), which is concluded by LE HASARD of the main theme. But *comme si* is also taken up by the expression beginning on Page 10, *Comme si rien n'aura eu lieu que le lieu* ("As if nothing will have taken place but the place"), which is in turn completed in the conclusion on Page 11, *Excepté peut-être une constellation* ("Except perhaps a constellation"). Constellations in smaller type are interspersed and clustered around the larger type. They have a meaning of their own and at the same time expand and explain and comment on the expressions in larger type. The syntactical complexity renders the poem difficult to interpret. Needless to say, the exegetes have again had a fine time with Mallarmé's poem. They have found the seasons of the year, the hours of the day, all of the sciences, Plato, a little Aristotle, lots of Hegel, and goodness only knows how many brands of metaphysics in the poem. All of these connotations may perfectly well be there, and even occasionally probably are, but they do not add much to the appreciation and the enjoyment of the poem.

The primary elements are the throw of the dice, which we have already noted in *Igitur;* the sea that is everywhere in Mallarmé's poetry; the shipwreck we saw in "Brise marine," "A la nue accablante tu," and *Igitur;* the Master of "Toast funèbre" and "Ses purs ongles . . ."; and the stars and constellations of the "Ouverture ancienne," "Hérodiade," "La chevelure vol d'une flamme," "Toast funèbre," "Ses purs ongles . . . ," and "Tombeau de Verlaine." Given these elements, what do the ideograms suggest? Page 1 with only its bold UN COUP DE DES suggests nothing so much as a title page which with its straight line of type leads the reader directly into the next Page. Page 2 gives us the calm sea but warns us verbally of a storm and a shipwreck. On

Page 3 the water washes down from left to right like a wave. We also see the constellation of the Big Dipper, which is mentioned later. The shipwreck at the bottom of Page 2 is repeated on this Page in a figure of speech involving the ship's hull. Page 4 resembles swirling waters that on Page 5 rise to formidable heights on the verso with the low level on the recto. Water again washes across Page 6 in a form reminiscent of Page 3 but not suggesting so much the shape of the Dipper. On Page 7 the water is again subsiding on the recto and suggests again the Dipper, although some prefer to see Hamlet's hat with its feather, which we noted in "Le Pitre châtié." On Pages 8 and 9 the water is again in movement but by Page 9 it is, under the weight of LE HASARD, beginning to subside. Page 10 is the Big Dipper, or, if you prefer, the pen in the inkwell. Page 11 is definitely the Big Dipper with on the recto a Little Dipper with which the poem closes. The auxiliary phrases might suggest other possibilities, but the basic elements limit us for the moment to these.

What then does the poem seem to be saying? Because of the limitations of space I shall have to stick disastrously close to a literal interpretation, not to say translation, which I put forth only as a springboard for possible flights of fancy. After the bold announcement of the subject on Page 1, "A throw of the dice," we are led to the neutral *Jamais* of Page 2, which may be "Ever" but which may be completed, as we know it will be, by *ne* and become "Never." The "cast" of "Even though cast in the eternal circumstances from the depths of a shipwreck" refers back to the throw of dice, but as on all Pages there is a carry-over from one page to the next so that it looks forward to the Master of Page 3.

This Page is a description of and a descent into the depths. "The Abyss," one of four capitalized words that include "Number" and "Spirit" on Page 4 and "Nuptials" on Page 5, recapitulates the preceding "depths of the shipwreck" and is described as "whitened" by the storm. It "spreads out furiously on an angle," the inclination being described visually by the descending line. It "hangs desperately by a wing, its own." Again, the ideogram of the verso describes visually a wing. But even as it hangs in the air it has "already fallen down again" because of the "difficulty of maintaining flight." Returning to the abyss as subject we find it "stifling the spurts" and "cutting level the leaps." In the long metaphor that follows, the dancing rim of the dark abyss is compared to the wobbling sail of the ship, whose hull in turn is compared to the trough of water: "Deep within itself it sums up the shadow buried in its depths by this alternate sail to the point of adapting to the spread of the sail its gaping depths like the shell of a ship listing to one side or the other." As the eye descends the Page the word *profondeur* describes the depths into which it is physically proceeding and is repeated to emphasize the movement.

With Page 4 a character is introduced, "The Master," who could be the master of the ship, the poet as Mallarmé has indicated in earlier poems, or everyman. This is the Page of swirling waters. The Master is described as "beyond ancient calculations in which the maneuvering has been forgotten with age," and "risen up," "concluding, formerly he grasped the tiller, from this conflagration at his feet," the conflagration being the reflection of the setting sun on the water, and "by the unanimous horizon that there is being prepared, agitating, and mingling in the fist which would grasp it, as one shakes his fist at destiny and the winds, the unique Number which cannot be another." The fist that formerly grasped the tiller, that is, seemed to direct its own destiny, is now the fist that is being shaken in the face of the storm as well as the fist that is being shaken at destiny as it shakes up the dice for a throw, another means of settling destiny. The one Number is the throw of the dice, which cannot be another number. "Spirit" in the middle of the Page can refer back to the Master as a thinking being and to the unique Number that has a spiritual being of its own. The "Spirit, in order to throw it into the tempest, to heal the division, and to pass proudly, hesitates," the fatal hesitation before the precipitous act. "To heal the division" could refer to the division between the Master and his destiny as represented by his sinking ship, or to the division between his ship and the elements as represented by the stormy sea. More generally, it refers to the division between conscious man and his blind destiny with an attempt to reconcile man to his fate so that he can die proudly.

The Master hesitates, a "cadaver by the arm isolated from the secret which he holds back." The throw of the dice, which he hesitates to make, could be fatal and he could become a cadaver, but he is isolated, separated from, just as the word "isolated" is physically separated from the word it modifies, "cadaver." The secret that the Master holds in his hand is the dice. He hesitates, "rather than to play, like a hoary maniac, the game in the name of the waves." "One" of them, that is, the waves, "floods over his head, flows in his subdued beard." The conclusion to this scene is summed up in the statement: "All of which is the direct shipwreck of the man without a ship, useless." *N'importe* may be combined with *où* to form the expression "no matter where," indicating that man's destiny could be settled anywhere on the ocean or anywhere in the world. The "in which" refers to the shipwreck while "vain" can mean that all has been done in vain, or that the shipwreck or death of any man is a vain threat of destiny since from his death will rise "his puerile shadow," as we find on the next Page. This is also the third Page to end with a ship or shipwreck.

The ideogram of Page 5 is in the form of the high flank of the restrained wave, which on Page 6 will flow again across the Page. Just as the wave is suspended so the Master hesitates to throw the dice. In not casting the dice he is "like his ancestors, not opening the fist clenched above the useless head," useless because not making the decision and thus not ready to accept the consequences of the throw of the dice. Such indecision is a "legacy at death to someone ambiguous," ambiguous because the son remains an unknown quantity to the father. Here we arrive at the subject of the sentence, "the later, immemorial demon" that drives man to do what he does, "having from worthless countries led the old man towards this supreme conjunction with probability," led him to this throw of the dice. Such countries were worthless because his destiny was not decided there. "The one" refers to the "someone ambiguous" who is the son. "His childish shadow" is "caressed and polished and made presentable and washed, broken in by the wave and drawn from the hard bones lost between the planks." This birth is summarized by "born from a frolic, the sea tempting the grandfather or the grandfather against the sea, an idle chance." In this line, *la mer par l'aïeul tentant ou l'aïeul contre la mer,* Mallarmé uses for the last time the doubling of words, *la mer–la mer* and *l'aïeul–l'aïeul.* Because of the central position of *tentant* it can refer to both the preceding and the following phrases. Because of its double meaning, to tempt and to attempt, it lends itself to multiple interpretations one of which might be, "the sea attempting an idle chance through the grandfather or the grandfather attempting an idle chance against the sea." The chance is idle because the grandfather will die in any event.

The idea of the birth is also summarized by "Nuptials, whose thrown back veil of illusion, their obsession, is just like the phantom gesture." In order for marriage to be consummated the veil of modesty must be thrown back. The idea of this dropping of the veil is an obsession and the phantom of a gesture like the throwing of the dice. One gesture symbolizes birth, the other death. The one who was born "will falter, will be bewildered," which is a "folly" as the act of Igitur

was a folly. It "will not abolish" probability or chance or the consequences to come in the new life that is the birth that was also a throw
of the dice. On this Page the Master becomes everyman and the poem
takes on broader connotations.

Page 6 is a parenthetical thought, "A simple insinuation," contained
between two large "As if"s, one at top left, the other at bottom right.
Although there is no punctuation in the poem, Mallarmé uses a capital
letter here and there to indicate a new sentence. This is then "A simple
insinuation wrapped up with irony in silence or the mystery hurled,
howled in some nearby whirlpool of hilarity and horror," the comedy
and tragedy of the human condition. The insinuation or the mystery
"flutters around the abyss" (*gouffre* can also mean whirlpool), "without
strewing it nor fleeing, and rocks its virgin sign," which is the white
foam around its edges, "as if." The circular movement on this Page
describes the circular movement of the whirlpool and leads to a further
description of the foam on the following page.

On Page 7 we learn that the "virgin sign" of the wave, its foam, has
become high on the left and isolated, a "feather solitary and frantic
unless a toque of midnight [the dark wave] encounters it or brushes
against it and immobilizes on the rumpled velvet by a somber guffaw
this rigid whiteness," which brings us back to the feather. It is rigid
only insofar as it appears to be a thin line and is "derisory" in its
fragility and instability. It is by its location "in opposition to the sky,
too much so as not to mark, in the slightest detail, anyone," that is,
even though it is but a fragile spray of foam or delicate feather, this
sign of destiny marks any wave or man that wears it. On the human
level, the "bitter prince of the reef" who might be Hamlet but who
could just as well be the Master, "puts it on his head as if in an heroic
act, irresistible but contained by his small virile reason in lightning
[in an enlightened moment]." This Page, in addition to the Big Dipper, describes Hamlet's toque with its feather, if you wish. The vacil-
lating Hamlet well epitomizes mankind, which hesitates but in the
end with its "small virile reason" bravely assumes its destiny.

The basic relationship between Pages 7 and 8 is that between "a
somber guffaw" and the "anxious, expiatory and pubescent, mute
laugh," which in turn is connected directly to the thought on Page 9
by the large "if." The howl of the storm becomes the hideous laugh of
fate that derides man's puny efforts. A new sentence interrupts, however, to describe the foam become feather: "The lucid and lordly egret
of vertigo, on the invisible forehead, glitters then shades, a dainty

shadowy stature, standing up in its siren-like twisting, just long enough to slap with impatient ultimate bifurcated scales a rock, a false manor-house immediately evaporated into mist which imposed a limit on infinity." As the foam slaps against the rock and is cut in two, bifurcated like the tail of the siren, it is also endowed with the scales of the siren. The rock becomes a manor house that reminds us of the chateau of Igitur, and, although it disappears immediately into the fog and is "false" because a figment of our imagination, it serves as a limit to the endless sea, a limit to infinity, and end to chance.

Page 9, continuing from the "if" of the preceding page, returns to the idea of the Number on Page 4, to state clearly that "if it were the Number, it would be chance," the chance of the main theme, the chance number of the throw of the dice. The "it were" is described as "born of the stars" and by its position high and isolated on the page both gives the impression of a small constellation and introduces the important idea of the stars. Between the "if it were the Number" and "it would be" there is a secondary development utilizing a series of verbs in the imperfect subjunctive, each with its own commentary, all referring to the Number: "If it had existed, other than as a scattered, dying hallucination, if it had begun and if it had ceased, arising although denied and closed when it finally appeared through some profusion spread out thinly, if it had added itself up, if it had illuminated, evidence of the sum as a unique total," then "this would be no worse and no better but just the same as chance." The casting of the dice and the accidental number that results have been equated with the stars scattered at random in the sky. They determine the destiny of man as much by chance as does the Number turned up by chance on the dice.

The foregoing action takes place on the upper, sky level of the Page. Beneath it begins a new sentence according to which "The feather, rhythmic suspension of the fatal, falls, burying itself in the original foam, from which its frenzy recently leaped up to the very summit, withered by the identical neutrality of the abyss." We are back to the shipwreck and abyss of Pages 2 and 4. The rise and fall of the foam is of course conditioned by the rise and fall of the waves, which are all identical and whose very rise and fall are identical.

On Page 10 the conclusion begins with the word "Nothing," which is completed by the idea "will have taken place except the place," all we have in this endless stormy sea. "Nothing of the memorable crisis or the event with no human result in view might have been accomplished, will have taken place, a normal elevation pours out absence,

except the place, an inferior ordinary lapping as if to dissipate the
empty act abruptly, which otherwise by its lie might have founded
perdition in this region of the vague in which all reality dissolves."
The important expression is "with no human result in view" for the
seascape without the Master is only "a normal elevation [which] pours
out absence," "an inferior ordinary lapping." Without the presence of
human consciousness tragedy cannot take place, nothing can take place
but the place, "this region of the vague in which all reality dissolves"
because there is no awareness to give it reality.

The pessimism is relieved by the magnificent constellation of Page
11 and the final exception, "except perhaps a constellation." The "Except on high" is high on the left page and followed by a conditioning
"perhaps," all of which is "so far away that a place blends with the
beyond." The space between subject and verb, *endroit* and *fusionne*, indicates the effort necessary for fusion. We note that this is the point
where the handle joins the dipper to become something else. All of
this is so far away that it is "beyond the interest which is generally
given it according to such obliquity through such a declivity of fires,
towards, it must be, the North." Mallarmé uses obliquity and declivity
to indicate the angles of the sextant, fires for the light of the stars, and
the expression *Septentrion aussi Nord* to indicate the seven stars of the
Dipper that point to the North Star, which is, as he says, "a constellation." The group of stars is "cold with forgetfulness and desuetude,
not so much that it does not enumerate on some empty and superior
surface the successive shock, as stars do, of a total reckoning in formation." The "shock" is the throw of the dice or the conjunction of
the stars. The "total reckoning in formation" is the number composed
by the dice but it is also the last Dipper formed on the page with a
handle composed of magnificent descending present participles,
"watching, doubting, rolling, shining and meditating, before stop-
ping at some last point which consecrates it." The poem is consecrated
only when it has come to an end. The throw of the dice has meaning
only when completed. The final sentence of the poem, "Every Thought
emits a Throw of the Dice" takes us back to the beginning of the poem
at the same time as it says that while a throw of the dice never will
abolish chance, every thought has infinite possibilities and in each
thought we must remember that if we act on it, we have done nothing
more than submit ourselves to the chance of a throw of the dice. As
Igitur put it, "Infinity is finally *fixed*."

By way of recapitulation, what then has the poem said? The idea that a throw of the dice never will abolish chance is a truism cleverly stated. That every thought emits a throw of the dice is much more original although even with the development Mallarmé provides in the poem, such an idea can hardly be arrogated into an epistemology. Every thought offers, as we have seen, myriad possibilities while acting on any one of the possibilities does not eliminate chance, it merely fixes it. The decor of the poem, the endless sea and the infinite constellations, those "reciprocal voids" of *Igitur,* are two abysses, one into which man may sink, the other to which man may rise. The sea from which we came can hardly help us any more than the faraway stars, "cold with forgetfulness and desuetude," to which we aspire. In the story of the Master, Mallarmé recapitulates the story of mankind. In that story chance plays as great a role as in any other aspect of human endeavor, yet the continuing generation of mankind is perhaps the only answer to chance.

In the conclusion of his preface to *Un Coup de Dés* Mallarmé wrote that in the poem he had treated "subjects of pure and complex imagination or intellect: not a single reason remains to exclude them from Poetry—unique source."[5] Mallarmé has already been quoted as saying that sonnets are made of words, not ideas. *Un Coup de Dés* is far from being a sonnet, but perhaps Mallarmé would have done well to remember his own dictum. The poetic beauty of the descriptions of the stormy sea and the cold stars, of the bearded Master aboard the sinking ship, throwing the dice in the face of the storm, is unsurpassed in French literature. The exquisite delicacy and precision of the parenthetical expressions are unparalleled. The attempt at intermingling several thoughts on various harmonic levels has never been equalled. The suggestiveness of the position of the type on the page, as well as the ambiguity of much that is said, create a multiplicity of impressions open to many interpretations. Yet all of these factors combine to defeat the poem. The development is too tenuous, the effort overextended. The individual developments are like planets revolving around the sun of the central idea. The system can be observed and the "internal mirage of the words themselves" in the separate parts do create a "cabalistic sensation." The system as a whole, however, is difficult to grasp. The sequence of sensations does finally add up to the poem that is *Un Coup de Dés,* yet the reader can arrive at the sensation only after long and patient study. By then his interest in *Un Coup de Dés* has dissipated itself and Mallarmé has defeated himself. Nevertheless, the experiment was one that had to be made and only Mallarmé could and did attempt it. Perhaps we could say of *Un Coup de Dés* what T. S. Eliot said about Joyce's *Finnegans Wake:* "one book like this is enough."[6] In any event, almost one hundred years later the poem remains a challenge to every poet of any language.

Chapter Nine
Conclusion: A Certain Unexpected Music

Two more disparate personalities than those of Jean-Paul Sartre and Stéphane Mallarmé would be difficult to imagine. The brilliant, provocative, long-winded philosopher would hardly seem the type to take an interest in the reserved, withdrawn, and reticent poet, yet Sartre produced another of his psycho-socio-politico philosophical treatises about Mallarmé in which he called him "hero, prophet, wizard, tragedian."[1] Sartre thus deftly encapsulated the major aspects of Mallarmé's character and career.

Certainly Mallarmé was something of all these, particularly in his later, greater poetry. He was heroic in his exalted concept of the role of the poet and of poetry, and more than heroic in his personal endeavor to live up to his own almost impossibly high standards. As his biographer put it, Mallarmé eschewed the facile, the declamatory, the immodest, the sentimental, and the purely descriptive.[2] He did not seek difficulty for difficulty's sake but he did scrupulously avoid the easy lyricism of many of his predecessors and, alas, successors. His goal was something quite other. As one critic put it, the distinction Mallarmé made between chance—that is, the very vocabulary the poet has at his disposal through education, experience, and preference—and structure—that is, the form into which that vocabulary must be forced and which has "an absolute rather than a fortuitous existence"—"constitutes a basic division, on which by analogy, a view of the world can be built."[3] In the end he attempted to create something more than just "a view of the world." Another critic stated it this way: "From the *what* to write to the *how* to write, this obstinate—and sometimes smiling—search should result in an authentification and justification of man's terrestrial sojourn."[4] In short, Mallarmé's goal was not only to offer a view of the world but also to seek a justification for our life here on earth through a choice of words within a structure created by the intellect and the will, no small task.

Mallarmé never simply stated nor attempted to convert his readers by his oratory. In a very subtle way he involves the attention and the intelligence of the reader simultaneously in the process of creating the poem and creating the effect desired. Never can Mallarmé be found intruding into his poems with his personal feelings or troubles, and yet his poetry, because of its style, remains uniquely his. While many of his poems have about them a nostalgic aura, Mallarmé never comes near mawkish sentimentality in any of its forms. While his poems are frequently descriptive, his inspired impressionism is far from the coldly calculated and impersonal poetry of his contemporaries, the Parnassians.

Even in his own day Mallarmé was a prophet. One of his contemporaries called him the initiator and the master of the artistic and philosophical thought of the younger generation;[5] "our spiritual master," said one of them.[6] That generation included Mallarmé's truest disciple, Paul Valéry, who remains perhaps the greatest French poet of the twentieth century. Mallarmé's poetry inspired both musical composition as early as Debussy's "Prélude à l'après-midi d'un faune" of 1894 and the choreography of Nijinsky in 1912, and continues to do so today.[7] His influence permeated the symbolist theater and can be found as well in contemporary avant-garde plays. He is "a distant prophet of the new theater" as one critic put it.[8] Another critic defined the debt of both the surrealists and the theater of the absurd when he wrote that "the distrust of language—and by implication of literature—in Mallarmé anticipates the atmosphere of suspicion which characterizes an important body of 20th century literature—particularly the work of the Surrealists, of Kafka, Ionesco, Genet, and Beckett."[9]

We have to remember that "Mallarmé was the first modern poet fully to articulate the page"[10] and that through "the spatial configuration of *Un Coup de dés,* Mallarmé bestows upon his reader the experience of poetic creation and offers visual, concrete, material evidence of the presence of Poetry as the ultimate sign of human value, dignity, and salvation."[11] Without going quite that far one can nevertheless find in the complicated precision with which the New Novelists organized their works, their willed ambiguity, the typographical experiments of Michel Butor, for example, more than mere traces of Mallarmé's influence. The idea that "Every time there is an effort at style, there is versification,"[12] set down by Mallarmé in 1891, comes as near to defining present-day poetics as any statement since. T. S. Eliot[13] and

Wallace Stevens[14] are two of many poets who attest to Mallarmé's wide and enduring influence.

Mallarmé can also safely be called a wizard with words. "By dismantling the opposition between subject and object and by tilting the fragile equilibrium which would sustain the subject in control of the other(s) and its other, the text affirms shifting division of consciousness."[15] By means of this shift of consciousness Mallarmé creates a space "whose only possible sense is that of an impossible essence, whose only possible structure is that of an impossible figure—which are both . . . the ideal, and whose final proof is that they affect as such the instinct of the careful reader."[16] As a result of these "irreducible syntheses," as Sartre called them,[17] Mallarmé's poetry remains unequalled in its dizzying eminence and its dazzling purity. His star was beauty, its perfect embodiment poetry, and his faith in the two never wavered. He went to great lengths to realize his vision and suffered in the attempt.

Mallarmé was thus undoubtedly something of the tragedian also. The grand gesture marks *Un Coup de dés* just as a certain grandiloquent posturing pervades his later prose. Nevertheless, this "unique spiritual product we call Mallarmé," as Sartre's translator put it,[18] daily played out the tragedy of his life, which reveals, according to one critic, "the cruel refinement of the modern imagination."[19] His plight is one with that of the modern poet in "his frustrating attempt to strike a balance between the demands of his ideal with his creative powers."[20] As a result "he created self-sustaining flowers of language surviving beyond transcience" that triumph "over silence and darkness" and represent "the poet's victory . . . over reality itself." His only refuge was his unfailing modesty, his exquisite reserve, his quiet determination. As a tragic actor he lived the knowledge that his dream of "The Book" could never be fulfilled, his only stage, his "Tuesdays," his only consolation, the few poems he published, his only reward, immortality.

Ironically, almost a hundred years after Mallarmé's death, a critic writes, "If we speak of Mallarmé's revolutionary position in the history of literature, it may be precisely those qualities which make his writing seem hopelessly remote from the Book as an 'orphic explanation of the Earth' which define his most revolutionary accomplishment."[21] As in the case of Rimbaud, the poetry of Mallarmé is in danger of disappearing beneath the weight of the "myth" of Mallarmé. His poems are the important thing and it is they, not his life, which led a commentator to say of Mallarmé, "Unique, like some bilingual inscription, he seems to be the key to something,"[22] one is not yet sure just what. We can say of his works as a whole what one of the best Mallarmé critics said about the prose poems: "what we retain most of all is an intimate late-Romantic temperament gingerly experiencing a world that is as mysterious as it is present, vivacious, and varied; almost too sensitive to live but going on anyway with what Joyce called 'timid courage,' rewarded now and then by privileged moments including an almost Tolstoyan love of life."[23] Mallarmé's poetry is a phenomenon in literary history, and whether or not one considers him "the incontestable Rector of modern letters" in French literature one can agree that "anyone who has listened to him, dates from him."[24] In listening to him carefully one hears a "certain unexpected music,"[25] not to be encountered in any other poetry. In analyzing that music we have been able, for a moment, to hear it a bit more clearly.

Notes and References

To simplify notation Mallarmé's *Oeuvres complètes* are indicated by *OC* and his *Correspondance* 1 and 2 by *C* 1 and *C* 2, plus the page number(s). All translations of Mallarmé are my own.

Chapter One

1. Henri Mondor, *Vie de Mallarmé* (Paris: Gallimard, 1941), 7.
2. Quoted by Mondor, *Vie*, 667.
3. Ernst Fischer, *The Necessity of Art, A Marxist Approach*, trans. Anne Bostock (Harmondsworth, England: Penguin Books, 1963), 70.
4. G. S. Fraser, *The Modern Writer and His World* (Harmondsworth: Penguin Books, 1964), 41.
5. Quoted by Paul Valéry in *Degas Danse Dessin* (1938; Paris: Gallimard, 1965), 140.
6. Sir Herbert Read, preface, "The Resurrection of the Word," to *Abraxas* by Arlene Zekowski (New York: Wittenborn, 1964), 5.
7. *C* 1:137.
8. Stendhal, *Vie de Henry Brulard* (Paris: Union Générale d'Editions, 1964), 170.
9. Northrop Frye, *Anatomy of Criticism* (Princeton: Princeton University Press, 1957), 81.
10. Thibaudet, *La Poésie de Stéphane Mallarmé* (1912; Paris: Gallimard, 1926, 1959), 116.
11. Frye, *Anatomy of Criticism*, 80, 81.
12. *C* 1:166.
13. *OC*, 312–23.
14. *C* 1:195.
15. *OC*, 662–63.
16. *OC*, 541.
17. Mondor, *Vie*, 186.
18. *C* 1:242.
19. Arthur Rimbaud, *Oeuvres complètes*, introduction and annotations by Antoine Adam (Paris: Gallimard, 1972), 248–54.
20. *C* 1:243.
21. Mondor, *Vie*, 238, n. 3.
22. Henri Peyre, *Connaissance de Baudelaire* (Paris: Corti, 1951), p. 108 ff. The whole chapter on Baudelaire and Poe, pp. 104–16, is well worth reading in this connection.

23. Mondor, *Vie*, 325.
24. *OC*, 866–72.
25. *OC*, 306.
26. *C* 1:278.
27. Thibaudet, *La Poésie*, 378.

Chapter Two

1. *OC*, 662.
2. *Dieu bon écoutez-moi: un horrible attentat*, seven lines of which are reproduced in Henri Mondor, *Mallarmé plus intime* (1944; Paris: Gallimard, 1947), 18–19.
3. *Ce que disaient les Trois Cigognes*, reprinted in Mondor, *Mallarmé plus intime*, 22–42, and in Mondor, *Mallarmé lycéen* (Paris: Gallimard, 1954), 338–56.
4. Lloyd James Austin, "Les 'Années d'apprentissage' de Stéphane Mallarmé," *Revue d'Histoire Littéraire de la France* (January–March 1956), 83.
5. Mondor, *Mallarmé lycéen*, 125–225 and 297–309.
6. Mondor, *Mallarmé lycéen*, 295.
7. *OC*, 1387.
8. *OC*, 1389.
9. *OC*, 1392–93.

Chapter Three

1. *OC*, 1409.
2. Robert Greer Cohn, *Toward the Poems of Mallarmé* (1965; Berkeley: University of California Press, 1980), 39.
3. *Mallarmé*, ed. and trans. Anthony Hartley (Baltimore: Penquin Books, 1965), 14.
4. Yves-Gérard Le Dantec, quoted in *OC*, 1421–22.
5. André Fontainas, quoted in *OC*, 1424.
6. *OC*, 1426.
7. *OC*, 1428.
8. *C* 1:103.
9. *OC*, 1432.
10. *OC*, 1433.
11. *C* 1:200.
12. *OC*, 1439.
13. Cohn, *Toward the Poems*, 47.
14. Cohn, *Toward the Poems*, 48.

Chapter Four

1. Helen Grace Zagona gives an excellent account of the phenomenon in *The Legend of Salomé and the Principle of Art for Art's Sake* (Geneva: Droz, 1960).

2. *Noces d'Hérodiade*, 51.

3. *OC*, 154.

4. In the Pléiade edition the expression reads *une étoile encensée*. Other editions read *une toile encensée*, which makes much better sense.

5. *OC*, 251.

6. Thibaudet, *La Poésie*, 387.

7. Mondor, *Vie*, 792.

8. Mario Praz, *The Romantic Agony*, trans. Angus Davidson (London: Oxford University Press, 1951), 303.

9. Clark Mills, "Commentary" in *Hérodias*, Prairie City, Ill.: James A. Decker, 1940), 37.

10. Yves Bonnefoy, *L'Improbable* (Paris: Mercure de France, 1959), 160.

Chapter Five

1. *C* 1:166.

2. I am indebted to the commentaries of Wallace Fowlie, *Mallarmé* (Chicago: University of Chicago Press, 1953), 148–70, and A. R. Chisholm, *Mallarmé's "L'Après-midi d'un Faune"* (Melbourne: Melbourne University Press, 1958). A great deal can be learned by comparing the two studies as well as from the contrast between two translations: C. F. MacIntyre, *Selected Poems* (Berkeley: University of California Press, 1959), 46–55, and Hartley, *Mallarmé*, 51–56. Cohn, *Toward the Poems*, 13–32, is thought-provoking, particularly where the verbal music of the poem is concerned. The commentary of Pierre Beausire in his glosses of the *Poésies* (Lausanne: Mermod, 1945), 95–105, is straightforward, while the much older analysis by Thibaudet in *La Poésie*, 393–402, remains a valuable introduction, as does the more recent study of Bernard Weinberg, *The Limits of Symbolism* (Chicago: University of Chicago Press, 1966), 127–69.

3. MacIntyre, *Selected Poems*, 51.

4. Cohn, *Toward the Poems*, 26.

5. Fowlie, *Mallarmé*, 159.

6. Chisholm, *Mallarmé's "L'Après-midi d'un Faune,"* 20–21.

Chapter Six

1. Thibaudet, *La Poésie*, 164.

2. Cohn, *Toward the Poems*, 148.

3. *C* 2:37.

4. J.-K. Huysmans, *Against Nature*, trans. Robert Baldick (Baltimore: Penguin Books, 1959), 89, 115.
5. *OC*, 1474.
6. *OC*, 1475.
7. Jean Pierre Richard, *L'Univers imaginaire de Mallarmé* (Paris: Seuil, 1961), 122.
8. Cohn, *Toward the Poems*, 136.
9. *C* 1:179.

Chapter Seven

1. *C* 1:259.
2. Davies, *Les "Tombeaux" de Mallarmé* (Paris: Corti, 1950), 167.
3. Davies, *Les "Tombeaux,"* 168.
4. Cohn, *Toward the Poems*, 160.
5. A comparison of the following interpretations of "Le Tombeau de Charles Baudelaire" is very instructive: Beausire, *Poésies*, 175; Davies, *Les "Tombeaux,"* 164–87; Fowlie, *Mallarmé*, 65–68; Charles Chassé, *Les Clefs de Mallarmé* (Paris: Editions Montaigne, 1954), 230–34; Cohn, *Toward the Poems*, 158–69.
6. Davies, *Les "Tombeaux,"* 196.
7. Cohn, *Toward the Poems*, 172, 173.
8. *C* 2:290.
9. *OC*, 541.
10. Léon Cellier, *Mallarmé et la Morte qui parle* (Paris: Presses Universitaires de France, 1950), 208.
11. Cellier, *Mallarmé*, 211.
12. Cellier, *Mallarmé*, 221.
13. Thibaudet, *La Poésie*, 110.
14. Mondor, *Vie*, 785.
15. *OC*, 869.
16. Michaud, *Mallarmé*, 62.
17. *OC*, 368.
18. Cohn, *Toward the Poems*, 220.
19. Emile Noulet, *Dix Poèmes de Stéphane Mallarmé* (Geneva: Droz, 1948), 116.
20. Walter A. Strauss, "The Reconciliation of Opposites in Orphic Poetry: Rilke and Mallarmé," *Centennial Review*, (Spring 1966):235.

Chapter Eight

1. *OC*, 1559.
2. *C* 1:313.
3. *Igitur*, 33.

4. *C* 1:342.
5. *OC,* 456.
6. T. S. Eliot, *On Poetry and Poets* (New York: Noonday Press, 1961), 119.

Chapter Nine

1. Jean-Paul Sartre, *Mallarmé or the Poet of Nothingness,* trans. with introduction by Ernest Sturm (University Park: Pennsylvania State University Press, 1988), 145.
2. Mondor, *Vie,* 19.
3. John Porter Houston, *Patterns of Thought in Rimbaud and Mallarmé* (Lexington, Ky.: French Forum, 1986), 127.
4. Robert Giroux, *Désir de synthèse chez Mallarmé* (Sherbrooke, Quebec: Editions Naaman, 1978), 265.
5. Verlaine in *Hommes d'aujourd'hui,* quoted by Mondor, *Vie,* 480.
6. Stuart Merrill, quoted by Marjorie H. Ilsley, "Four Unpublished Letters of Stéphane Mallarmé to Stuart Merrill," *Yale French Studies,* 9 (1952):161.
7. For example: Paul Hindemith, *Hérodiade de Stéphane Mallarmé,* Récitation orchestrale. New York: Associated Music Publishers, 1944; Serge Nigg, *Le chant du dépossédé,* d'après des notes poétiques de Stéphane Mallarmé. Editions Jobert, 1961; Pierre Boulez, *Pli selon pli.* London: Universal Edition, 1977; Christopher Wilmarth, *Breath,* inspired by seven poems of Stéphane Mallarmé. New York: C. Wilmarth, 1982; Charles Wine, *Dialogue & Fugue: A Peace in Progress,* hommage à Stéphane Mallarmé and Leonard Bernstein. Washington, D.C.: Sun & Moon Press, 1984. And for the dance: Baron Adolf de Meyer, *L'Après-midi d'un faune: Vaslav Nijinsky, 1912,* 33 photographs. New York: Dance Horizons, 1983. And all of Nijinsky's successors.
8. Calvin Evans, "Mallarméan Antecedents of the Avant-Garde Theater," *Modern Drama* 6 (Summer 1963):13.
9. Strauss, "Reconciliation of Opposites," *Centennial Review,* 236.
10. David Scott, "Mallarmé: Un Coup de Dés," in *Pictorialist Poetics* (Cambridge: Cambridge University Press, 1988), 138.
11. Virginia A. La Charité, *Dynamics of Space* (Lexington, Ky.: French Forum, 1987), 175.
12. *OC,* 867.
13. Raymond Preston, *"Four Quartets" Rehearsed* (New York: Sheed & Ward, 1947), 16.
14. Joan Richardson, *Wallace Stevens: The Early Years 1879–1923* (New York: Morrow, 1986), 21, 65, 197.
15. Nathaniel Wing, "False Confusions," in *The Limits of Narrative* (Cambridge: Cambridge University Press, 1986), 112.

16. Peter Dayan, *Mallarmé's "Divine Transposition"* (Oxford: Clarendon Press, 1986), 219.

17. Sartre, *Mallarmé or the Poet of Nothingness,* 24.

18. Ernest Sturm, "Notes to the Introduction," Sartre, *Mallarmé,* 147.

19. Kurt Weinberg, "Heine, Baudelaire, Mallarmé: Atavism and Urbanity," *Western Review,* 21 (Winter 1957):134.

20. Philip Knight, "Mallarmé," in *Flower Poetics* in *Nineteenth-Century France* (Oxford: Clarendon Press, 1986), 219.

21. Leo Bersani, *The Death of Stéphane Mallarmé* (Cambridge: Cambridge University Press, 1982), 46.

22. Maud Mannoni, "Mallarmé relu," *Les Temps Modernes,* no. 198 (November 1957):864.

23. Robert Greer Cohn, *Mallarmé's Prose Poems: A Critical Study* (Cambridge: Cambridge University Press, 1987), 120.

24. Charles Morice, in *Portraits du Prochain Siècle,* quoted by Mondor, *Vie,* 686.

25. Thibaudet, *La Poésie,* 10.

Bibliography

PRIMARY WORKS

French Editions

Correspondance. 11 vols. Edited by Henri Mondor, Jean-Pierre Richard, and Lloyd J. Austin. Paris: Gallimard, 1959–85. Covers the years 1862–98.

Correspondance avec Henri Cazalis (1862–97). Edited by Lawrence A. Joseph. Paris: Nizet, 1977.

Mallarmé–Whistler, *Correspondance.* Edited by Carl Paul Barbier. Paris: Nizet, 1964.

Un coup de dés jamais n'abolira le hasard. Edited by Claude Roulet. Neuchâtel: Messeiller, 1960.

Divagations. Edited by E. M. Souffrin. Paris: Charpentier, 1949.

Ecrits sur le livre. Edited by Henri Meschonnic, with his essay "Mallarmé au-delà du silence." Paris: Editions de l'Éclat, 1985.

Les "gossips" de Mallarmé, Athanaeum 1875–1876. Edited by Henri Mondor and Lloyd J. Austin. Paris: Gallimard, 1962.

Igiture ou La Folie d'Elbehnon. Edited by Dr. Edmond Bonniot. 1925; Paris: Gallimard, 1952.

Les Noces d'Hérodiade, Mystère. Edited by Gardner Davies. Paris: Gallimard, 1959.

Oeuvres complètes. Edited by Henri Mondor and G. Jean-Aubry. 1945; Paris: Gallimard, 1984.

Pages choisies. Edited by Guy Delfel. Paris: Hachette, 1954.

Poésies. Edited by É[milie]. Noulet. Mexico: Edition Quetzal, 1944.

Poésies. Edited by Pierre Beausire. Lausanne: Mermod, 1945.

Poésies. Preface by Jean-Paul Sartre. Paris: Gallimard, 1966.

Le manuscrit autographe des "Poésies" de Mallarmé. Paris: Editions Ramsay, 1981.

Pour un tombeau d'Anatole. Edited by Jean-Pierre Richard. Paris: Seuil, 1961.

Translations

Die Thrown Never Will Annul Chance. Translated by Brian Goffey. London: Oxford University Press, 1965.

Herodias. Translated by Clark Mills. Prairie City, [Ill.]: James A. Decker, 1940.

Igitur. Translated by Jack Hirschman. Los Angeles: Press of the Pegacycle Lady, 1974.

Mallarmé. Edited and translated by Anthony Hartley. Baltimore: Penguin Books, 1965.
Poems. Translated by Roger Fry. London: Vision Press, 1951.
Pour un tombeau d'Anatole/A Tomb for Anatole. Translated by Paul Auster. San Francisco: North Point Press, 1983.
Selected Poems. Translated by C. F. MacIntyre. Berkeley and Los Angeles: University of California Press, 1959.
Mallarmé: Selected Poetry and Prose. Edited by Mary Ann Caws. New York: New Directions, 1982.
Selected Prose Poems, Essays and Letters. Translated by Brad Cook. Baltimore: Johns Hopkins Press, 1956.

SECONDARY WORKS

Books

Abastado, Claude. *Expérience et théorie de la création poétique chez Mallarmé.* Paris: Minard, 1970. A sound analysis of the point where theory and practice meet in the creation of poetry.
Aish, Deborah A. K. *La Métaphore dans l'oeuvre de Mallarmé.* Paris: Droz, 1938. An early study of the role of metaphor in the poetry of Mallarmé. Now somewhat outdated, but still informative.
Ayda, Adile. *Le Drame intérieur de Mallarmé ou l'Origine des symboles mallarméens.* Istanbul: Editions La Turquie Moderne, 1955. The author's method is questionable and her conclusion debatable, but she often has interesting things to say about Mallarmé's use of specific words.
Barbier, Carl P. *Documents Stéphane Mallarmé.* 7 vols. Paris: Nizet, 1968–81. Important contributions to the study and appreciation of Mallarmé's life and poetry.
Beausire, Pierre. *Mallarmé, Poésie et Poétique.* Lausanne: Mermod, 1949. The theoretical part of this book is excellent. One might have wished for a more direct and above all more detailed application of the theory to the poetry.
Bernard, Suzanne. *Mallarmé et la musique.* Paris: Nizet, 1959. A clear and careful analysis of the relationship between the theories of Wagner and Mallarmé followed by a study of the "musicality" of the latter's poems. No mention of one of the most interesting musical experiments, Hindemith's "Hérodiade" of 1944.
Bersani, Leo. *The Death of Stéphane Mallarmé.* Cambridge: Cambridge University Press, 1982. One of the best and most profound studies in recent Mallarmé criticism.
Bird, Edward A. *L'Univers poétique de Stéphane Mallarmé.* Paris: Nizet, 1962. A good general introduction to the times and works of Mallarmé.

Block, Haskell M. *Mallarmé and the Symbolist Drama.* Detroit: Wayne State University Press, 1963. A brief but coherent analysis of Mallarmé's concept of the theater and his enduring influence on the theater.

Boulay, Daniel. *L'Obscurité esthétique de Mallarmé et "La Prose pour des Esseintes."* Paris: Boulay, 1960; Nizet, 1973. An interesting and often convincing exegesis according to which the "sister" of the poem is Platonic memory.

Bowie, Malcolm. *Mallarmé and the Art of Being Difficult.* Cambridge: Cambridge University Press, 1978. Reveals the true "art" hidden in Mallarmé's supposedly "difficult" poetry.

Cellier, Léon. *Mallarmé et la Morte qui parle.* Paris: Presses Universitaires de France, 1950. The author demonstrates in detail the influence of Hugo and Gautier on Mallarmé. His interpretations of the poems are not always convincing, but his analyses of various themes—the mirror, the feather, etc.—are informative.

Chadwick, Charles. *Mallarmé, sa pensée dans sa poésie.* Paris: Corti, 1962. A chronological (biographical) interpretation of Mallarmé's works that sometimes results in a too close identification of the poet with too many details of the poems. An insistence on Christian symbolism somewhat detracts from otherwise sensitive and intelligent exegeses.

Chassé, Charles. *Lueurs sur Mallarmé.* Paris: Nouvelle Revue Critique, 1947. Six articles published between 1912 and 1946 that focus on Mallarmé as a teacher and on his friendship with Mistral. Includes some sidelights on his biography.

———. *Les Clefs de Mallarmé.* Paris: Editions Montaigne, 1954. Chassé's interpretations of Mallarmé's poems based on etymologies found in Littré frequently produce interesting possibilities, but he too often mistakes the makings of a poem for the poem itself.

Chisholm, A. R. *Towards "Hérodiade": A Literary Genealogy.* Melbourne: Melbourne University Press, 1934. With great erudition and subtlety Professor Chisholm demonstrates how the works of Mallarmé were the culmination of poetic and philosophical tendencies in nineteenth-century French literature. The nature of the thesis precludes showing how they were the beginning of something even more important.

———. *Mallarmé's "L'Après-Midi d'un Faune."* Melbourne: Melbourne University Press, 1958. A brief but sensitive and intelligent interpretation of Mallarmé's poem.

———. *Mallarmé's "Grand Oeuvre."* Manchester, England: Manchester University Press, 1962. A strangely disappointing book. I do not find, for example, a clock in *"Ses purs ongles . . ."* Nevertheless the author has many interesting and worthwhile things to say about Mallarmé's poetry.

Cohn, Robert Greer. *Mallarmé's "Un Coup de Dés."* New Haven, Conn.: Yale French Studies, 1949.

———. *L'Oeuvre de Mallarmé: "Un Coup de Dés."* Paris: Librairie les Lettres, 1951.

————. *Toward the Poems of Mallarmé.* 1965; Berkeley and Los Angeles: University of California Press, 1980.

————. *Mallarmé's Masterwork: New Findings.* The Hague: Mouton, 1966.

————. *Mallarmé's "Igitur."* Berkeley and Los Angeles: University of California Press, 1981.

————. *Mallarmé's Prose Poems: A Critical Study.* Cambridge: Cambridge University Press, 1987.

Every student owes a debt of gratitude to Professor Cohn. His books reveal an amazing erudition, a global knowledge of the works of Mallarmé, and a sensitivity and an intelligence in interpreting those works equalled by few.

Cooperman, Hasye. *The Aesthetics of Stéphane Mallarmé.* New York: Koffern Press, 1933. One of the earliest attempts by an American to interpret Mallarmé, with particular attention to Wagner, *Igitur,* and *Un Coup de Dés.* Some of the judgments are no longer valid and a few of the translations are inaccurate, but the book remains a good general introduction with an excellent bibliography of earlier works.

Davies, Gardner. *Les "Tombeaux" de Mallarmé, essai d'exégèse raisonnée.* Paris: Corti, 1950.

————. *Vers une explication rationnelle du "Coup de Dés," essai d'exégèse mallarméenne.* Paris: Corti, 1953.

————. *Mallarmé et le drame solaire, essai d'exégèse raisonnée.* Paris: Corti, 1959.

————. *Mallarmé et le rêve d' "Hérodiade."* Paris: Corti, 1978.

The author has used the same approach in the first three volumes: he has compared Mallarmé's use of words and expressions throughout his works to illuminate their use in a particular poem. The results are instructive until the approach is tied too closely to a theme, that of the solar drama, for example, in the third volume. Certainly it is a recurring theme in Mallarmé's poetry, but the author is led to force too many associations by this mixture of devices. His clear and scholarly account of what the unfinished manuscript of *Les Noces d'Hérodiade* tells us about the poem "Hérodiade" and its relationship with many other works by Mallarmé is both informative and helpful.

Dayan, Peter. *Mallarmé's "Divine Transposition": Real and Apparent Sources of Literary Value.* Oxford: Clarendon Press, 1986. A complex study of how Mallarmé gets to the essence of literary value through the transposition of space and structure to arrive at the ideal.

Delfel, Guy. *L'Esthétique de Stéphane Mallarmé.* Paris: Flammarion, 1951. This book, written primarily for the philosopher and aesthetician, gives clear and sound ideas concerning Mallarmé's aesthetics. The author possibly does a disservice to the poet by claiming too much for him in his conclusion: "There is hardly any domain in the kingdom of Esthetics where he has not totally upset the usual way of thinking and left some brilliant traces of his passing."

Dujardin, Edouard. *Mallarmé par un des siens.* Paris: Messein, 1936. Reminiscences of Mallarmé, symbolism, free verse, and the *Revue Wagnérienne* by a writer and editor who was involved with all of them. These collected articles are somewhat disparate but they do re-create the atmosphere of the times.

Erwin, John F. *Mallarmé and Claudel: An Intellectual Encounter.* Ann Arbor, Mich.: University Microfilms, 1970. A study of one of the most fruitful encounters for twentieth-century French literature.

Fabureau, Hubert. *Stéphane Mallarmé, son oeuvre.* Paris: Nouvelle Revue Critique, 1933. Although subtitled *son oeuvre,* half of this little book is spent recounting Mallarmé's life, and not always accurately. The second half offers a cursory glimpse at the works.

Faure, Gabriel. *Mallarmé à Tournon.* Paris: Horizons de France, 1946. Mondor's *Vie de Mallarmé* and the publication of the correspondence have deprived this little volume of much of its interest and importance, except for the photographs of Tournon.

Florence, Penny. *Mallarmé, Monet and Redon: Visual and Aural Signs and the Generation of Meaning.* Cambridge: Cambridge University Press, 1986. Demonstrates that "The idea of reading *Un Coup de Dés* as an *illustrated* text is not an easy one to assimilate" and in fact an unthinkable one for all those who revere the text as printed.

Fowlie, Wallace. *Mallarmé.* Chicago: University of Chicago Press, 1953. Still one of the best general introductions to the works of Mallarmé in English.

Fraenkel, Ernest. *Les Dessins transconscients de Stéphane Mallarmé: A propos de "Un Coup de Dés."* Paris: Nizet, 1960. *Un Coup de Dés* as a sort of Rorschach test, interesting but in the end extraliterary.

Franklin, Ursula. *"Divagations": An Anatomy of Poésis: The Prose Poems of Stéphane Mallarmé.* Chapel Hill: University of North Carolina Press, 1976. A sound study of the central importance of *Divagations* in Mallarmé's works.

Gengoux, Jacques. *Le Symbolisme de Mallarmé.* Paris: Nizet, 1950. According to Gengoux, Mallarmé's metaphysics is polarized on time or life or life and eternity or thought. Before the union of life as dispersion and thought as synthesis there is a prior unity followed by scission followed at last by unity regained. Although the demonstration is accompanied by an interpretation of almost all the poems, the explanations do not always help with the real difficulties of Mallarmé's poetry.

Gill, Austin. *Mallarmé's Poem: "La chevelure vol d'une flamme."* Glasgow: University of Glasgow Press, 1971.

———. *The Early Mallarmé.* Oxford: Clarendon Press, 1979. A fascinating study of one of Mallarmé's most difficult poems followed by a careful analysis of the early works.

Giroux, Robert. *Désir de synthèse chez Mallarmé.* Sherbrooke, Quebec: Editions Naaman, 1978. How Mallarmé synthesized the "what" and the "how" of poetic creation into a message of universal significance.

Goffin, Robert. *Mallarmé vivant.* Paris: Nizet, 1956. According to Goffin, Mallarmé's hermeticism resulted from his attempts to hide his unrequited love for Méry Laurent. The author provides interesting details about Laurent's life and fortunes but not too much that is illuminating about Mallarmé's poetry.

Goodkin, Richard E. *The Symbolist Home and the Tragic Home: Mallarmé and Oedipus.* Philadelphia: John Benjamins, 1984. Interesting analyses of six poems based on the structuring unit of the home. Goodkin concludes that "Tragedy and Symbolism are both predicated upon the need for struggle and resistance, upon the existence of a negating mechanism within the human spirit which can also be an affirmation of that spirit."

Hayman, David. *Joyce et Mallarmé:* Vol. 1, *Stylistique de la suggestion;* Vol. 2, *Les Eléments mallarméens dans l'oeuvre de Joyce.* Paris: Les Lettres Modernes, 1956. A splendid piece of scholarship. Although such excellent, ready-made subjects are rare, there is still much to be done on Mallarmé's influence on other writers.

Huot, Sylviane. *Le "Mythe d'Hérodiade" chez Mallarmé: Genèse et évolution.* Paris: Nizet, 1977. A scrupulous analysis of *Les Noces d'Hérodiade* tied closely to the poet's biography that reveals a great deal about the role of the "Myth of Hérodiade" in the evolution of Mallarmé's creative process. The work suffers only by comparison with that of Davies which appeared the following year.

Jones, Henri. *Mallarmé chez Gabrielle Séailles: vues esthétiques sur la poésie de synthèse.* Toulouse: University of Toulouse-Le Mirail, 1975. Another encounter that this time deepened Mallarmé's concept of the aesthetics of synthesis.

Kravis, Judy. *The Prose of Mallarmé: The Evolution of a Literary Language.* Cambridge: Cambridge University Press, 1976. Another revealing study of the evolution of Mallarmé's prose so necessary for an understanding of his poetry.

La Charité, Virginia A. *The Dynamics of Space: Mallarmé's "Un Coup de dés jamais n'abolira le hasard."* Lexington, Ky.: French Forum, 1987. A sound study of the dynamics of space as exemplified in Mallarmé's great poem.

Laflèche, Guy. *Mallarmé: Grammaire générative des "Contes indiens."* Montreal: University of Montreal Press, 1975. A useful analysis of how the grammar of one of Mallarmé's less studied texts generated itself, so to speak, into the final product, significant for an analysis of the grammar of the poetry.

Langan, Janine D. *Hegel and Mallarmé.* Lanham, Maryland: University Press of America, 1986. The role of Hegel in Mallarmé's thought has perhaps been overemphasized, but Langan's study is sound and convincing.

Lewis, Paula G. *The Aesthetics of Mallarmé in Relation to His Public.* Rutherford, N.J.: Fairleigh Dickinson University Press, 1975. An informative study of a relationship that has been scanted in much Mallarmé criticism.

Lloyd, Rosemary. *Mallarmé: Poésies.* London: Grant & Cutler, 1984. A helpful introduction.

Marvick, Louis Wirth. *Mallarmé and the Sublime.* Albany: State University of New York Press, 1986. An interesting and exhaustive study of one of Mallarmé's basic concepts.

Mauclair, Camille. *Mallarmé chez lui.* Paris: Grasset, 1935. Pious reminiscences in which Madame Mallarmé is twice mistakenly named Blanche-Flore d'Heilly (my edition is the eighth) and Gustave Kahn is termed "cet israélite." Illuminating verbal portraits of many of the Tuesday faithfuls along with interesting details and misinformation in about equal parts.

Mauron, Charles. *Mallarmé l'obscur.* Paris: Denoël, 1941.

———. *Introduction à la psychanalyse de Mallarmé.* Neuchâtel: La Baconnière, 1950.

———. *Mallarmé par lui-même.* 1954; Paris: Seuil, 1964.

———. *Des métaphores obsédantes au mythe personnel.* Paris: Corti, 1964.

———. *Mallarmé.* Paris: Seuil, 1977.

In his psychoanalysis of Mallarmé Mauron puts forth the theory that the decollation of John the Baptist symbolizes the castration complex, which tells us more perhaps about Mallarmé than his poem "Salut." His method has, nevertheless, some revealing things to say about Mallarmé's recurrent symbols. If the author repeats some of the points he made in his earlier works, he also gives a brief and clear psychological portrait of Mallarmé. *Mallarmé par lui-même* also contains many interesting photographs and illustrations.

Michaud, Guy. *Mallarmé.* 1953; Paris: Hatier, 1958. The author's desire was to propose "an introduction to the reading and the knowledge of Mallarmé." He has done just that although the reader may not always agree with his interpretations nor find that he is always helpful with the more difficult passages in Mallarmé's poetry.

Michon, Jacques. *Mallarmé et les mots anglais.* Montreal: University of Montreal Press, 1978. An instructive study of a subject that has not received the attention it deserves.

Miomandre, Francis de. *Mallarmé.* Paris: Bader-Dufour, 1948. The recollections of the effect of Mallarmé's poems at the time of their appearance on a group of young men deep in the provinces make informative reading. Otherwise the book offers little that is new about the life and even less about the works.

Mondor, Henri. *Vie de Mallarmé.* Paris: Gallimard, 1941.

————. *Mallarmé plus intime.* Paris: 1944; Gallimard, 1947.

————. *Mallarmé: Documents iconographiques.* Geneva: Cailler, 1947.

————. *L'Heureuse Rencontre de Valéry et Mallarmé.* Lausanne: La Guilde du Livre, 1947.

————. *"Histoire d'un faune," avec un état inédit de "L'Après-Midi d'un faune."* Paris: Gallimard, 1948.

————. *Mallarmé lycéen.* Paris: Gallimard, 1954.

————. *Autres Précisions sur Mallarmé et inédits.* Paris: Gallimard, 1961.

Over twenty years this indefatigable Mallarmé scholar gave us first the definitive biography according to what was known in 1941—it still remains a valuable source. He next published sometimes interesting but frequently not very important details about Mallarmé's life, his early publications, the death of his sister, his choice of profession, his love of cats, his lecture tour in Belgium, his friendship with Villiers de l'Isle-Adam, the genesis of the *Contes indiens,* and his friendship with Méry Laurent. That was followed by photographs of Mallarmé, his family, his friends, his manuscripts and publications which turned out to be a disappointing collection. His account of the meeting of Valéry and Mallarmé included Valéry and Pierre Louÿs, Valéry and Gide, Mallarmé and *Un Coup de Dés,* and a little about these last two and Valéry. Perhaps Valéry is the one to consult on the subject. His volume on the possible sources plus the three existing versions of *L'Après-Midi* provides an important and fascinating opportunity to observe Mallarmé's development. Then came the discovery and publication of four of Mallarmé's "hundred little notebooks" containing forty-one of his early poems, as well as the names of favorite poets and their poems that Mallarmé had written down. More precise details would have been desirable but the early poems provide an important source study. Mondor's final contribution contains fourteen chapters on Mallarmé's publications, his friends, and events in his life. Several are in part Mondor's prefaces to the books of others. Otherwise one gets the impression these are the last gleanings from Mondor's huge Mallarmé collection, repetitive, not very important, but sometimes interesting. Not to be forgotten is the fact that Mondor provided a major impulse for Mallarmé studies.

Morris, Drewry. *Stéphane Mallarmé: 20th Century Criticism.* University, Miss.: Romance Monographs, 1977. A vital source for those interested in the development of Mallarmé criticism.

Nicholas, H., ed. *Mallarmé et le symbolisme: Documentation thématique.* Paris: Larousse, 1972. A careful outline of the themes of Mallarmé's poetry.

Noulet, Emilie. *L'Oeuvre poétique de Stéphane Mallarmé.* Paris: Droz, 1940; Brussels: Jacques Antoine, 1974.

————. *Études littéraires.* Mexico: Talleres Gráficos, 1944.

————. *Dix poèmes de Stéphane Mallarmé.* Geneva: Droz, 1948.

————. *Suite mallarméenne.* Paris: Editions des Artistes, 1959.

————. *Vingt poèmes de Stéphane Mallarmé.* Paris: Minard, 1967. Noulet's first volume consisted of the "chronology of an intellectual adventure," a classic in Mallarmé criticism that provides an excellent general introduction to the works of Mallarmé as well as detailed analyses of the poems. That was followed by a study of hermeticism in Poe, and Poe's influence on modern French poetry, with many references to Mallarmé that are intelligent, clear, and helpful. It includes exegeses of three poems republished in *Dix poèmes.* Although one cannot, after forty years, always agree with Madame Noulet in that volume, her "literal and literary interpretation" continues to be one of the primary source works in the exegesis of Mallarmé's poetry. The analyses of twenty poems drawn from *L'Oeuvre poétique,* beginning chronologically with "Toast funèbre" and including *Dix poèmes,* make available again Noulet's pertinent commentaries on some of Mallarmé's most difficult poems. Cognizance was taken of most of the advances in Mallarmé scholarship since 1940 so that this final volume exhibits all of the virtues and few of the faults of its predecessors. Noulet's contributions to Mallarmé studies cannot be underestimated.

Olds, Marshall C. *Desire Seeking Expression: Mallarmé's "Prose pour des Esseintes."* Lexington, Ky.: French Forum, 1983. A convincing analysis of one of Mallarmé's most complex poems.

Orliac, Antoine. *La Cathédrale symboliste:* Vol. 2, *Mallarmé tel qu'en lui-même.* 1932; Paris: Mercure de France, 1948. A highly philosophical study in which the author notes similarities between Mallarmé's thought and that of Keats, the German romantics, Balzac, Plato, Wagner, the *Baghavad-Gita,* and a host of others. Using all of these sources Mallarmé arrived at the "simple and logical relationship of cause and effect," which is, as the author himself says, "a somewhat rudimentary system." The more than fifty years that have passed since the book's first publication have witnessed neither the rediscovery of the poet René Ghil nor the slow sinking of impressionist art "into a gray uniformity" as the author predicted.

Pancrazi, Jean-Noël. *Mallarmé.* Paris: Hatier, 1973. A helpful introduction to Mallarmé.

Park, Ynhui. *L' "Idée" chez Mallarmé ou Conférence rêvée.* Paris: Centre de Documentation Universitaire, 1966. A clear and convincing analysis of Mallarmé's concept of the idea and all its implications. If Mallarmé was defeated by the very nature of his concept, it was a magnificent defeat that resulted in more than man has a right to expect. The book is unfortunately marred by numerous typographical errors but the bibliography is useful up to 1966.

Paxton, Norman. *The Development of Mallarmé's Prose Style.* Geneva: Droz, 1968. A careful study of the evolution of Mallarmé's prose style, which has great relevance for his poetry.

Richard, Jean-Pierre. *L'Univers imaginaire de Mallarmé.* Paris: Seuil, 1961. A monstrous book that is difficult to read but also rich in suggestions with an important bibliography, 623–44.

Rietman, L. E. *Vision et mouvement chez Stéphane Mallarmé*. Paris: Presses Modernes, 1932. An early attempt to counteract the impression of stasis so many critics found in Mallarmé's poetry.

Roulet, Claude. *Elucidation du poème de Stéphane Mallarmé*. Neuchâtel: Ides et Calendes, 1943.

————. *Eléments de poétique mallarméenne*. Neuchâtel: Editions du Griffon, 1947.

————. *Version du poème de Mallarmé "Un Coup de Dés jamais n'abolira le hasard."* Neuchâtel: Editions du Griffon, 1949.

————. *Nouveaux éléments de poétique mallarméenne d'après le poème "Un Coup de Dés jamais n'abolira le hasard."* Neuchâtel: Editions du Griffon, 1950.

————. *Traité de poétique supérieure: "Un Coup de Dés jamais n'abolira le hasard."* Neuchâtel: Messeiller, 1956. Roulet's long poem of twenty-eight pages with many a "Ho!," a "Ha!," and a "Ha! Ha!" has as its point of departure *Un Coup de Dés* and is intended as a commentary on that poem. The general observations of the "postface," although somewhat abstract and much too "religious" in nature, constitute a better commentary on Mallarmé's poetic art then does Roulet's poem. In his volumes on poetics Roulet has constructed a higher poetics, somewhat as we speak of higher mathematics, in order to interpret Mallarmé's poem. He finds it to be a Bible, the Bible, another Bible, a mass, the classical tragedy of the Atridae, an ode, "a modern *De natura rerum,*" a symphony, a fugue, in short, "the most difficult work in the world, also the most beautiful that has ever been written." He also points out many details that are useful in studying the poem.

Royère, Jean. *Mallarmé*. Paris: Messein, 1931. In this early study the author finds Mallarmé's sensitivity controlled by two "fervors": his "physicism," that is, the "extreme humanization of things"; and his "erotology," that is, "a mystique of the feminine sentiment which, at every moment, is transformed into another exaltation." Mallarmé's "irony" is the proof of these fervors. As a result, "poetry becomes the profound meaning of life realized through expression." A complicated and at the same time somewhat oversimplified point of view.

Ruchon, François. *L'Amitié de Stéphane Mallarmé et de Georges Rodenbach*. Geneva: Cailler, 1959. The pleasant account of an exemplary friendship that reveals another aspect of Mallarmé, his unfailing consideration for younger poets.

Sartre, Jean-Paul. *Mallarmé: la lucidité et sa face d'ombre*. Edited by Arlette Elkaïn-Sartre. Paris: Gallimard, 1986.

————. *Mallarmé or the Poet of Nothingness*. Translated and introduced by Ernest Sturm. University Park: Pennsylvania State University Press, 1988.

Whatever one may think of Sartre's literary criticism, he nevertheless illuminates certain aspects of Mallarmé's world as no one else has.

Scherer, Jacques. *L'Expression littéraire dans l'oeuvre de Mallarmé*. Paris: Nizet, 1947.

———. *Le "Livre" de Mallarmé*. 1957; Paris: Gallimard, 1977.

———. *Grammaire de Mallarmé*. Paris: Nizet, 1977.

Scherer's first volume is a detailed, one could almost say scientific, study of Mallarmé's style that confirms one's impressions of Mallarmé's use of adverbs, conjunctions, etc., after one has read ten poems. Such well-documented confirmations are necessary and useful. In Scherer's second volume a great deal can be learned about what Mallarmé did accomplish by the study of what he did not accomplish. Scherer's presentation of and commentary on the many pages of notes Mallarmé accumulated in view of "the Book" help us to appreciate the enormity of his concept and to understand better why it was never realized. Scherer's "Grammar" gives careful attention to that aspect of Mallarmé's works.

Soula, Camille. *La Poésie et la pensée de Stéphane Mallarmé: Essai sur le symbole de la chevelure*. Paris: Champion, 1926.

———. *Notes sur "Toast funèbre."* Paris: Champion, 1929.

———. *Gloses sur Mallarmé*. Paris: Diderot, 1945. Informative and useful early studies of Mallarmé's poetry.

Steland, Dieter. *Dialektische Gedanken in Stéphane Mallarmés "Divagations."* Munich: Wilhelm Fink Verlag, 1965. The author attempts to demonstrate that "many of the obscurities in Mallarmé's critical prose are nothing other than the abridged precision of a dialectical thought." The proof is not sufficiently inclusive to be conclusive and while such a demonstration says something about the prose, it is not designed to say much about the poetry.

Thibaudet, Albert. *La Poésie de Stéphane Mallarmé*. 1912; Paris: Gallimard, 1926, 1959. One of the earliest and still one of the best general introductions to the works of Mallarmé.

Valéry, Paul. *Écrits divers sur Stéphane Mallarmé*. Paris: Gallimard, 1950. Almost all of Valéry's writings on Mallarmé brought together conveniently in one volume, thus providing the book on Mallarmé Valéry could never bring himself to write. One almost inevitably learns more about Valéry than Mallarmé but the book does reveal clearly the role of one great poet in the life of another.

Verin, Simone. *Stéphane Mallarmé, le presque contradictoire*. Paris: Nizet 1975. How Mallarmé seems to contradict himself with special attention to the variants that substantiate the idea.

Vial, André-Marc. *Mallarmé: Tétralogie pour un enfant mort*. Paris: Corti, 1976. How the early death of Mallarmé's son influenced his poetry.

Wais, Kurt. *Mallarmé: Dichtung—Weisheit—Haltung*. Munich: Beck, 1952. A

formidable study of the life, times, and works of Mallarmé with many of
the best and few of the worst characteristics generally described as "Ger-
manic": a meticulous attention to detail that is only occasionally over-
whelming, a philosophical approach that only now and then tends too
much to the tragic. Because of its insights and erudition this book should
be translated into English.

Walzer, Pierre-Oliver. *Essai sur Stéphane Mallarmé.* Paris: Seghers, 1963. A
good, general introduction to Mallarmé in which each work is considered
briefly but clearly.

Williams, Thomas A. *Mallarmé and the Language of Mysticism.* Athens: University of Georgia Press, 1970. Illuminates the significant role of mysticism in Mallarmé's poetry, an aspect not always given its just attention.

Wolf, Mary E. *Eros under Glass: Psychoanalysis and Mallarmé's "Hérodiade."* Co-
lumbus: Ohio State University Press, 1987. Demonstrates how much a
psychoanalytic approach can reveal about Mallarmé and his great poem.

Woolley, Grange. *Stéphane Mallarmé.* Madison, N.J.: Drew University Press,
1942. An early study now perhaps somewhat outdated, but still useful.

Wyzewa, Téodor. *Mallarmé: notes.* Paris: La Vogue, 1886. One of the very
earliest Mallarmé critiques and as such important in the study of Mallarmé criticism.

Zurowski, Maceij. *Les Poèmes hermétiques de Stéphane Mallarmé.* Warsaw: Sem-
inaria Jezykow I Literatur Romanskich, 1947. These very brief interpretations of nine of Mallarmé's poems, dated June 1939, are too sketchy to
be of much help but they do reveal a certain sensitivity to the poetry and
an interest in Mallarmé in Poland almost fifty years ago.

Selected Articles and Essays

Anderson, Richard C. "Hindu Myth in Mallarmé: *Un Coup de Dés.*" *Compar-
ative Literature* (Winter 1967):28–35.

Austin, Lloyd J. "Mallarmé critique d'art." In *The Artist and Writer in France,*
edited by Francis Haskell et al., 153–62. Oxford: Clarendon Press, 1974.

———. Thirteen essays on Mallarmé, sixteen reviews of books about Mallarmé. In *Poetic Principles and Practice: Occasional Papers on Baudelaire, Mallarmé and Valéry,* 19–229; 299–330. Cambridge: Cambridge University
Press, 1987.

Austin, Lloyd J. "Mallarmé's Reshaping of 'Le Pitre châtié'"; Austin Gill.
"Mallarmé's Use of Christian Imagery for Post-Christian Concepts"; Albert Sonnenfeld. "Eros and Poetry: Mallarmé's Disappearing Visions." In
Order and Adventure in French Post-Romantic Poetry, edited by E. M. Beau-
mont et al., 56–71, 72–88, 89–98. Oxford: Oxford University Press,
1976.

Bernard, Suzanne. "Mallarmé et la Métaphysique du langage." In *Le Poème en
prose de Baudelaire jusqu'à nos jours,* 253–330. Paris: Nizet, 1959.

————. "La clef de Mallarmé, est-elle dans Littré?" *Revue d'Histoire de la Littérature Française*, no. 1(January–March 1956):85–93.

Blanchot, Maurice. "Le mythe de Mallarmé." In *La Part du feu*, 35–48. Paris: Gallimard, 1949 [1972].

————. "Mallarmé's Experience"; "The *Igitur* Experience." In *The Space of Literature*, translated by Ann Smock, 38–48, 108–19. Lincoln: University of Nebraska Press, 1982. First published as *L'Espace littéraire*. Paris: Gallimard, 1955.

————. "Mallarmé and Literary Space." In *The Siren's Song*, edited by Gabriel Josipovici, translanted by Sacha Rabinovitch, 110–20. Bloomington: Indiana University Press, 1982.

Bonnefoy, Yves. "La Poétique de Mallarmé." In *Le Nuage rouge*, 183–211. Paris: Mercure de France, 1977.

Brereton, Geoffrey. "Stéphane Mallarmé." In *An Introduction to the French Poets*, 201–16. London: Methuen, 1956.

Butor, Michel. "Mallarmé selon Boulez." In *Essais sur les modernes*, 95–109. Paris: Gallimard, 1960 [1964].

Cornulier, Benoît de. "L'alexandrin chez Verlaine, Rimbaud, Mallarmé." In *Théorie du vers*, 145–209. Paris: Seuil, 1982.

Crow, Christine, et al. Ten essays about Mallarmé. In *Baudelaire, Mallarmé, Valéry*, edited by Malcolm Bowie, et al, 1–23, 142–313. Cambridge: Cambridge University Press, 1982.

Derrida, Jacques. "Mallarmé." In *Tableau de la littérature française de Madame de Staël à Rimbaud*, Vol. 3, preface by Dominique Aury, 368–79. Paris: Gallimard, 1974.

Fowlie, Wallace. "Mallarmé and the Aesthetics of the Theater." In *Dionysus in Paris*, 265–76. New York: Meridian Books, 1960.

Genette, Gérard. "Bonheur de Mallarmé?" In *Figures I*, 91–100. Paris: Seuil, 1966.

————. "Au défaut des langues." In *Mimologique: voyage en Cratylie*, 257–314. Paris: Seuil, 1976.

Glauser, Alfred. "Du satyre de Hugo au faune de Mallarmé." In *Le Poème-symbole de Scève à Valléry*, 151–62. Paris: Nizet, 1967.

Gourmont, Remy de. "Stéphane Mallarmé." In *Selected Writings*, edited and translated by Glenn S. Burne, 183–90. Ann Arbor: University of Michigan Press, 1966.

Houston, John Porter. "Mallarmé in the 1860s," "Mallarmé's Later Work." In *Patterns of Thought in Rimbaud and Mallarmé*, 88–130. Lexington, Ky.: French Forum, 1986.

Jones, Rhys S. "Mallarmé and Valéry: Imitation or Continuation?" In *Gallica*, edited by R. H. Spencer, 201–17. Cardiff: University of Wales Press, 1969.

Joseph, Lawrence A. *Henri Cazalis, sa vie, son oeuvre, son amitié avec Stéphane Mallarmé*. Paris: Nizet, 1972.

Kaufman, Vincent. "Mallarmé." In *Le Livre et ses adresses*, 19–111. Paris: Méridiens Klincksieck, 1986.

Knight, Philip. "Mallarmé." In *Flower Poetics in Nineteenth-Century France*, 204–19. Oxford: Clarendon Press, 1986.

Kristeva, Julia. "Quelques problèmes de sémiotique à propos d'un poème de Mallarmé: 'Un Coup de dés.'" In *Essais de sémiotique poétique*, edited by A. J. Greimas, 207–34. Paris: Larousse, 1972.

———. "The Expenditure of a Logical Conclusion: *Igitur.*" In *Revolution in Poetic Language*, translated by Margaret Weller, 226–34. New York: Columbia University Press, 1984.

Lawler, James. "Mallarmé and the 'Monstre d'or.'" In *The Language of French Symbolism*, 3–20. Princeton: Princeton University Press, 1969.

———. "Reading as Explication: Mallarmé's 'Toast funèbre.'" In *Textual Analysis: Some Readers Reading*, edited by Mary Ann Caws, 34–44. New York: Modern Language Association, 1986.

Lehmann, A. G. "Schopenhauer and Mallarmé"; "Mallarmé"; "Mallarmé and the 'Music' of Poetry." In *The Symbolist Aesthetic in France 1885–1895*, 60–66, 88–92, 149–67. Oxford: Blackwell, 1950.

Martino, Pierre. "Mallarmé." In *Parnasse et Symbolisme (1850–1900)*, 119–29. Paris: Armand Colin, 1928.

Mazel, Henri. "Verlaine et Mallarmé." In *Aux beaux temps du symbolisme: 1890–1895*, 35–49. Paris: Mercure de France, 1934.

Mitchell, Robert L. "Stéphane Mallarmé." In *Corbière, Mallarmé, Valéry*, 38–57, 102–29. Saratoga [Calif.]: Anma Libri, 1981.

Mockel, Albert. "Stéphane Mallarmé, un héros (1899)." In *Esthétique du Symbolisme*, edited by Michel Otten, 177–207. Brussels: Palais des Académies, 1962.

Pelletier, Anne-Marie. "Description et fonctionnement de la syntaxe de Mallarmé." In *Fonctions poétiques*, 93–105. Paris: Klincksieck, 1977.

Poizat, Alfred. "Mallarmé." In *Le Symbolisme de Baudelaire à Claudel*, 70–105. Paris: Renaissance du Livre, 1919.

Poulet, Georges. "Mallarmé." In *Etudes sur le temps humain*, 298–355. Paris: Plon, 1952.

———. "La 'Prose' de Mallarmé." In *Les Métamorphoses du circle*, 439–56. Paris: Flammarion, 1979.

Rastier, F. "Systématique des isotopies ['Salut']." In *Essais de sémiotique poétique*, edited by A. J. Greimas, 80–106. Paris: Larousse, 1972.

Richard, Jean-Pierre. "Feu rué, fue scintillé." In *Microlectures*, 109–34. Paris: Seuil, 1979.

Scott, David, "Mallarmé: Un Coup de Dés." In *Pictorialist Poetics: Poetry & the Visual Arts in Nineteenth-Century France*, 138–69. Cambridge: Cambridge University Press, 1988.

Steinmetz, Jean-Luc. "Mallarmé: sens et réticences." In *Le Champ d'écoute: Essais critiques*, 179–229. Neuchâtel: La Baconnière, 1985.

Weinberg, Bernard. "'L'Après-midi d'un faune', 'Le Vierge, le vivace et le bel aujourd'hui,' 'Toast funèbre,' 'Le Tombeau de Poe,' 'Un Coup de dés jamais n'abolira le hasard.'" In *The Limits of Symbolism*, 127–321. Chicago: University of Chicago Press, 1966.

Welch, Cyril and Liliane Welch. "Mallarmé's Poetic Transformation"; "Mallarmé and the Experience of Art." In *Emergence: Baudelaire, Mallarmé, Rimbaud:* 67–78, 79–89. State College [Penn.]: Bald Eagle Press, 1973.

Welch, Liliane and Cyril Welch. "Mallarmé and Finite Transcendence." In *Address: Rimbaud, Mallarmé, Butor,* 61–168. Victoria [British Columbia]: Sono Nis Press, 1979.

Wing, Nathaniel. "False Confusions: Fictions of Masculine Desire in Mallarmé's 'L'Après-midi d'un faune.'" In *The Limits of Narrative: Essays on Baudelaire, Flaubert, Rimbaud & Mallarmé*, 96–113. Cambridge: Cambridge University Press, 1986.

York, R. A. "Mallarmé." In *The Poem as Utterance*, 47–60. London: Methuen, 1986.

Zagona, Helen G. "Salomé as the Image of an Esoteric Principle." In *The Legend of Salomé and the Principle of Art for Art's Sake*, 41–68. Geneva: Droz, 1960.

Periodicals

Cahiers du Sud: "Autour de Mallarmé," no. 378—379 (July–October 1964).
Les Lettres: "Stéphane Mallarmé (1842–1898)," no. 9–10–11 (1948).
Le Point: "Mallarmé," no. 29–30 (February–April 1944).
Yale French Studies: "Mallarmé," no. 54 (1977).

Index